Ludwig Engel (ed.)

Zamp Kelp
Prospector
Casting an Eye on Haus-Rucker-Co and Post-Haus-Rucker

Spector Books

for Lilly

We find ourselves in a time that unhinges the rehearsed relationships between man and machine, city and nature, perception and truth, and makes our present actions appear as exercises of a new life practice that we must navigate blindly. The world seems so confusing, complex, uncertain, and incomprehensible that we no longer try to understand it with our instruments but instead strive to experience and explore it. In today's global simultaneity of spaces and times, pervaded by digital data streams, technology seems to both be a tool for freedom and an undertaker, the salvation of the world only possible with the latest technology and in the rejection of it. Looking at Zamp Kelp's work, one meets a researcher who, since the 1960s, has encountered this state with a curious architectural-artistic practice. Zamp completes his training as an architect at a time when the idea of architecture and what an architect is capable of is fragmented by utopias that are liberated from work by new technological possibilities and fans out into countless strands of a constructive-critical practices. The explosive power of these liberated possibilities of spatial intervention and the alternative handling of buildings and yet-to-be-built constructions shines through Zamp's works. Kinetic sculptures, performances, happenings, cakes, T-shirts, posters, films, play equipment, lamps, and texts are created with the same implicitness as sketches, plans, models, furniture, and buildings as an expression of architectural thinking. All of this, and with the still world-famous group Haus-Rucker-Co above all, though also alone, as well as in changing roles—as university assistant, professor, artist, architect, activist, and utopian—Zamp's life and work appears both dazzling and wobbling. His story is one that can be told from front to back, but also from right to left, from top to bottom, and again from back to front. And so, the structure of this book is not told in a linear and clearly straightforward manner, but rather takes a derive, as Guy Debord calls it, into the world of Professor DI Günter Zamp Kelp. In the newly written science-fiction stories, Zamp once again questions his ideas on the genre's relevance to the present day and, in a selection of recently edited essays, shows the range of possibilities for manifesting what is thought—accompanied by the biographical notes that relentlessly keep the course of events in line with the times. In Zamp's fragments of space and time documented here, it becomes clear how relative time and how flexible space (and its perception) ultimately are and how the result—the real thing—is ultimately only one possibility. What Zamp is always concerned with is the idea, which finds a different aesthetic and formal repeater in each time. This book is thus also dedicated to the castle in the sky—the idea itself—and shows Zamp's work as a workshop of concepts woven into time-loops, and Zamp himself as a prospector, always searching for stimulating ideas to reflect on architecture, city, landscape, space, and virtuality.

Ludwig Engel

15 ANNO 2186
Igor Inside the Architrainer

    23   Gravity Contragravity
    32   Jules Verne, Georges Méliès, and NASA

39 ANNO 2170
Francis's Dramatic Weekend

    45   Skin: The Medium of Surface
    60   Tools of Perception

77 ANNO 2222
Sylvia in the Dome

    84   At the Table of the 21st Century
    93   Climate and Landscape

117 ANNO 2172
Balthazar Plays the Piano

    123   Aura, Network, Node
    134   Fluxus and the World of Provisional Architecture
    144   Art and Society

161 ANNO 2255
Carla and Carlo at the Euracle

    170   Space-time
    177   Sisters of Imagination
    186   Hagia Sophia, Ronchamp, St. Elijah

193   *Ludwig Engel in conversation with Zamp Kelp*

199   *Kristin Feireiss in conversation with Zamp Kelp*

205   *Utopia and Function* by Christoph Kelp

211   Register chronology
235   Vita Zamp Kelp / Haus-Rucker-Co
238   Imprint

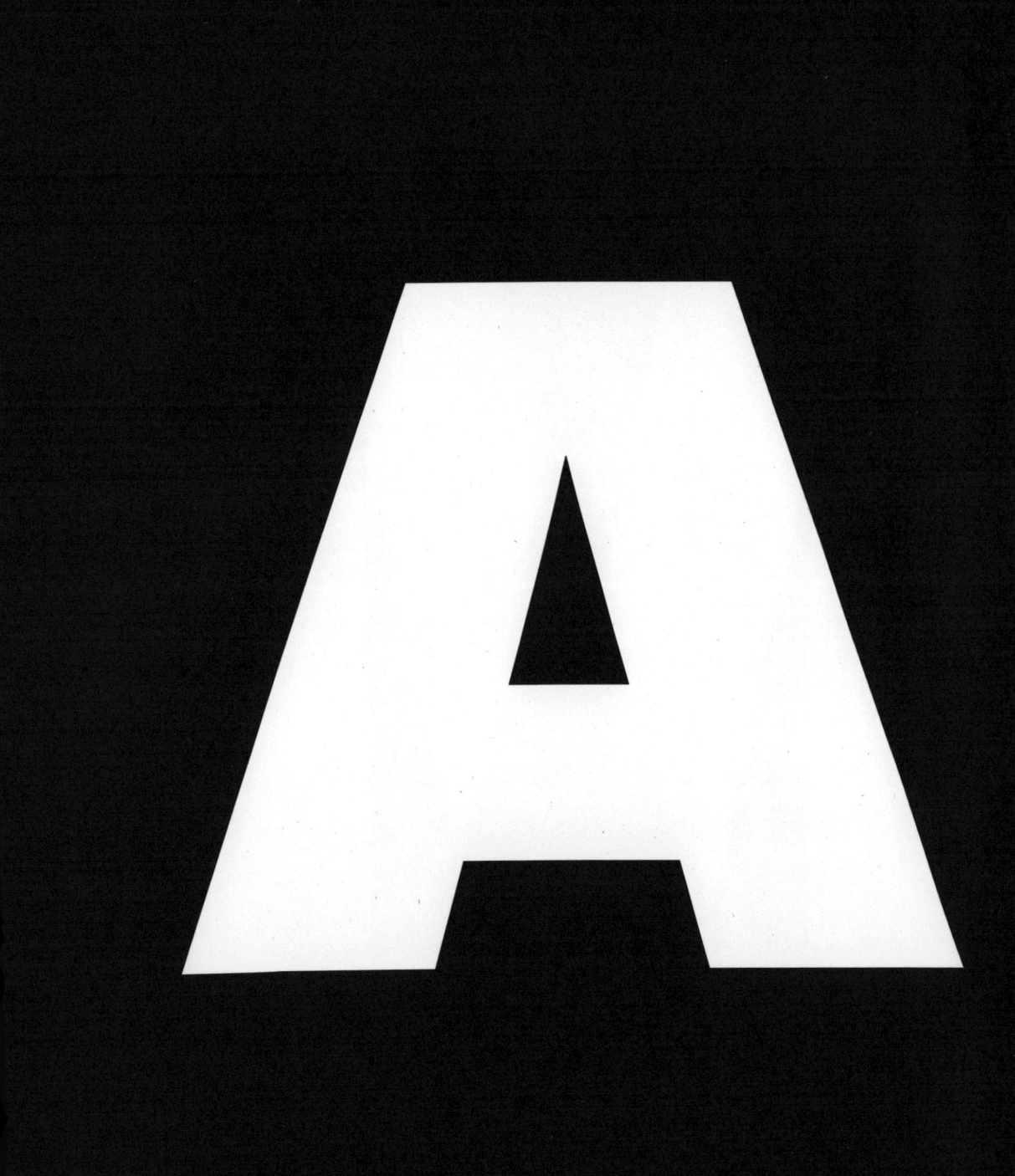

1964 — 2255

IN THE YEAR 2186

Igor Inside

the Archi-trainer

Igor is in the final phase of his architecture degree. He has just completed his master's project: a "Palace of Perfumes" for the 201st Burning Man Festival. Igor's Palace design consists of an agglomeration of spherical spaces filled with oxygen and added fragrances and essences that offer physical and mental regeneration to the festival's party crowd.

Sitting in one of the Architrainer's individualized cells, in which he developed the digital plans and three-dimensional animations for his "Palace of Perfumes," Igor is now preparing to present his project to the diploma jury. Overall, he has spent less than a month in the Architrainer, an edifice on stilts that appears to hover at about 100 feet above a steep Danube river gorge, and which has served as a training facility for architects since its construction.

Earning an architecture degree used to take three to five years and was supervised by professors and their assistants. In the Architrainer, the program has been condensed to one month of mind programming by means of instructive force fields, which transfer all required specialist knowledge into the students' consciousnesses. Igor's rapid studies were very intense and covered various specialisms. The transfers of knowledge took place in several stages, each ending in a period spent under a helmet-like apparatus that stabilized and calmed Igor's cortex, freshly imbued and stimulated with insights into architecture. He slept little over the past weeks and when he would finally fall asleep, he had wild dreams.

In one of these troubled dreams, he was walking with a group of famous architects through the ancient city of Palmyra, which had been destroyed more than a hundred years ago. There they met Pliny the Elder, who complained bitterly about the destruction of the historical site and called for its reconstruction. Minoru Yamasaki, on the other hand, wanted to rebuild Manhattan's World Trade Center from the 1970s on the edge of Palmyra's urban fragments. Fischer von Erlach mused on the importance of duplicating Vienna's Karlskirche as a mosque, while Zaha Hadid wanted to build a mausoleum for herself. In the dream, Igor desperately tried to argue against these outrageous plans but even his assumed ally Pliny seemed to sympathize with his colleagues' ideas. As so often with nightmares, Igor saved himself by waking up.

Now Igor sits in front of his "Palace of Perfumes" and thinks about how he can best sell the project to the jury. He leaves his cell and moves to the central hub of the Architrainer, where he will present and defend his project in front of the

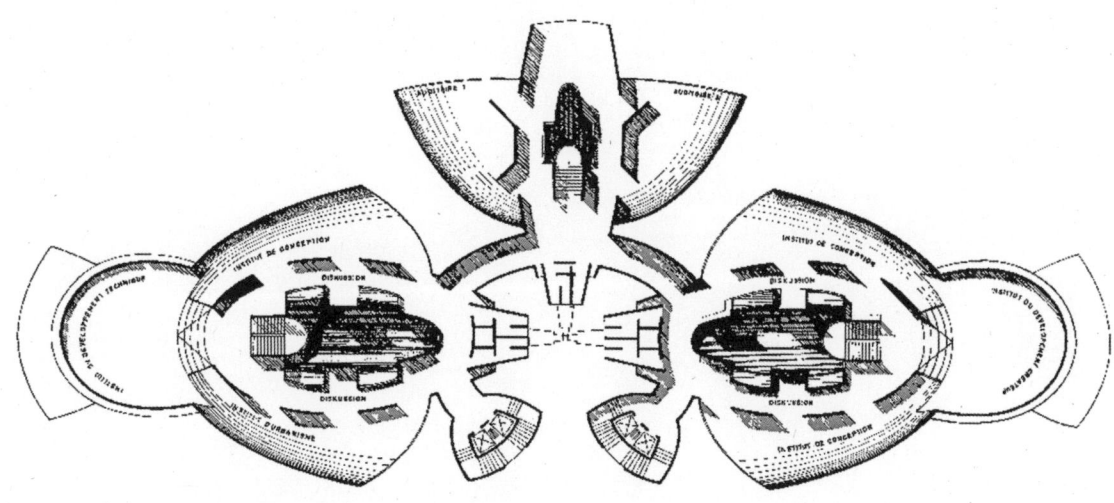

Architrainer, ground section, project TU Vienna, delegated by Institute of Architectural Design 2, for the UIA Competition, Paris, 1965

designated jury. When he enters the auditorium, most of the other postgrads are already there. Igor hands the data for his presentation to the head of media facilities, who tells him that he will be fifth in line. After a while, the jury arrives with an air of sovereignty and the presentations begin. After Igor finishes his presentation, he receives feedback from individual jurors. Some are critical, while others are supportive. One juror asks him how he intends to solve the problem of mixing different scents in a spatial context. Igor explains his concept in greater detail, pointing out the spherical helmets arranged within the larger spheres for individuals or small

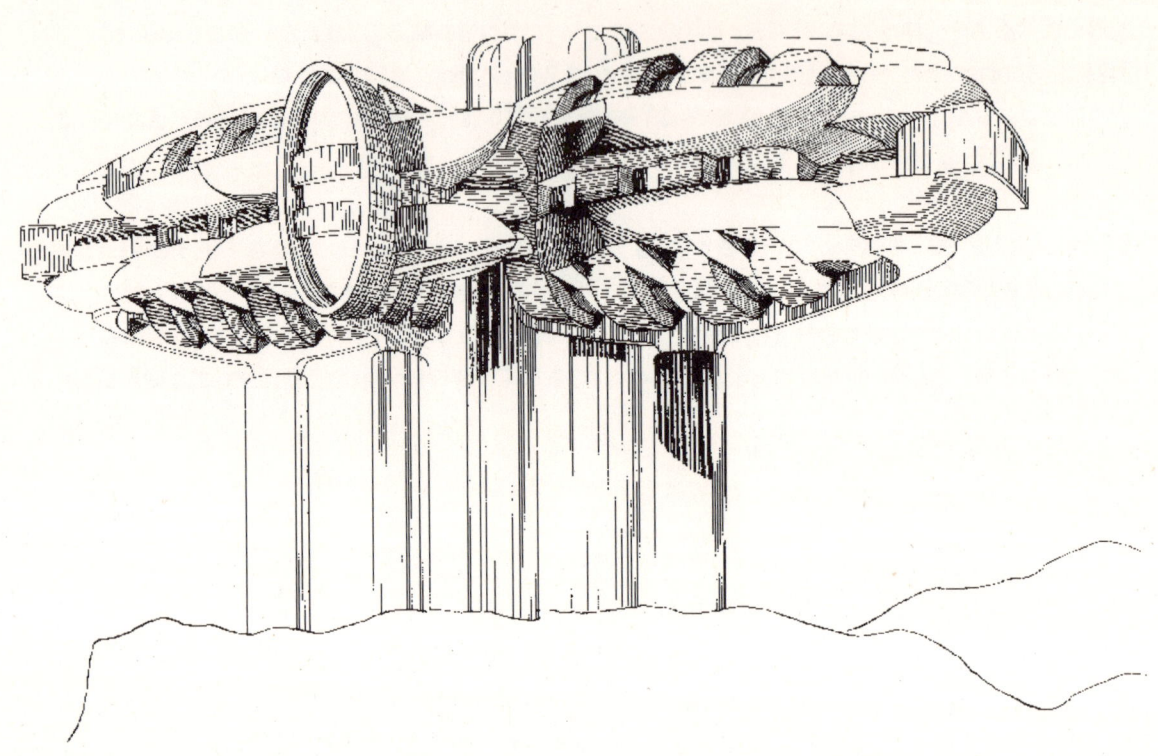
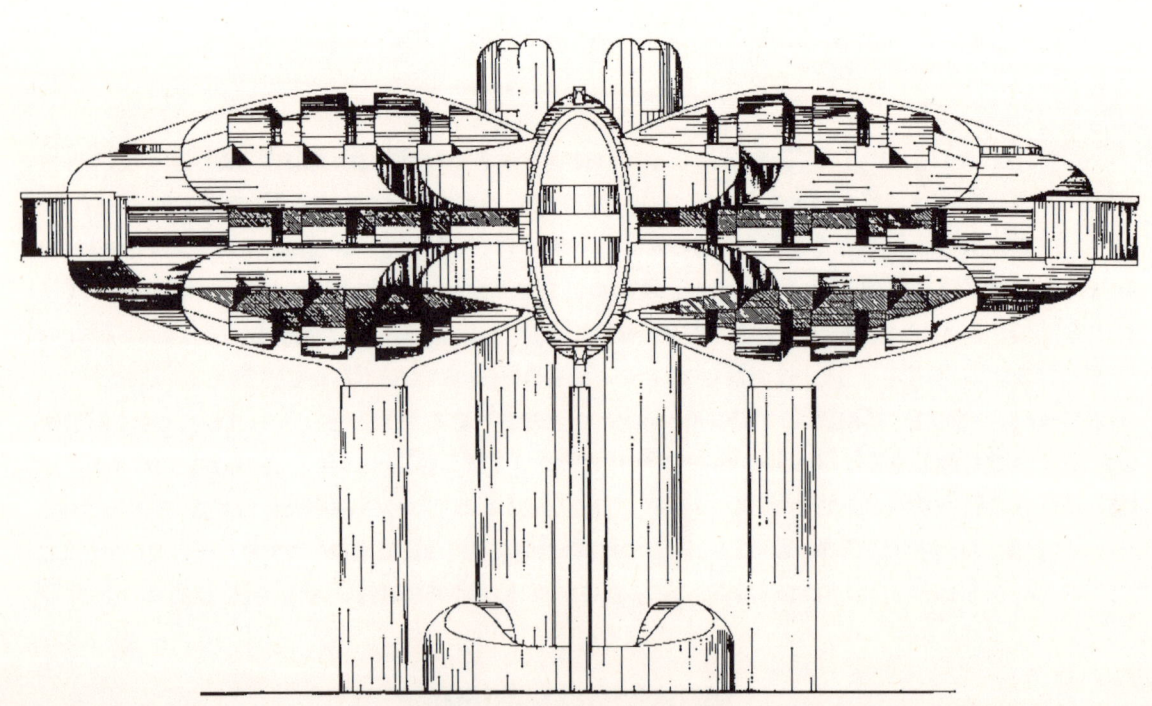

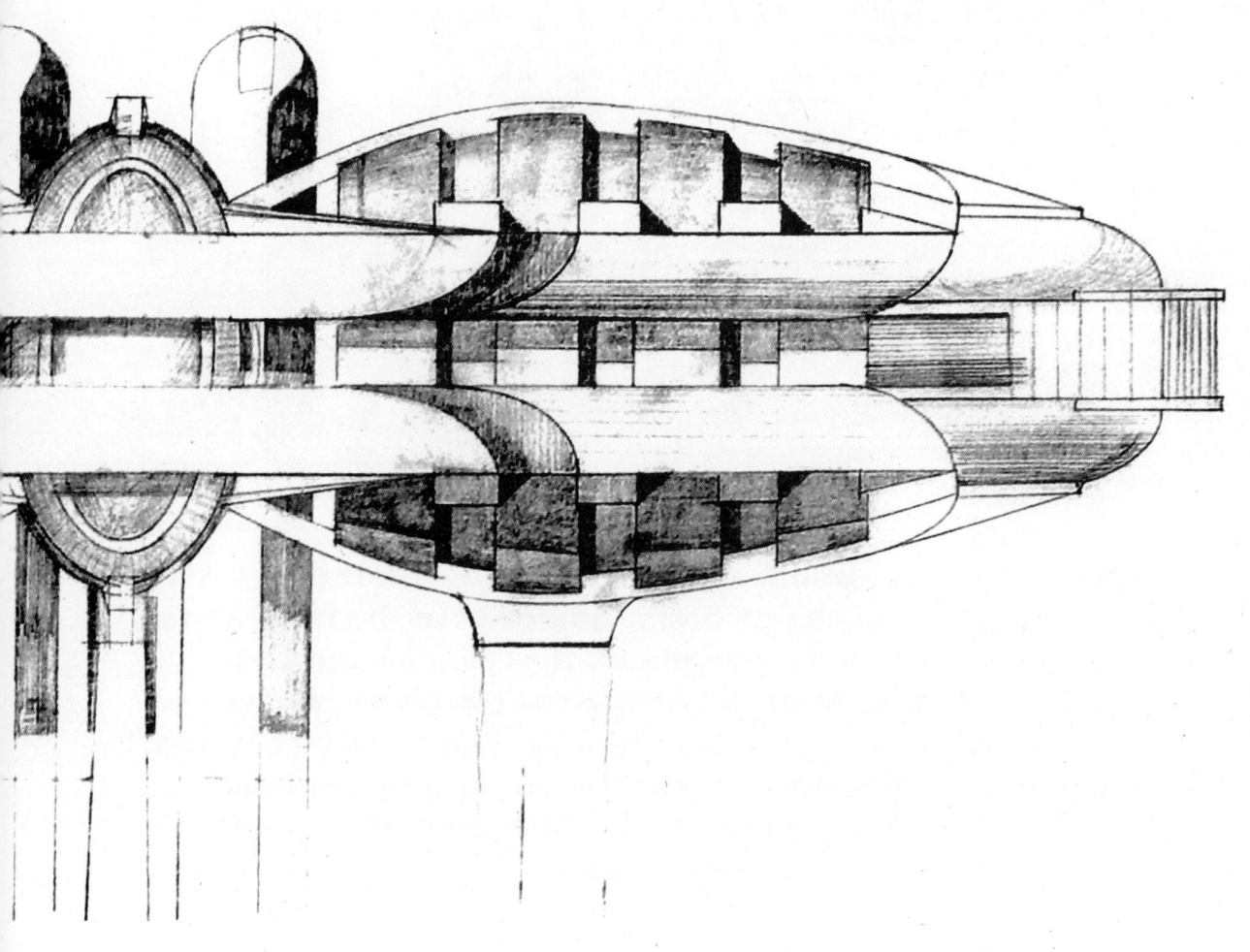

groups to breathe specifically scented air. Another question concerns the atmospheric enhancements to the fragrances offered in the Palace. Igor explains that there would be different atmospheric variables, with light and acoustic effects supplementing the fragrances. The number of people in a sphere would also be taken into account by the control elements. Finally, there is also the offer of optical scent supplementation via scenic projections.

The jurors agree on a positive verdict and Igor feels ready to start his career. But he still has to wait for the diploma ceremony the next day. After the intensive time of his programming to become an architect, he soon surrenders to the need for rest and seeks early sleep in his cell.

The next morning greets Igor with a cloudless sky. For the last time, he wanders through the floating structure. He has grown fond of the homely atmosphere inside. The rich yellow of the building's interior continues to have a positive, soothing effect on his mind. The large spaces of the left and right wings of the building remind him of the inside of a mammal's rib cage. Inside the rooms with their organically constructive atmosphere, the various elements capable of shaping consciousness seem to float. Only the central hub of the three-part building constellation and the panoramic boxes at the outer endpoints of the wings have window surfaces that open up a view of the surrounding landscape. Otherwise, the transfer of knowledge from the trainer's digital archives into the recipients' mental faculties is a task that demands great concentration from all involved—any distraction would only endanger the quality of the transfusion processes.

The graduation is ceremonial. Igor, like the other graduating students, is given a graduation certificate, which declares him a Master of Architecture. He also receives a wingsuit. Like all Masters trained in the Architrainer, he will exit the building by jumping out the central window. For this purpose, there is a protruding platform without railings on a central open floor of the vertical ellipse, where all the freshly graduated students gather in their wingsuits and discuss the ritual's risks. Suddenly, a whistle sounds and at the same time, a draught of air is felt, which quickly develops storm-like force and sweeps the new Masters of Architecture into the sky.

Igor starts sailing towards the nearby city of Linz. He realizes that the use of flying and gliding apparatuses has also been implanted into his cerebellum, as he soars quite naturally over the landscape below him, thanks to the force of aerodynamic lift. When he senses a certain atmospheric updraft, he opens the ram-air parachute and his flight becomes calmer. Fascinated, he steers his wing-suit-turned-paraglide along the course of the Danube and finally approaches Linz, where he lands on a bridge that is over 250 years old and links the two parts of the city.

Gravity Contragravity

Legend has it that in the 17th century, while sitting in his garden under a tree, Isaac Newton was hit on the head by a falling apple. This triggered the first ideas about his law of universal gravitation, whereupon he cooperated with scientists Robert Hooke and John Flamsteed to come to a ground-breaking conclusion. The scientists discovered that, based on Johannes Kepler's insights on planetary orbits, each point mass impacts other point masses with a force of attraction. This force, gravitation, is known to be an essential component on which the universe, space, and Earth's living conditions are based. As a force that codetermines life on Earth, human development, animals, and plants, it influences the tectonics of natural landscapes and the architecture of our cities. It is part of evolution. It ensures that liquids remain in their containers and that rain falls down onto Earth. It is a means of order and an ever-present force. Its existence stabilizes our atmosphere, which provides oxygen and protects us from cosmic radiation.

1964 The excursion participants of the TU Wien (Technische Universität Wien) gather in Vienna International Airport's departure lounge. A short time later, we board the Swiss Air Boeing 707 en route to New York City. Everyone, even Karl Schwanzer, is in very good spirits. In anticipation of experiencing the American way of life, I drink a whiskey on the rocks with Götz Hagmüller, Laurids Ortner, Diether Hoppe, and others. I think about Antonín Dvořák's *New World Symphony* as the excursion draws closer to the new, unknown cultural environment with each second.

***Melancholia*, dystopian movie, Lars von Trier, 2011**

However, gravity also has its downsides. In his film *Melancholia* (2011), Lars von Trier stages our Earth's downfall as a result of an enormous planet whose gravitational field begins to gradually interfere with that of the Earth. Both planets eventually attract one another, and, as the Earth's inhabitants watch, the foreign planet and its point mass hurtle towards Earth at an increasing speed due to the developing of gravitational forces.

Zamp Kelp and Ludwig Engel in discussion at the *Table of Zero Gravity*

At the end of the film, the planets collide. This cinematic dystopia demonstrates the ambivalent characteristics of gravitational forces in space. The history of the Earth tells us a lot about the impacts of meteorites, meteors, and asteroids that were attracted to it. This selectively changed the topography of Earth's surface and negatively impacted the global climate in the long run, while also severely transforming the habitat conditions of many animal species. Gravitation serves as a factor that shapes a sense of home and down-to-earthness in our conscious minds and signposts the way back for humans when they return from space. After all, gravity is in balance with the centrifugal forces that stabilize the moon's orbit around Earth. Gravity, however, is also what kindles a desire to free ourselves from it, to leave the levels of earthly landscapes in order to experience the feeling of weightlessness in new spaces. In this sense, the movie *A Trip to Mars* (1910) by Thomas A. Edison makes the overcoming of gravity easy: an adventurous alchemist mixes two pulverized substances and accidentally invents "reverse gravity," before floating out of his laboratory to voyage to Mars. To this day, contragravity has been an element of science fiction and an important design medium in the respective narratives.

Achieving moments of weightlessness during parabolic flights in a jet requires considerable efforts, in terms of aircraft maneuvers and the associated energy that these flights require. Surely, the so-called body flight is the more favorable and less elaborate alternative. It allows hovering in a specialized suit above a vertically positioned wind tunnel, defying gravity while holding the body steady over an airflow of 250 km/h winds. Those willing to take risks plunge from steep alpine cliffs and hurl themselves into an abyss, wearing only a wing suit, and eventually gently land with a parachute.

In the world of images, gravity manages without technical auxiliary constructions. An example is the retrofuturistic images of classic automobiles by photographer Renaud Marion, where cars are freed from their four wheels and float above the pavement. The cars display no new utopian shapes, such as the vehicles in Star Wars. Instead, they are simply classics without wheels, hovering and conjuring memories of a possible future for private transportation. The future meets the past and thus issues a warning about the state of Western societies—one which allows a saturated awareness of a successful past to head full speed towards a future fraught with changes and uncertainties.

But back to the ordinary and its constant companion: gravity. For years I have been eating breakfast at a "zero gravity table," a piece of furniture in my home that I made in 1977 in Düsseldorf. The steel construction of angled sections supports a tabletop with a mirror mounted to it, and this creates a visual indentation that reflects and thus inverts the surrounding space.

The elements positioned on the mirror's surface reside in the threshold between real space and fictively mirrored space and are doubled. This creates the optical illusion that real objects and their inverted mirror images are weightless.

Around twenty years later, *Zero Gravity Space* was developed through a project of extending the entrance to the Mutter-Ey-Strasse gallery building in Düsseldorf, which was built for Alfred Schmela by Aldo van Eyck in 1971. This space conceptually assumes the characteristics of a space capsule. The two walls, floor, and ceiling are cased in gray stained maple parquet and can be used functionally in the speculative case of gravity suspension, analogous to the walls in space vehicles. This terrestrial paraphrase on space-travel conditions was transferred into urban dimensions through the project *Zero Gravity Town* (2000), allowing the project to transform into a dimension of an urban utopia. A certain analogy of this principle is found in a sequence from the movie *Inception* (2010), which speculates that the human conscience can be influenced by a manipulator through various levels of dreams. In this sequence, architecture student Ariadne is told to confuse the subconscious of a targeted person, who is having a dream about Paris. In doing so, she enables the potential manipulator to intervene in this person's dream,

Circle Line

1964 At 4 p.m. local time, we land and arrive at the John F. Kennedy Airport in New York. After going through customs and picking up our luggage, we meet Günther Feuerstein in one of the arrivals halls. He has been in the US for a while in order to prepare for our visit. The bus ride to the Manhattan hotel conveys a first impression of the city. Here, everything is bigger than in European urbanities. Even the suburbs superficially bespeak a generous unkemptness. There is a harsh visual climate present, which I perceive with a certain sympathy. After checking into the Empire Hotel on Broadway and discussing the program for the coming days at the reception, we take our first tours around Manhattan. The height of the buildings seems bearable to me as I was expecting more spatial pressure. Despite the massiveness of the development, the urban space appears harmonious, and at times, this first walk is even pleasant. While strolling around, we come up with the idea to rent a car as a group of four and immediately make the plan a reality. I have the rather ambivalent pleasure of acting as our driver. The metallic vehicle is not particularly large by US standards, but is considered a mid-sized, high-class car in European terms. So, Wolf Pont, Götz Hagmüller, Laurids Ortner, and I get in the car, roll the windows down, turn the radio up as loud as possible and off we go down Broadway towards downtown. Now we feel like we have arrived in the US, and sometimes we even run red lights on our way. After the initial excitement, the coin flips and we have problems finding a parking spot. It is almost impossible to park your car on the side of the road and paid parking is expensive. The police sirens permanently accentuate the atmosphere in the streets. Compared to the sirens of Austrian police cars, they sound like the calls of exotic animals.

Statue of Liberty

1964 Upon arriving at the Austrian embassy, we meet Kiki Kogelnik, an Austrian artist living in New York. She joins us as our little group visits Trude Heller's, a trendy club in Greenwich Village on the corner of 6th Avenue and West 9th Street. Inside, there are go-go dancers and the crowd is swinging to the sound of Roy Orbison's "Pretty Woman."

Zero Gravity Space, space extension in the doorway of Schmela Gallery, Düsseldorf (maple parquet, glass, aluminum)

and thus, conscience. Ariadne's method of confusion is to vertically bend and fold a city district of the Paris-inspired dreamscape. The movie's script leaves the open possibility that the transformation could lead to another bend, which would result in a space-creating unfolding of the district. The dream stops abruptly, and the events are catapulted into the next scenario.

The space-creating unfolding of urbanity is the theme of *Zero Gravity Town*. While in *Inception*, this process receives its conceptual legitimation through the dream, in *Zero Gravity Town*, it

GRAVITY CONTRAGRAVITY

Zero Gravity Town, collage, Zamp Kelp, Berlin, 2011

1964 In the Seagram Building, we visit Philip Johnson, who speaks perfect German, and discuss the end of his collaboration with Ludwig Mies van der Rohe after completing a skyscraper and what the diversity of his new architectural strategies entail. The New York World's Fair in Flushing Meadows; Frank L. Wright's Guggenheim Museum near Central Park; the Miller Shoe Salon by Victor Lundy; the Lincoln Center; the Lever Building of Skidmore, Owings & Merrill; and the Museum of Modern Art are only a few of the objects and institutions we intensively examine. We spend our last night in New York in the most fitting way: four hundred meters above ground on the Empire State Building's observation deck, the then-tallest building in the world. As the day transforms into dusk and darkness, my gaze wanders into the depths of the space before me, with its viewing radius of around eight hundred kilometers, and returns to the island that, in the well-tempered Indian summer draft, seems to emerge from the darkness and shine artificially.

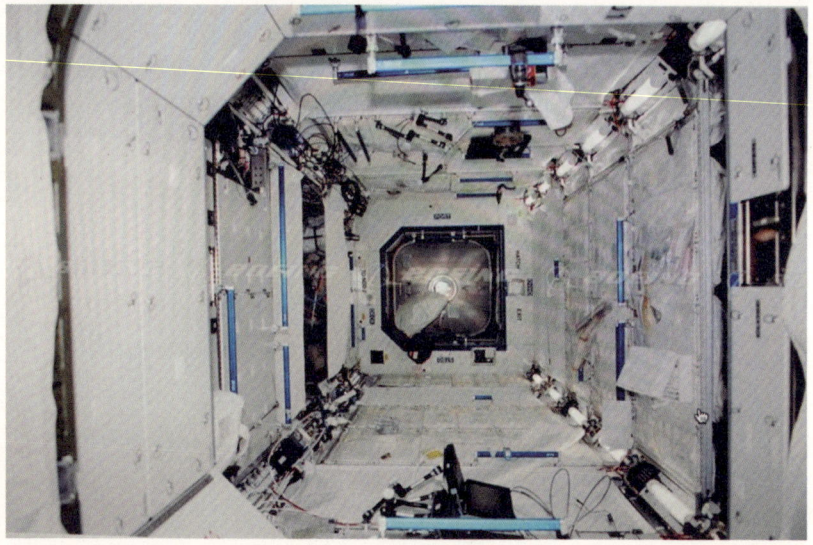

International Space Station, inside view

is the weightlessness and/or absence of gravity. This creates the speculative outlook that humans are able to travel through space with shuttles in order to reach spatial landscapes that are folded analogies of urban districts on Earth, i.e. travel through space with a sense of home.

The National Aeronautics and Space Administration's goal was to land on the moon and to delve into spaces outside of the Earth. For this purpose, exotic transportation capsules were developed, providing the agency with a high level of appeal.

Inception, screen still, science-fiction thriller, Christopher Nolan, 2010

Haus-Rucker-Co, on the other hand, took the everyday space in Earth's natural and urban landscapes to task. They did this in order to perceive them anew through enactments of empirically produced spatial adventures, and to test their effect on passers-by and users. The zero-gravity simulation was an element that Haus-Rucker-Co was concerned with early on. Accordingly, the architects created the *Balloon for 2*—a spherical, transparent structure that appears to be floating in front of a house façade in the Apollogasse in Vienna.

Similarly, Haus-Rucker-Co's *Yellow Heart*, a pulsating space for two, floats as an airborne construction roughly one meter above the ground. The impression of hovering is achieved by a construction of steel tubes that keep the object in the air against the forces of gravity. Its appearance is shaped by artificiality, and thus seems rather like a mythical creature that has escaped from the ocean or an ark destined for space. The breathing capsule is built for two people and can be accessed through an airlock made of three yellow rings that are full of air. Users that enter *Yellow Heart* immediately feel a slight swaying of the apparatus, triggered by their weight. It is part of the experience, which forms a sharp contrast to any typical ambience, allowing a brief withdrawal from the reality of everyday life. It is an experience of meditative tranquility for two. The pair hovers in a horizontal position, surrounded by sounds and aromas, in a space that expands and contracts through control of the air supply. *Yellow Heart* thus develops its own calming rhythm, ideally passing it on to its passengers.

Zero Gravity Town with H₂O Spiral, Zamp Kelp, Berlin, 2012

1964 Bus ride to New Canaan, Connecticut to see Philip Johnson's Glass House, with its almost invisible glass walls bathed in autumnal yellow from the nearby deciduous trees, and the nearby stylistic counterpoint that was realized later on: an introverted guest house with a postmodern approach. We continue our journey to Yale University in New Haven, where we talk to Paul Rudolph in his Art and Architecture Building and study the details with admiration. That night, we chat with American students in the Old Heidelberg, a student restaurant on campus. Visiting the Married Students Housing by Eero Saarinen— a village for married couples studying at Yale—is impressive. Even though I am in no way considering getting married at twenty-three, I note and admire the comfort of the apartments and refrain from comparing it to the possibilities in Vienna. Our plans to drive to Boston with a bus full of students and visit Walter Gropius in his stone house in a neighborhood of stately mansions falls through. Gropius was not convinced enough by the delegation of Karl Schwanzer and Günther Feuerstein, who meet him in his house that day, to talk to us. Unsatisfied and subdued, we leave the place that we, agog with expectation, had headed to.

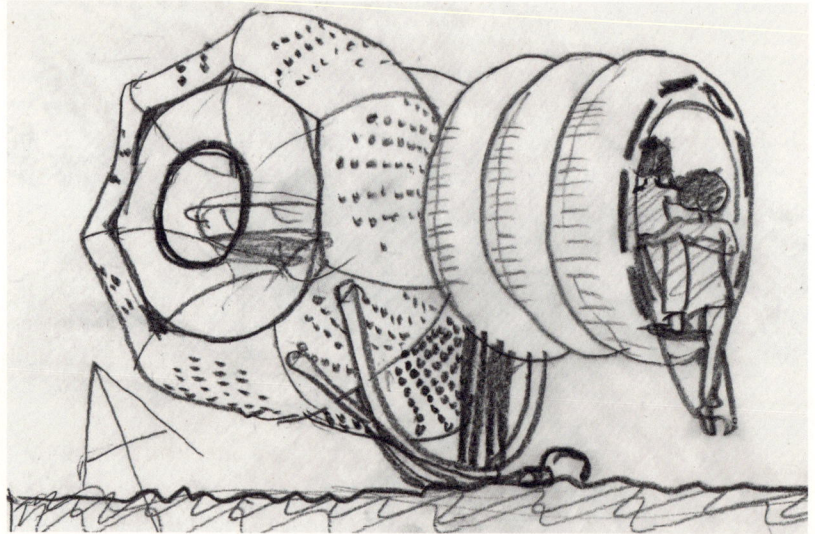

Yellow Heart + Environment Transformer, Super-drawing, Zamp Kelp, Berlin, 2017

Yellow Heart+Environment Transformer, Haus-Rucker-Co, Laurids Ortner, Zamp Kelp, Klaus Pinter, Wieselburg, 1968

Yellow Heart, travelling under water

GRAVITY CONTRAGRAVITY

Jules Verne, Georges Méliès, and NASA

Mustang

1964 We move on to Detroit. The Motor City is still vital and going strong; its demise is yet to come. We visit General Motors, a spacious open-air facility with a mighty water tower, which has a reflective metal surface to serve as an identity-forming element of Eero Saarinen. At Ford, we witness the assembly of a Mustang in just under fifty minutes. Visiting the adjoining steel mill of the auto manufacturer was especially impressive to me. Everything here is of phenomenally large dimensions and imposingly represents the "think big" mentality of this nation.

In 1902, Georges Méliès shot the movie *Le Voyage dans la Lune* (A Trip to the Moon). Sixty-seven years later, the dream of a moon landing became a reality with the help of the National Aeronautics and Space Administration astronauts.

In Méliès's film, he uses fairytale-like images to depict the way people were imagining such a trip. Six scientists, presumably astronomers, enter the cavity of a swiftly produced, oversized projectile, which is then pushed into a massive barrel. The fuse is lit, and the missile is launched to embark on its journey. The film adopts elements from Jules Verne's 1865 novel *De la Terre à la Lune: trajet direct en 97 heures 20 minutes* (From the Earth to the Moon: A Direct Route in 97 Hours, 20 minutes), though it does not address the author's constructive thoughts as described in the book. The lack of an oxygen-enriched atmosphere, for instance, is completely ignored. The moon visitors travel in casual clothing without putting on any spacesuits. Still, the film manages to account for the overcoming of gravity and the distance of 384,400 km traveled via a cannon shot of a projectile-shaped transportation capsule. The moon then presents itself as a landscape of surreal vegetation, in which peculiar

Le voyage dans la Lune (A Trip to the Moon), screen still, George Méliès, Paris, 1902

Piece of Moon and *Viennese Heart*, event on the occasion of the first moon landing
Haus-Rucker-Co, Laurids Ortner, Zamp Kelp, Klaus Pinter, on the square Am Hof, Vienna, 1969

Chicago

1964 In Chicago, a cradle of modern architecture and the city where the first steel-framed skyscrapers were built, we are staying at the Croydon Hotel, located between the city center and an entertainment district. Our first activity is a visit to Mies van der Rohe's office. Unfortunately, the master—seventy-eight years old at the time—is not present. At least we can visit his study and get an overview of the office's current tasks. The next day, we visit his Crown Hall at the Illinois Institute of Technology, where he taught for years. We enter a room with an unsupported ceiling where young architects, urban planners, and designers work together and most likely inspire

moon inhabitants, who explode once they are hit by punches and umbrellas, argue with the newcomers. Eventually, the expedition of the terrestrials has to concede to the superior forces of the moon dwellers. The astronomers flee and withdraw to their vehicle. One of them pulls the capsule over the edge and falls back to Earth with it, while a moon inhabitant clings onto the capsule's back.

Above all, the film's capsule launch and landing process are visionary. The return of the astronauts, at least those from the Apollo program, is almost identical to that of the projectile in Méliès's film. Both the capsule dropping down to Earth—full of astronomers in the silent movie—and the conical shuttle of the 1969 Apollo program land in the ocean on their return from the moon. From there, they are each transported to solid ground by ships and aircrafts.

In 1906, Hermann Oberth, one of the founding fathers of space travel, received Jules Verne's novel as a Christmas gift. He later considered this to be a crucial inspiration for why he devoted himself to rocket technology. Oberth is responsible for develop-

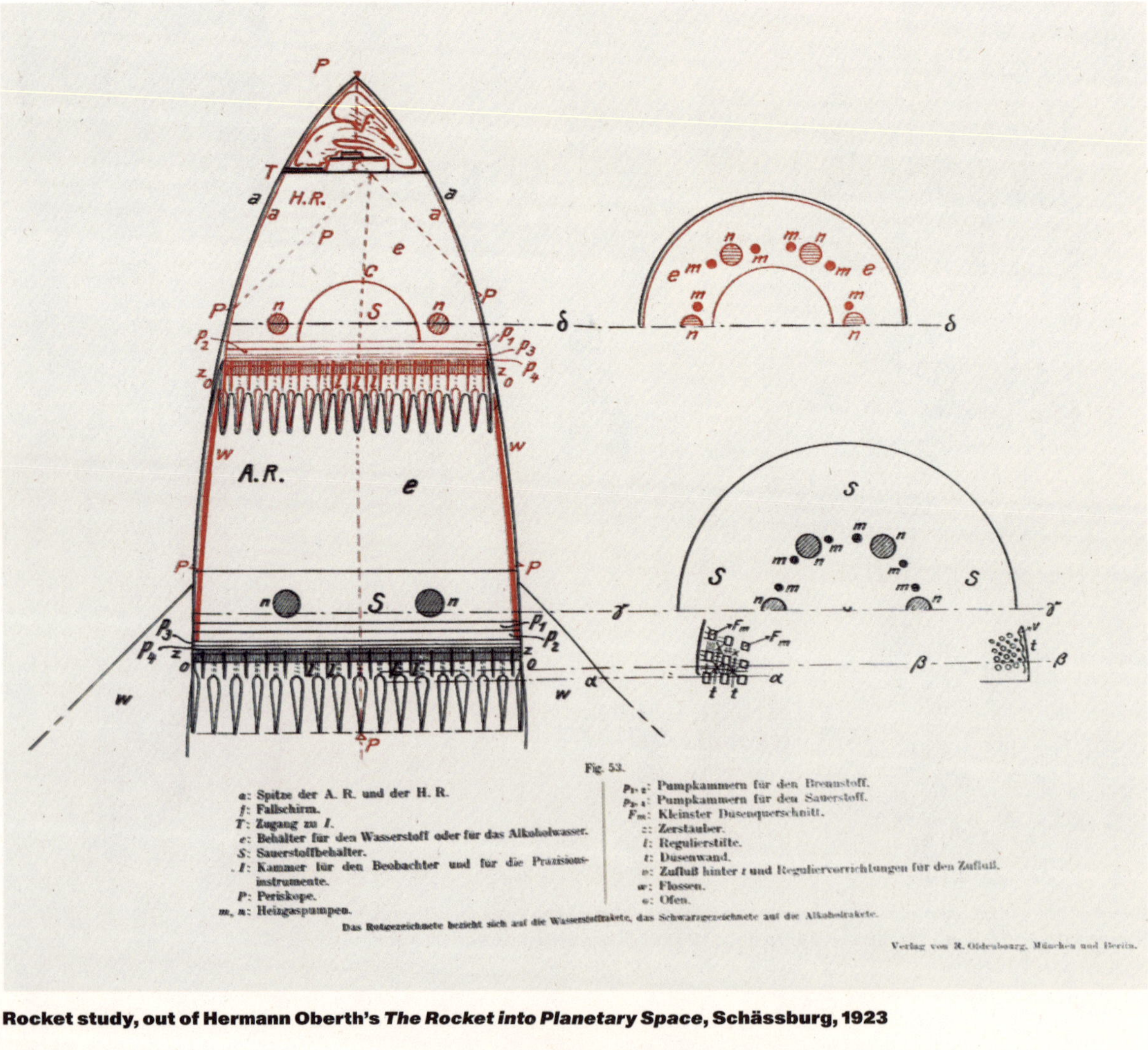

Rocket study, out of Hermann Oberth's *The Rocket into Planetary Space*, Schässburg, 1923

Eating the Moon, Haus-Rucker-Co event, Laurids Ortner, Zamp Kelp, Klaus Pinter, Am Hof, Vienna, 1969

ing the basics of rocket engineering, which eventually made moon travel possible in 1969. In 1923, Oberth published a book titled *The Rocket into Planetary Space*, in which he realized that, among other things, lunar travelers would not survive being shot to the moon because the contact pressure would crush the voyagers. However, the cannon shot in Jules Verne's narration still remains an initial incentive to deal with the overcoming of gravity and in this way, Oberth's book acts as a bridge between the utopia of the 19th century and the reality of the 20th century moon landing, which was accomplished under the direction of Wernher von Braun, Oberth's student.

In the spirit of this bridge, the first moon landing on July 21, 1969 became a fitting occasion for Haus-Rucker-Co to stage a corresponding event in the Vienna city center, with support from Österreichischer Rundfunk (ORF—Austrian Broadcasting Corporation):

"The woman walking past the square Am Hof this morning around 9 a.m. is confronted with an astronaut, a few musicians, a plastic cushion with a red heart on it, a crowd of people and a giant piece of cake with a lunar surface made from marzipan. She is especially impressed by the

one another. When we visit the office of Skidmore, Owings and Meril, I am particularly struck by the countless rows of continuous end-to-end desks with working stations that are in use around the clock. We devote our Saturday to Frank Lloyd Wright's Prairie Houses. Top priority is the empty Frederick C. Robie House from 1909. Both the outer appearance and the flow of interior concepts are closely related and create a compelling overall constellation for the building, in which one immediately feels comfortable. This is in spite of the fact that the wood paneling on the room's surfaces, combined with the shade of the trees outside, cannot meet the perceived need for sunlight. In any case, at the S.C. Johnson Wax Headquarters in Racine, Wisconsin, the interplay between translucent and opaque surfaces works perfectly, both atmospherically as well as technically, especially in the famous Great Workroom with its dendriform columns.

Louis Kahn

1964 We reach Washington by plane and spend the day in a bus heading towards Philadelphia—the city in which Louis Kahn's former office and one of his most important buildings, the so-called Medical Towers, are situated. With this building, Kahn proved that precast technology may well lead to outstanding architecture. In the afternoon, we have a plan to visit Louis Kahn himself. Naturally, the participants do not want to miss out on meeting him personally. The room where the discussion takes place is packed and Kahn's voice can hardly compete with the sound of all those present. He disregards our congratulations, conveyed by Feuerstein, for being honored with a medal from the Benjamin Franklin Institute, and begins a monologue, developing ideas ad hoc and trying to make the connections between architecture, art, and philosophy clear to us. The next day, we take the bus back to New York and go straight to JFK Airport. The last building that we visit is the Trans World Flight Center (TWA Flight Center) by Eero Saarinen, which seems considerably taller in publications than in reality, but still shines nonetheless in the consistency of its narrative appearance. Around 5 p.m., the TWA aircraft with all participants of the excursion takes off in the direction of Vienna. The journey has come to an end.

three-and-a-half-meter long pastry, so much so that she decides not to limit herself to whatever her hands can carry. She runs home to fetch her handcart in order to take her respective part of the oversized cake. When she returns twenty minutes later with her vehicle, all that is left of the dessert is tin foil and a pile of crumbs that run between her fingers. The woman misunderstood; she had mistaken the immediacy of a local festival in celebration of the first humans on the moon for a free meal provided by an aid agency. She was denied the culinary indulgence of a moon cake; instead, she had to settle for the Beatles imitators from the 16th district and the Schrammelmusik musicians present, sip on a glass of Afri-Cola and watch the Vienna heart cushion filled with hydrogen, as it made its way to the moon, disappearing behind the housetops." (Haus-Rucker-Co, 1976–1983, Journal, Vieweg, 1984)

Opposite page: *Viennese Heart*, hydrogen-filled PVC cushion with heart symbol, Haus-Rucker-Co, Laurids Ortner, Zamp Kelp, Klaus Pinter, Am Hof, Vienna, 1969

IN THE YEAR 2170

Francis's

Pneumacosm, living unit at Madison Ave, New York, montage, Haus-Rucker-Co, Laurids Ortner, Zamp Kelp, Klaus Pinter, Vienna, 1968

Dramatic Weekend

Francis Bacon lives in London during the 70s of the 22nd century. The only thing he has in common with the famous painter, who died in 1992, is his Irish roots. With the philosopher Francis Bacon, the father of Empiricism, he may only share a language. He came to London because here, in one of the largest seaports in Europe, he was offered the post of harbormaster, which he accepted after careful consideration.

Monocosm, study of virtual reality balloon for one person, sketch, Zamp Kelp, 2011

He has had an exhausting week and is looking forward to a regenerating weekend, which he intends to kick off in his apartment on Midhope Street near St. Pancras. The apartment is not overly large, as living space has become expensive due to the constantly growing population in the cities, especially in London. He has to set aside almost forty percent of his monthly income to pay for rent. Francis had originally thought about using the weekend to take a short

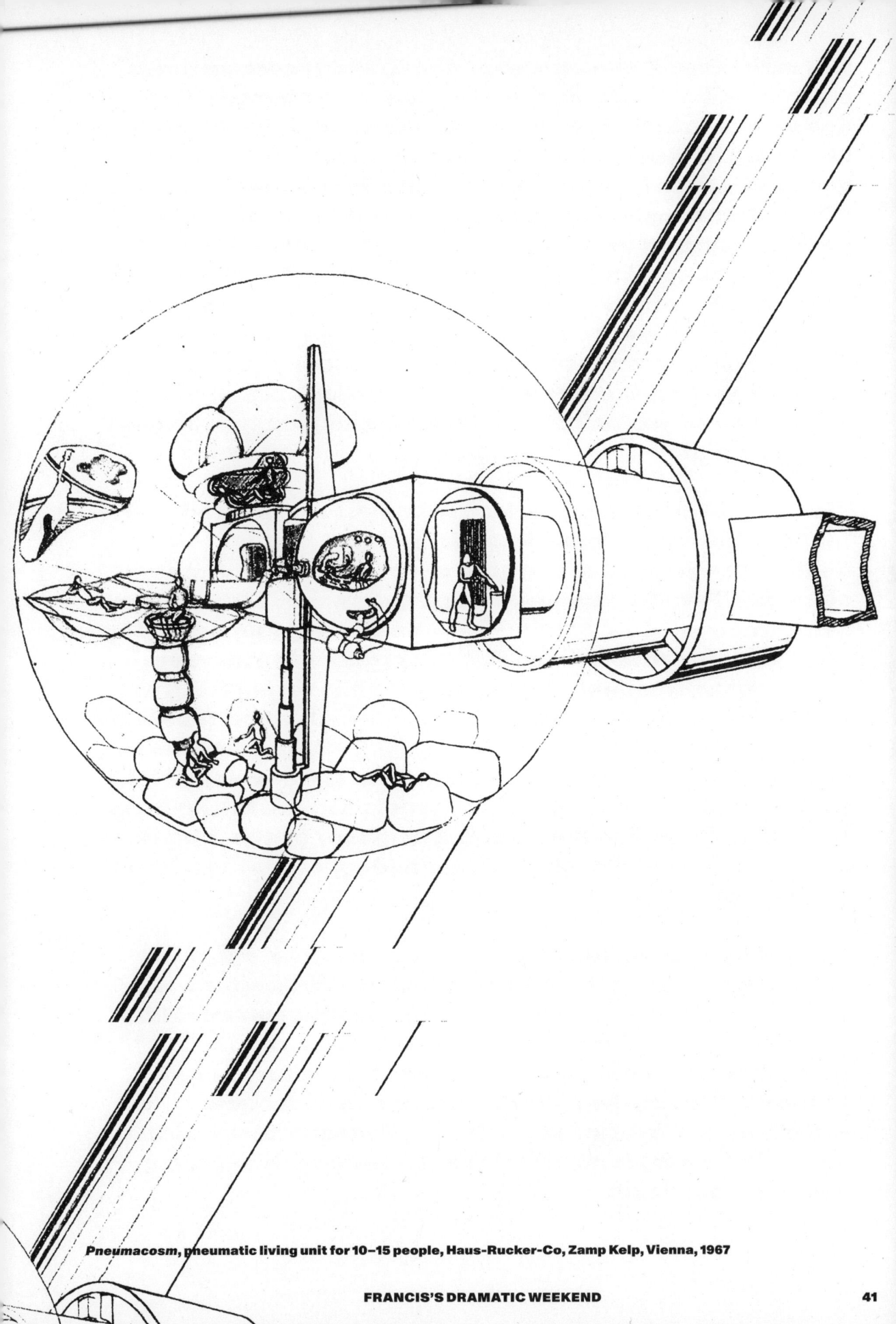

Pneumacosm, pneumatic living unit for 10–15 people, Haus-Rucker-Co, Zamp Kelp, Vienna, 1967

trip to the Caribbean. However, these are uncertain times and terrorist attacks cannot be ruled out anywhere. So he decided to stay in town and take an artificial minibreak instead. A device for this purpose has existed for a while now, and can be found in many private apartments. The "Traveller" consists of a collapsible, spherical air-supported room that functions as a temporary extension of an apartment's spatial realities. The "Traveller" protrudes from one of the apartment windows into the open space in front of the façade. Recently, the temporary use of open urban spaces by private individuals has been made legal, so on weekends, the streetscape in residential areas is animated by a profusion of spherical structures hovering in front of buildings.

This is also the case this Friday evening. Francis prepares for his trip in the balloon. Since it is winter, he slips into a boiler suit equipped with a network of sensors and heating elements. Francis's balloon has already expanded out of the living-room window as he sits downs on a seat supported by an articulated robotic arm. Francis presses the start button on the control module. The seat moves him through the window and out into the center of the spherical space. Inside the balloon, the air is enriched with oxygen, making him feel as if he were somewhere in the mountains. The envelope of the sphere is still transparent, and Francis can see the lights in the buildings across the street. A neighbor on the third floor across the street closes a window and switches the windowpane to opaque.

Francis briefly considers which experience category he should choose. He glances at the control module for a few seconds and then types in the categories "communication" and "adventure." After he presses the enter key, the initially transparent outer shell of the sphere slowly turns black. At the same time, the air he breathes fills with a scent reminiscent of exotic herbs. The two transmitters inside his auditory canals now emit the monotonously soothing sound of heavy rain.

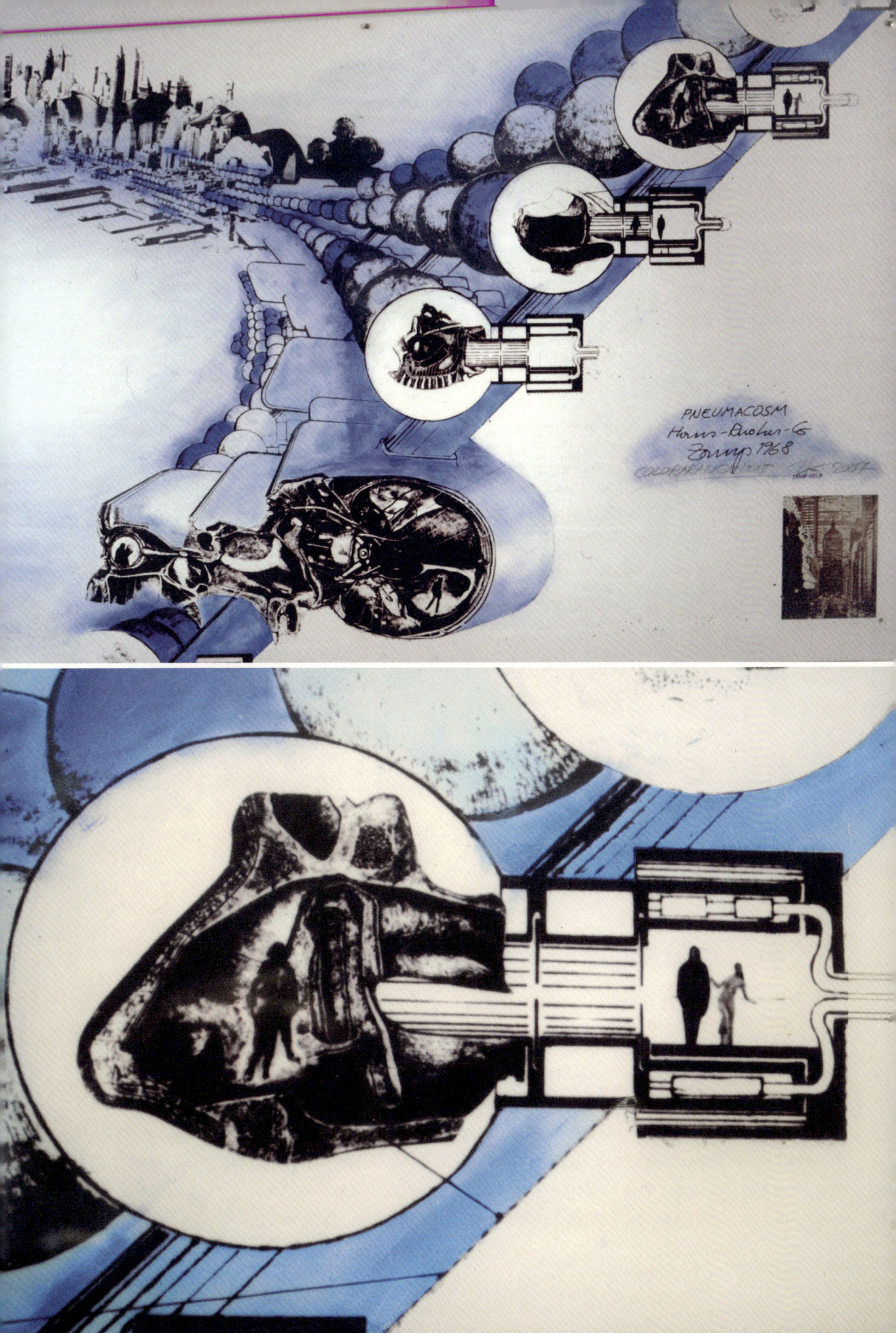

Although he is alone in the center of the balloon, Francis has the feeling that there is another person next to him whom he cannot identify at first. Only after a while does he realize that it must be a female movie star from the 1980s. After the scenery in the balloon begins to resemble a tropical forest, he concludes that he may have entered the real-life simulation of an almost two-hundred-year-old movie and is now

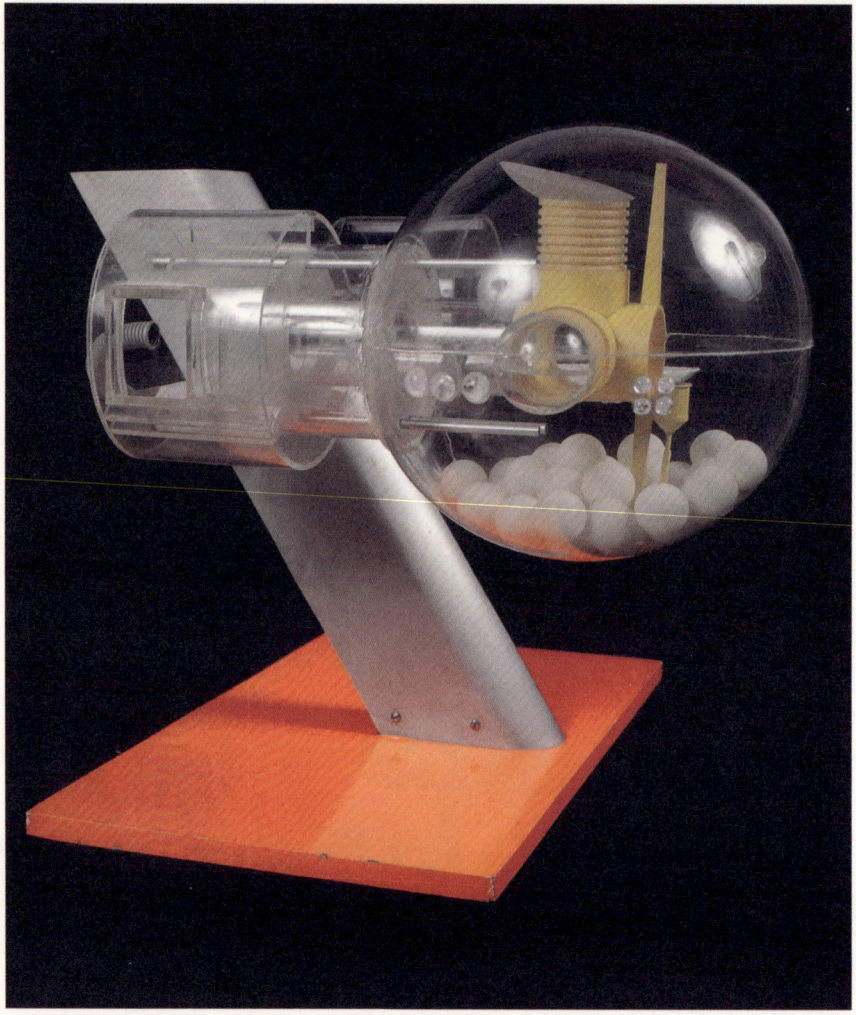

Pneumacosm, model 1:50, Haus-Rucker-Co, Vienna, 1967

himself beginning to act the part of the male lead from those days. He vaguely remembers watching the movie on a flight from Vancouver to Amsterdam and that it was an audacious encounter between a female and a male character who were hunting a precious stone. But before long, the story takes hold of him and he fully surrenders to the intensity of the events he himself is to help determine.

Skin: The Medium of Surface

In Issue 21 of *Isaac Asimov's Science Fiction Magazine*, Elizabeth A. Lynn tells the story of Illis, a young boy who accidentally catches on fire and burns large areas of his skin. Jana, his mother, happens to work in a research lab that studies the cultivation of artificial skin cells and applies this study to the boy with minimal success. His immune system quickly rejects the implants the doctors give him. Jana does not relent—she fights for her son's life with brute force, beginning to research the archives of the institute. However, one night she dreams about Illis turning into a shiny silver fish that she then swallows up. The fish, Illis, swims through her stomach, before she gives birth to him again. When Jana awakens, she becomes motivated by her dream and hunts down a silver liquid that's manufactured in the laboratory. It is based on fish scales and composed of proteins similar to those of human skin recently produced in a colleague's experiment. After successfully testing the liquid on her own forearm, she paints the skinless body of her son, whereupon he speedily recovers, gleaming with his scaly, hairless, and delicately speckled new skin, reminiscent to that of an eel.

1964 Being back in Vienna means we are back in Europe. For the first few days, the city seems slightly restrictive. I miss the colorfulness of American roads with their insistent advertisements. After three weeks in the US, the European population density and the old continent's confined, very serious-looking geographical space conditions need some getting used to. The scale is simply smaller, regardless of how spacious I still find Vienna's layout to be. In hindsight, one may say that we experienced the East Coast of the United States of America at its developmental peak. President Kennedy had started to support culture and academics, especially universities: hence, in 1964, we were able to sense how luxurious the features of these institutions were for that time. Another impressive aspect was experiencing the distances between the metropolises we visited and subsequently, the wealth of space and landscapes. We were also impressed by the inherently optimistic kindness of the people we talked to.

Isaac Asimov's Science Fiction Magazin, issue 21, Friedel Wahren (ed.), 1984

1965 One of the project themes for Design 2 is the draft of an architecture school: a task that will be advertised as an international student contest on occasion of the upcoming International Union of Architects (*Union internationale des Architectes*, UIA) congress in Paris in April. Five students from our university will contribute to the tendered procedure, which will be judged internally first. I am developing my project for the natural reserve Spatzenberg, located near Linz where the Danube breaks through the foothills of the Bohemian Massif, as a symbolic landmark that will seem to be floating above the city. Of course, I had seen Hans Hollein's study on "Communication Interchange" and was particularly amazed and inspired by the effect of this building's symmetry. In my symmetrical design, however, I stick to other atmospheric and graphic principles. While Hollein's *Interchanger* reminds me more of a South American cult building from the time of the Inca or Maya civilizations, I am creating my Architecture Trainer, as I call the draft, in the form of organic analogies followed by ideas on function, surface, and construction. The design convinces the internal jury and I receive one of the two prizes. My work is

This story of skin, written around 1980, combines poetry and utopia with a great deal of optimism. In today's world, researchers are asking similar questions to the ones posed by Lynn; they are gradually working step by step on the development of organic skin surfaces. Scientists worldwide are probing new methods of human skin production. The key technology in these kinds of processes is Inkjet or laser-based printing technology, which has only recently been developed and is being used in an increasing number of fields. This inspired a group at Harvard to develop a special organic "ink"—consisting of cells, enzymes, gelatin, blood vessels, and other ingredients—that forms skin fragments that are as thick as a finger and that stay alive for several weeks. It could only be a matter of time before printed-skin implants are used in reproductive medicine, and the utopian "fish skin drama" becomes an everyday reality in healing processes.

Human skin has long been considered as purely a protection mechanism against extrinsic impact. Only later was it acknowledged to be a complex, multilayered organ, without which the underlying organism is not viable. It weighs around twenty pounds, covering a surface of two square meters, and is an essential part of the human metabolism. At the same time, it is the organ responsible for the sense of touch, which transmits

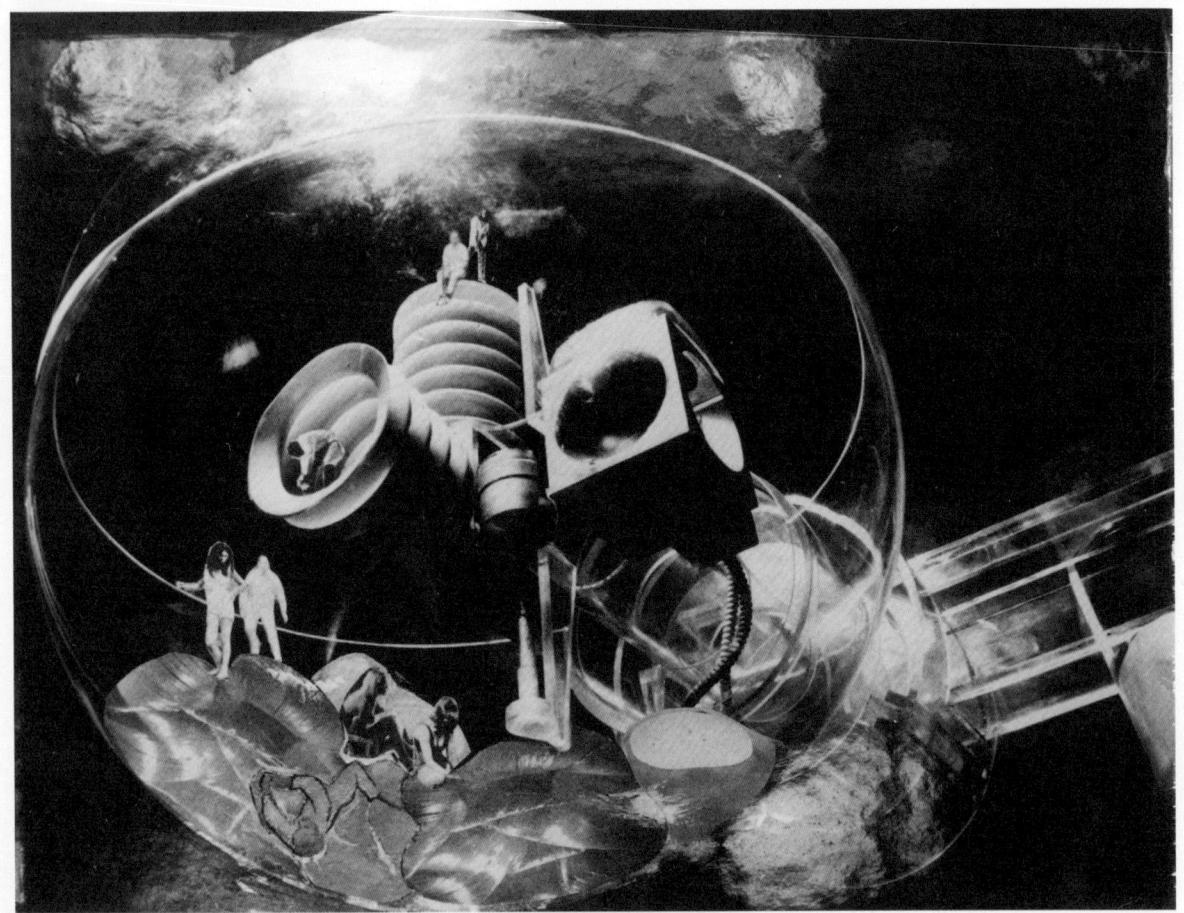

Pneumacosm, interior setting, montage, Haus-Rucker-Co, Zamp Kelp, 1968

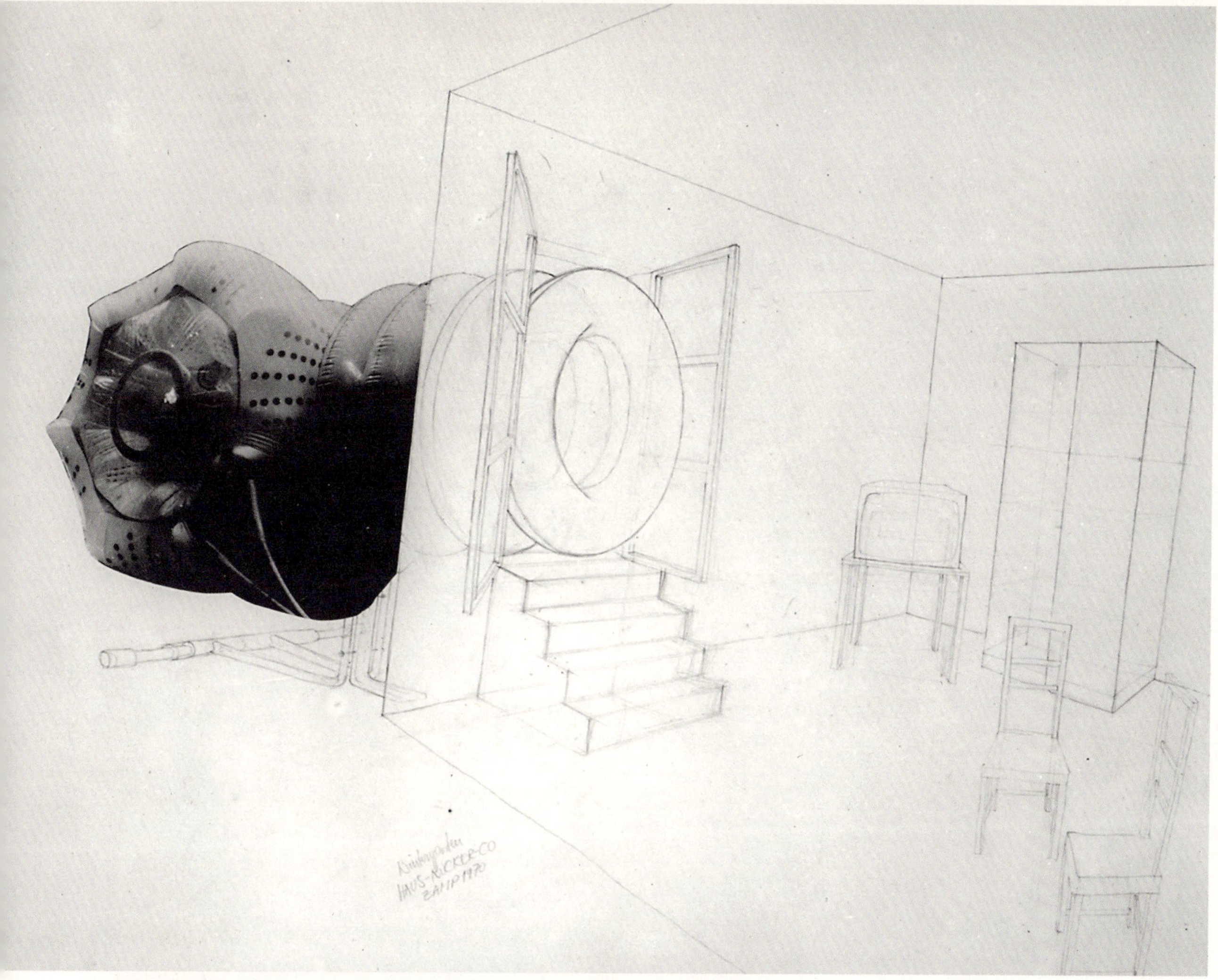

Yellow Heart, collage, Haus-Rucker-Co, Zamp Kelp, Düsseldorf, 1970

sent to Paris to participate in the international phase of the contest. Naturally, I participate in the excursion to Paris. During the afternoons, I work with Laurids Ortner and Helmut Grasberger in Günther Feuerstein's office, listening to Bob Dylan's *Highway 61 Revisited*.

Yellow Heart at a construction pit, Ringstrasse, Vienna, 1968

SKIN: THE MEDIUM OF SURFACE

Zero-Gravity-Heart, mixing technique, Post-Haus-Rucker, Zamp Kelp, Berlin, 2012

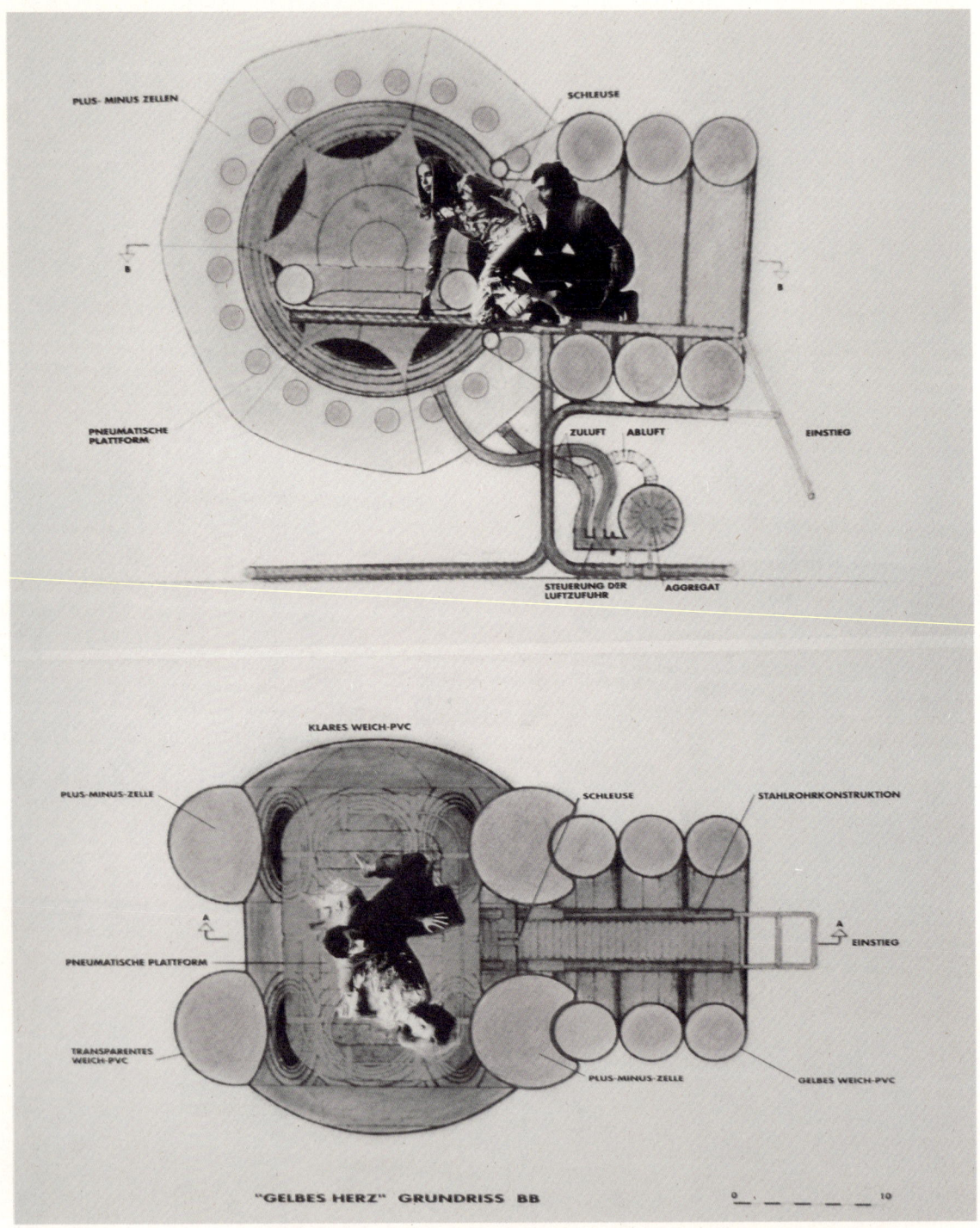

Yellow Heart, section and plan, Haus-Rucker-Co, Laurids Ortner, Zamp Kelp, Klaus Pinter, Vienna, 1968

Design-Post, stand for Austrian Institute of Design ÖIF, Trade Fair Vienna, Haus-Rucker-Co, Laurids Ortner, Zamp Kelp, Klaus Pinter, Vienna, 1969

Architecture Sling, 1966

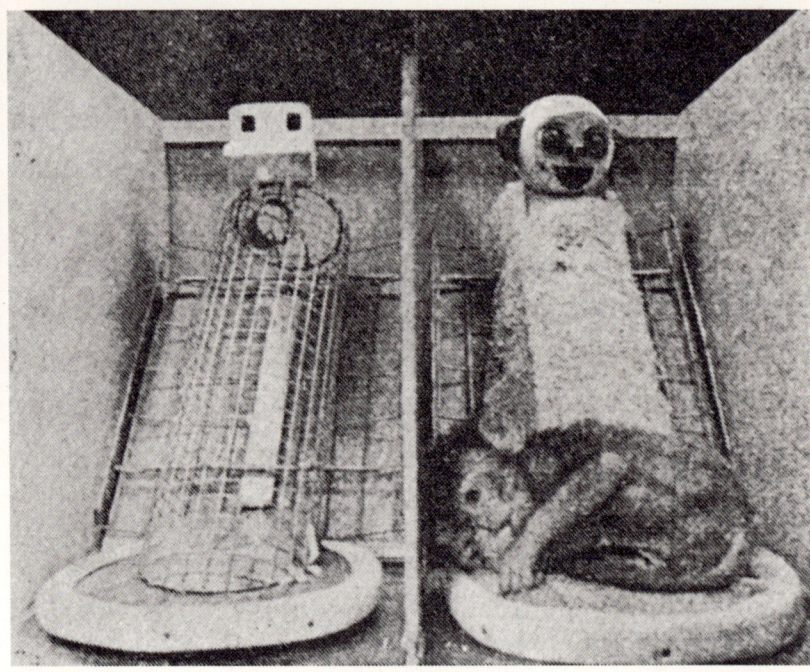

Nature of Love, experiment for the perception of surface, Harry S. Harlow, USA, 1959

1966 Initiated by Günther Feuerstein, Urban Fiction is taking place on the premises of the Galerie Nächst St. Florian in Vienna. Günther Feuerstein, Hans Hollein, Walter Pichler, the partnership Domenig & Huth, Raimund Abraham, Friedrich St. Florian, and others are participating. I had previously developed the *Architecture Sling*, and Laurids Ortner is here with his *City 47*. The *Architecture Sling* is a rotating, triangular construct composed of six mirror surfaces mounted on a piano stool. Using a Kodak carousel projector, slides of buildings and motifs from everyday life in Vienna are projected onto the rotating mirrors. One sunny afternoon, prior to finishing the piece, I was out with Gerd Winkler, a man with great photographic ambitions. We were walking through the Vienna Naschmarkt, the city's most popular outdoor market, and he took photos on a 35mm camera of everything offered at the market, and later of buildings around the area. The selection of eighty slides was then lined up in a tray and can now, whenever the *Architecture Sling* is activated, successively and in fifteen-second intervals be projected onto the reflecting rotating prism. The prism projects the image fragments onto two or three walls of the room, where they move along horizontally, slightly above eye level. For this purpose, sentences were documented on tape during one sociable evening in Edith Ortner's apartment on Gilgegasse—phrases like, "Only choose laser-based architecture ... whoosh, a house flew past and what did I do? I jumped ... Zamp Kelp just went outside and probably took his architecture spirit with him ... New houses will carry catapult towers and people will ask: who lived there? ... Images drift like in the stream of time. The eye follows, the body stays. ..." These sentences are played in a loop as an acoustic and musical backdrop while the object itself is in action.

information on temperature, pain, or tangibility to our center for perception, the brain. The skin is a pivotal element in communicative processes with our environment—for instance, in making emotions visible. It is part of the external appearance of a person when being perceived by others.

The importance of the surface and how humans and animals perceive it has been demonstrated in an experiment by the American psychologist Harry F. Harlow in 1958. Over the course of three years, Harlow confronted newborn baby macaques with two artificial mothers—one made of wire and one made of cloth. Taking turns, the baby monkeys received their food in close proximity to their cloth mother or wire mother. When stimulated by fear, the newborns exclusively sought refuge with the cloth mother, attempting to seek protection and shelter on her soft, furry, cloth surface. The experiment highlights the importance of touch as opposed to the visual.

However, in its function as a surface, the skin isn't an essential element for identification and appearance for humans and animals alone. Surfaces play a decisive role in the perception of the natural and artificial sceneries that make up our world as well. Objectivity always appears in spatial constellations. Space, on the other hand, is either completely or partially limited by surfaces. In his essay "The Principle of Cladding," Adolf Loos writes:

> "The architect's general task is to provide a warm and livable space. Carpets are warm and livable. He decides for this reason to spread out one carpet on the floor and to

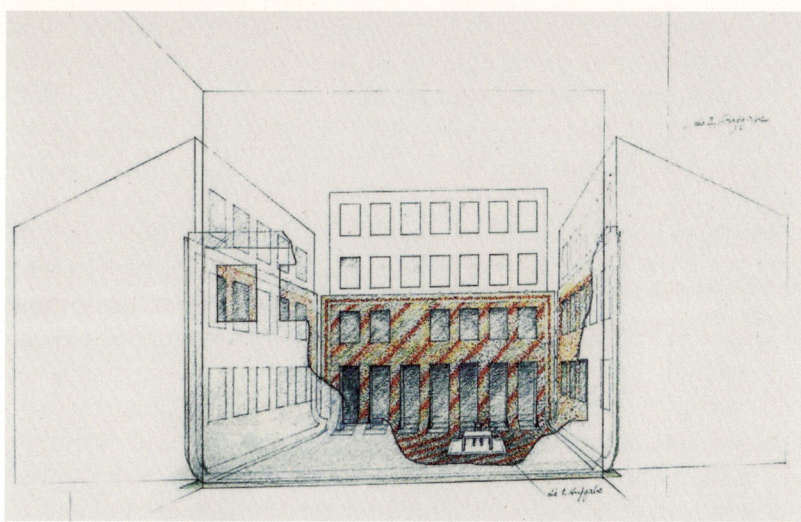

Construction and Surface, the second task of the architect according to Adolf Loos, drawing, Haus-Rucker-Co, Zamp Kelp, Düsseldorf, 1975

1966 I attempt to complete the second state-wide exam by the end of the year in order to finish my studies. Before the week-long test comes to an end, Karl Schwanzer swings by to set the task and to review my design of a school building before he travels to Montreal. There he will supervise the Austrian contribution to the World's Fair. He seemed to like the sculptural quality of my designed school—he had no objections at least—and I finish the work with a positive feeling. When the evaluation of the exams is published however, I realize, in dismay, that I did not pass. Later I am told that Schwanzer had absently marked the project as "excellent," but the nonuniversity judge had declared the light fields, vertically arranged for artistic reasons, unsuitable for classroom lighting in an academic context and insisted on my repeating the examination.

Balloon for 2, air-supported construction, Haus-Rucker-Co, Laurids Ortner, Zamp Kelp, Klaus Pinter, Vienna, 1967

1967 My studies end in March with the repetition of the second state exam and the reception of my diploma. I rent an attic atelier on Spengergasse 56 in Vienna's fifth district, overlooking the bed of the Wien River and the roofscape of the sixth and seventh district. In June, I land a job as an assistant at the Institute of Architecture and Design, an institute where I had worked as a tutor in the past.

1967 In the fall, Laurids-Zamp-Pinter, i.e., Laurids Ortner, Günter Zamp Kelp, and Klaus Pinter, found the architects-and-artists group Haus-Rucker-Co. We stay in my attic atelier on Spengergasse 56. Prior to the formation, two projects were developed in spring, which we submit to the Interdesign 2000 contest in Bavaria: *Mindexpander 1* and *Pneumacosm*. They are part of the *Mindexpanding Program* that Haus-Rucker-Co is starting to work on.

hang up four to form the four walls. But you cannot build a house out of carpets. Both the carpet on the floor and the tapestry on the wall require a structural frame to hold them in the correct place. To invent this frame is the architect's second task."

In his 2015 credo, Günther Feuerstein talks about "pneuma," the breath, as a God-given power. In Hinduism, it is a fifth element, along with fire, water, air, and earth, while in Christianity, most regard it as the spirit, identical to the air and mind. Religion as a construct is based on human consciousness or—in the sense of religious conviction—on faith, therefore on a material and immaterial quality. The air's oxygen provides the requirements for human thought and perception, and is thus a constructive element for the faith, awareness, and productivity of our minds. Air itself remains a prerequisite for the existence of terrestrial life and is both the structural and fundamental element for creating spaces with skin.

From 1967 to 1972, Haus-Rucker-Co used "pneuma" as the constructive principle of airborne constructions in general and of manufactured skins. In Vienna in 1967, there were several constellations of architects and artists who dealt with "pneuma" as a constructive medium. Initially, the question was, which group would first manage to place humans inside a vessel of airborne skin.

Bedroom of my Wife, whitewash, white curtains, white angora fur, Adolf Loos, 1903

In the end, Haus-Rucker-Co achieved this in November of that year with *Balloon for 2* in the Apollogasse of Vienna's 7th district. There were several factors that made this event noteworthy: 1. They used the window on the first floor of a *Gründerzeit* building as the location for the event. 2. The campaign consisted of various similar subevents, taking place hourly between two and six p.m. on a cloudy day. 3. The event was initially all about

1967 The first project we go public with after founding Haus-Rucker-Co is the *Balloon for 2*. Before its implementation, there are, of course, fundamental considerations for how the *Mindexpanding Program* could be further developed. It quickly becomes clear that it would be about airborne, interactive pieces that deal with space. Whether the planned object will be presented in a gallery, our own atelier, or out in the urban space is another item on the agenda. It takes a while until the object has been discussed conceptually from interior to urban space. Then the plans for its implementation can begin. However, before we can start, we have to decide on a location—which becomes Apollogasse 3 in the seventh district, in Ed Schulz's studio. First, we have to measure the window opening through which we want to push the balloon, its relation to the studio's floor and ceiling, and its position on the outside wall. Afterwards, the construction drawings for the mounted, moveable steel tube frame and balloon are created and discussed with the scaffolding rental company. They tell us that they can deliver the necessary pieces, but that we would have to assemble the construction ourselves. We adjust the balloon skin to fit the steel-tube construction and tattoo the surface with dynamic lines of force using colored, reflective tape. On a Monday in November, the *Balloon for 2* is officially presented and pushed out of the studio window on the second floor of the *Gründerzeit* building: inside sit a man and a woman, as the balloon fully expands with the help of a blower. The fact that this is happening in Apollogasse is rather coincidental, but nonetheless indicates a certain connection to the National Aeronautics and Space Administration's Apollo program, which is currently being developed and attracting lots of media attention. The situational stress that arises from the interplay of everyday life and intervention is important to us.

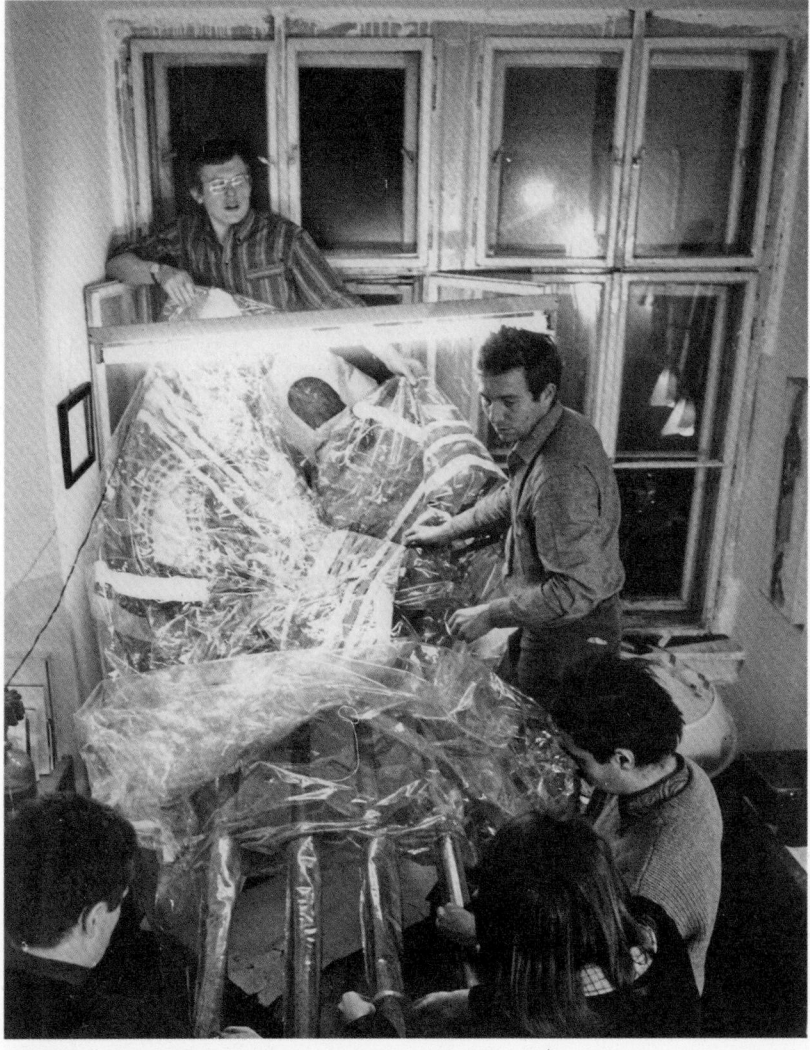

Balloon for 2, indoor preparation, Vienna, 1967

pushing the air-deprived skin object out of the building and into the urban open space in front of the façade, where it unfolded into a spherical shape of 3.5 meters in diameter by means of mechanically filling it with air. 4. The two people sitting in the heart of the ball-shaped balloon had a surreal experience for several moments before the balloon lost its "pneuma" and disappeared in the open window of the house once more.

The object affected the perception of the urbanites in two ways. To begin with, there were the "balloonists," who embarked on the adventure of perceiving the city from a vastly different per-

SKIN: THE MEDIUM OF SURFACE

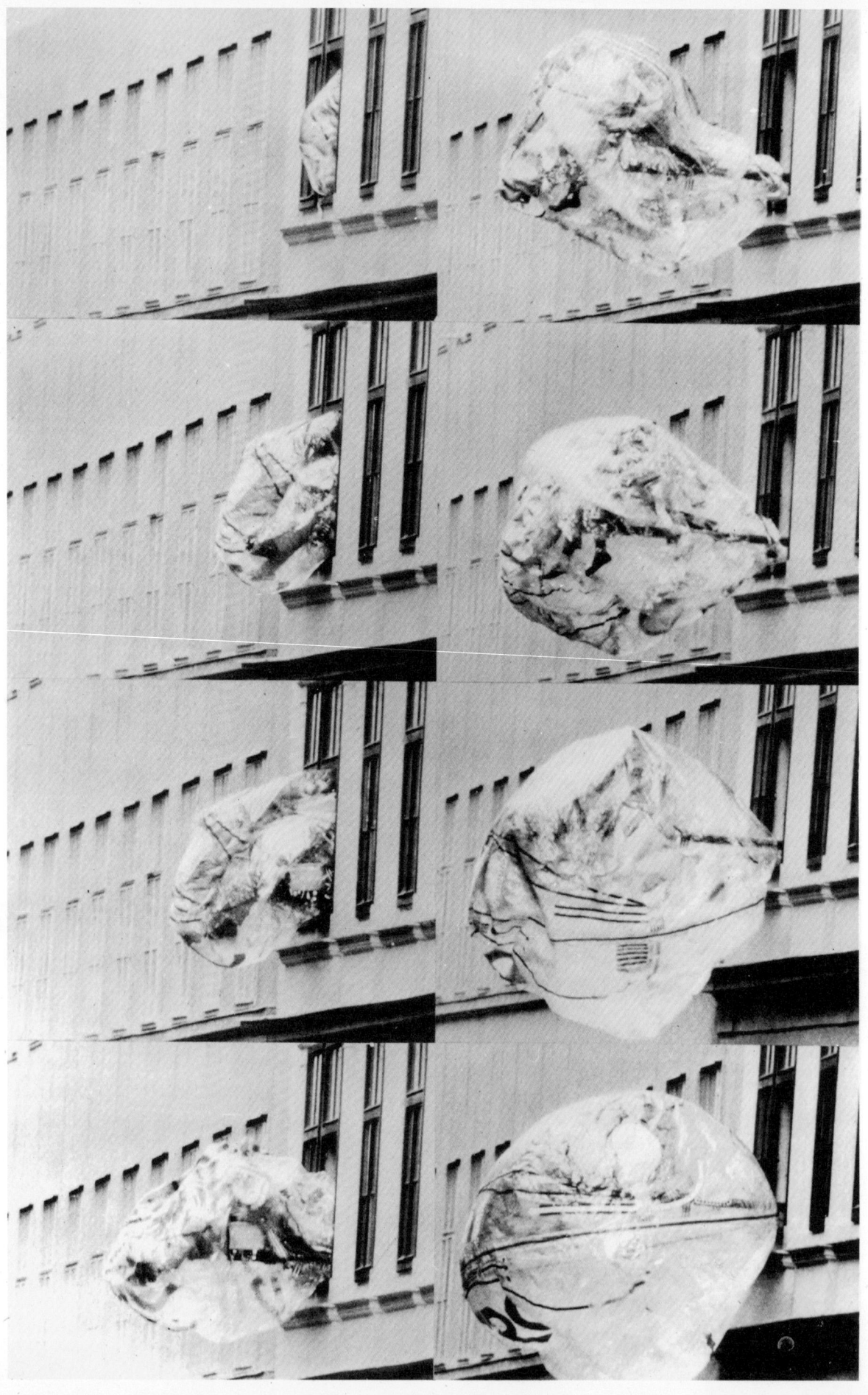

Opposite page:
Balloon for 2, sequences of unfolding, Haus-Rucker-Co, Laurids Ortner, Zamp Kelp, Klaus Pinter, Vienna, 1967

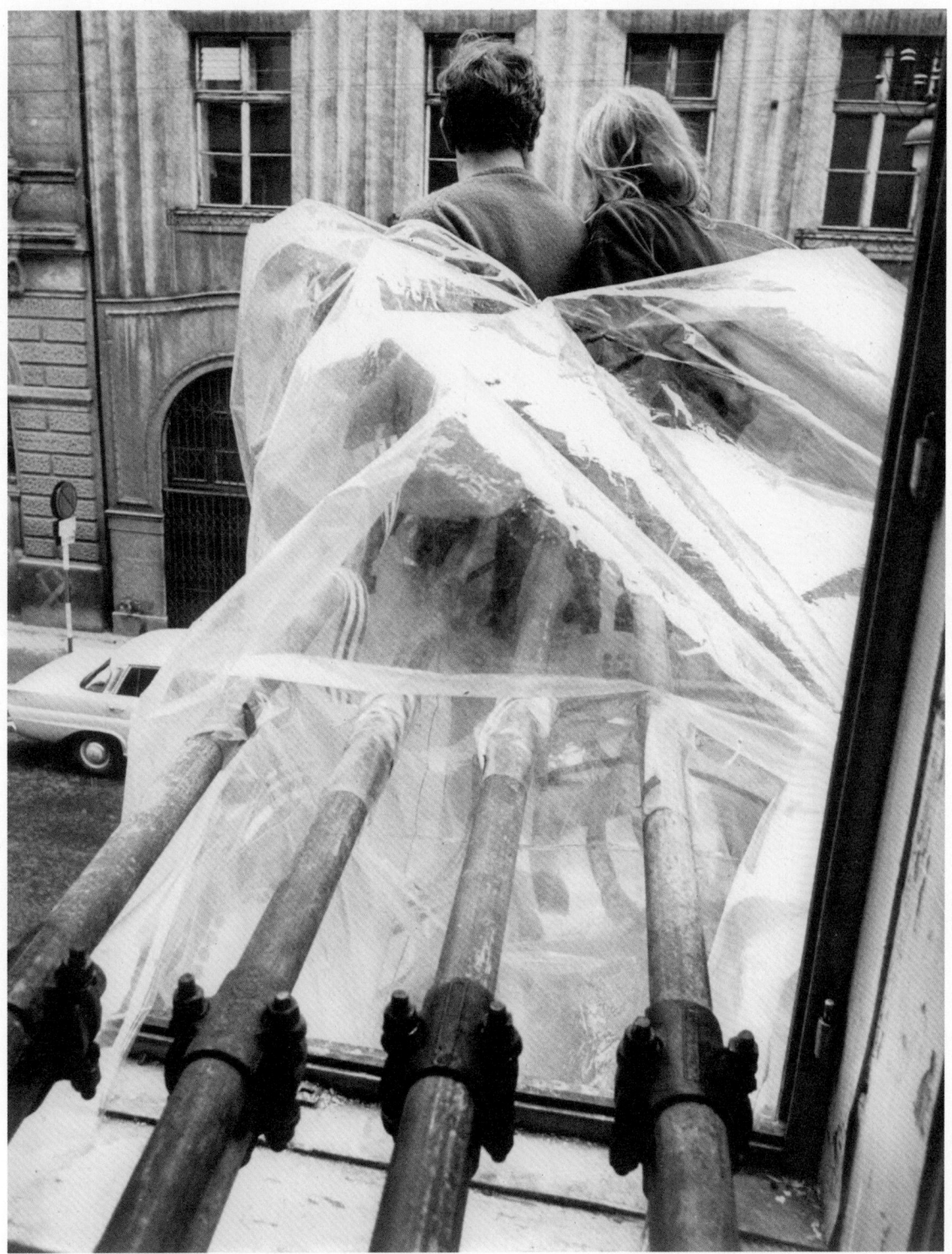

Balloon for 2, ready to be pulled back inside, Vienna, 1967

Connexionskin

1967 After dismantling the *Balloon for 2*, it is reconstructed and expanded into the so-called *Connexionskin*. The ball contains a cylindrically shaped annex that can be accessed via a crawl space. One fair day, we take the *Connexionskin*, Katrin Sarnitz, and the photographer Horst Wiedemann, who had arrived from Paris, and go to the Prater park to take pictures. Wiedmann positions the woman inside the larger balloon ball and the man inside the likewise airborne extension and takes several photos with his 6 × 6 Hasselblad. Later, Wiedemann takes a few photos of the skin's dismantling and transport as it is carried on the shoulders of one of its creators.

***Balloon for 2*, Apollogasse by night, Vienna, 1967**

spective. They inhaled, breathed the construction, and saw the local urban space through the transparent foil of the airborne balloon skin. They felt as if they were floating at the center of the balloon. This was made possible by a steel-tube construction that stabilized them from the inside. The colorful lines of the support and surfaces of the transparent balloon skin made the ball shape strongly visible. They simultaneously interfered with the perception of the urban surfaces in the surroundings and used this to irritate the viewing habits of the occupants. Passersby, who were perhaps out shopping or strolling around the Apollogasse for other reasons, were probably no less surprised by the appearance that thwarted the gray colors of the building's façade. Maybe they recognized the two people sitting inside the balloon. Maybe one of them waved from inside the balloon and someone from the street waved back. Some just shook their heads and walked on. Others looked out of their open windows, watching.

Tools of Perception

Fly Head / Environment Transformer, Haus-Rucker-Co, Laurids Ortner, Zamp Kelp, Klaus Pinter, Vienna, 1968

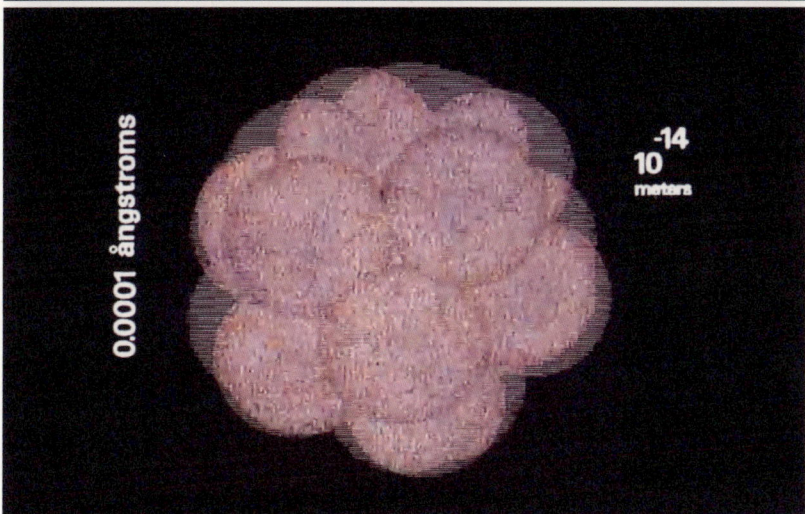

Powers of Ten, Charles and Ray Eames, final version, 1977 (9 minutes)

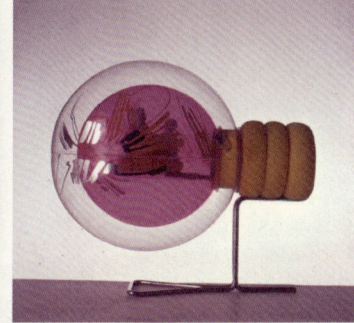

Yellow Heart, model

1967 With all the experience we have gained so far, we are now envisioning a more complex, expansive task: a space that breaths and is able to shrink and grow in a rhythm related to time. A first draft of the object that we will come to call *Yellow Heart* is drawn up during a conversation over lunch. The reference is to the first-ever heart transplant carried out by Christiaan Barnard in Cape Town, which fits this time frame. We build a model and, on a simple tire with dimensions of around 2×3×4, test how specialized colors can permanently be applied to PVC-foils. We give this prototype the working title *Livingroom in Room*. We take this model to the Vienna park Schweizergarten to present it to Werner Hofmann, the former director of the Museum of the 20th Century. Hofmann agrees to the sum required for building the object, provided that we hand over the model to the museum's collection—not a problem for us.

Living room in Room

Scientists use curiosity's spark to pursue the riddles of human existence in outer space. That spark drives them to explore the cosmic geography that is all around us. We do this in preparation for the moment when the growing number of humans creates unhabitable conditions on Earth, forcing us to find alternative living spaces. Since 1990, the Hubble Space Telescope has been orbiting Earth at 7.5 km per second at an altitude of 560, exploring objects and phenomena of the universe. Parallel to the Hubble, the Kepler space telescope went into operation in 2009 with the task of looking for extrasolar planets.

In 1977, Charles and Ray Eames wrote and directed a short film titled *Powers of Ten: A Film Dealing with the Relative Size of Things in the Universe and the Effect of Adding Another Zero*. In it, a tracking shot measures the universe from the microcosm of quarks to the macrocosm of quasars. Beginning with a picnic situation on Chicago's lakeside, the camera moves away towards space with a growing, square field of view, starting with a field of one meter. At first, Earth is depicted as a blue planet, only to

Environment Transformers: Fly Head, Viewatomizer, Drizzler, Haus-Rucker-Co, Laurids Ortner, Zamp Kelp, Klaus Pinter, Vienna, 1968

Environment Transformers, super-drawing, Zamp Kelp, 2017

disappear as a little dot in the vastness of the galaxies. Once the camera reaches the border between the unexplored and explored part of space, a reversal begins. The Earth reappears, the camera focuses on the lakeside meadow, and then enters the microcosm of the human body through the hand of the man sleeping on the picnic blanket. The clip documents these two fields of research in order to explain the connection of our existence.

Between these two extreme directions of exploratory perception stands the *Frame Building* of 1977, released the same year as *Powers of Ten*. The construction, with similar but fixed aspect ratios as the flying field of view in Charles and Ray Eames's clip, contrasts with the time-based frame gliding through space in the film's shots. The *Frame Building* has a static character. In the city of Kassel, it is a permanently installed tool to perceive landscapes, and acts as a border-creating space between the Friedrichsplatz to the Aue and the Orangerie.

Our senses, which have been sharpened by the perils of our environment throughout the course of evolution, now have new tasks in many parts of our habitat that are characterized by artificiality. The currently fluent and rapid change of environmental influences leads to stress and subsequently, to the flattening of everyday perception, resulting in the partial withdrawal of many contemporaries from ordinary life. At least, this was the conceptional assumption leading to the creation of the *Environment Transformers* series in Vienna in 1968: *Flyhead*,

1968 The first steps to realizing the *Yellow Heart* involve preparing construction plans, resolving the synergy between the steel-tube tripod and the tire components, as well as creating the plans for the metalworker and the manufacturing of foil parts. We decide on mainly yellow and orange radial dot patterns to foil segments before they are welded together to become the pulsating, pneumatic capsule. Along with the *Yellow Heart*, we create the *Electricskins* and *Environment Transformers*, which are photographed and documented during several campaigns for public relations.

Klaus Pinter, Laurids Ortner, and Zamp Kelp (from left) with *Environment Transformers* on Kärntnerstrasse, Vienna, 1968

TOOLS OF PERCEPTION

1968 The *Yellow Heart* is assembled for the first time in the foundation pit of the police headquarters, though the reference to the police does not play any conceptual role. Rather, it is the location on the Vienna ring road that evokes fascination. Walter Pichler and Heinz Frank also appear for the presentation. A guest drives his hydraulically suspended Citroën DS to the floor of the pit and parks the car at a respectful distance to the object. In general, the situation lives off of the foundation pit's impressive dimension and, in contrast, the seemingly miniaturized *Yellow Heart* that is thus showcased in its dominant yellow color.

View Atomizer, and *Drizzler* served as audiovisual filters, altering the environment of those wearing them. The fragmentation of the wearer's sensory impressions was realized in three different variations, aimed at initiating new perspectives and a new understanding of their surroundings.

Flyhead and its shape refer to the compound eyes of insects. When putting on the helmet, the wearer's atmosphere is fragmented by glass prisms before their eyes.

View Atomizer creates visual irritation through a colored lenticular air cushion, which is connected to a bellows by means of a tube. By activating the bellows, the gaps between the polyvinyl chloride blades of the lens change. Lines and dots on the outer lamellae withdraw and near the eyes of the user and thus distort the wearer's vision.

Laurids Ortner, Zamp Kelp, and Klaus Pinter with *Environment Transformers* at Wienfluss, Vienna, 1968

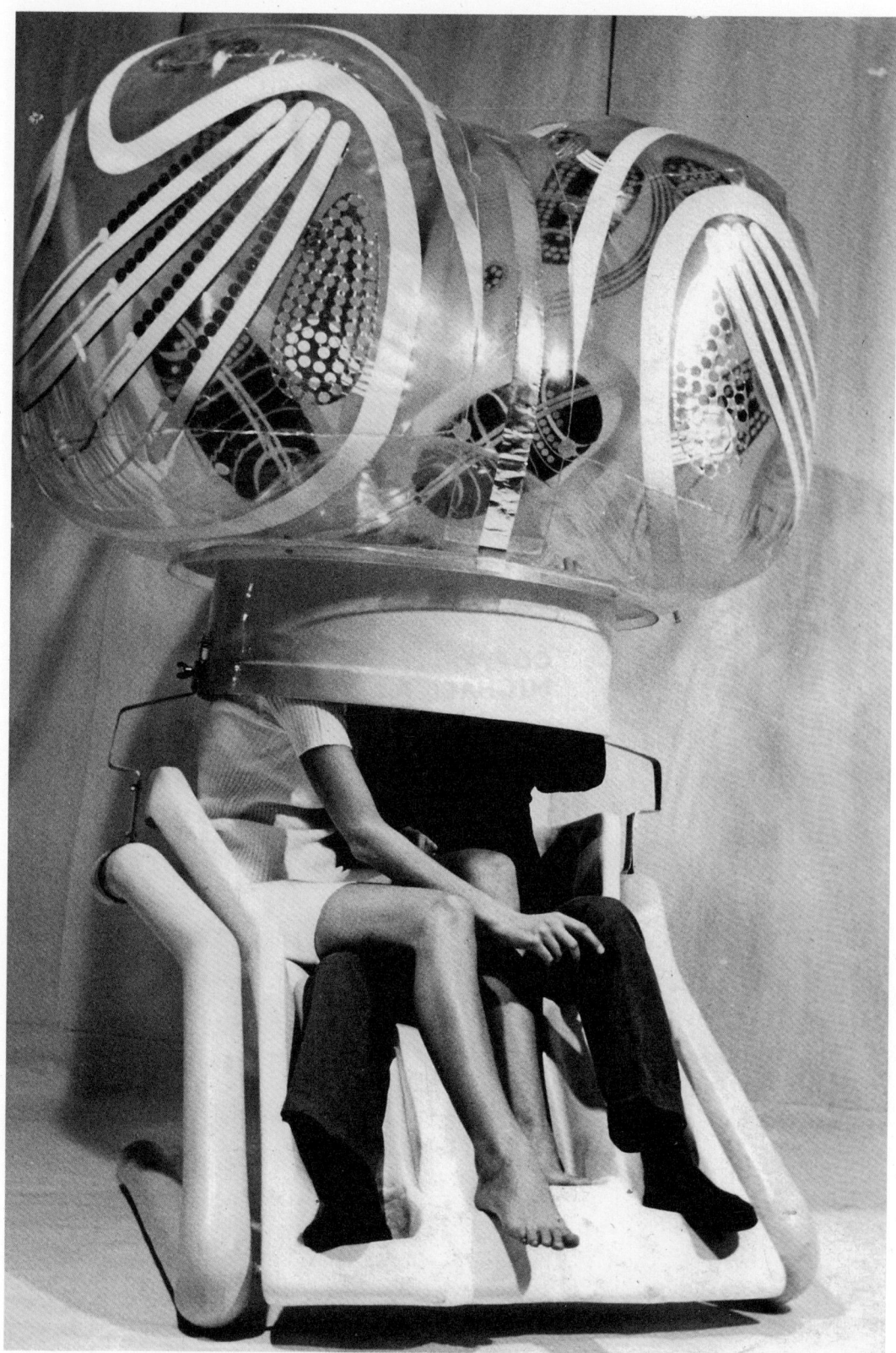
Mindexpander 1, Haus-Rucker-Co, Vienna, 1967

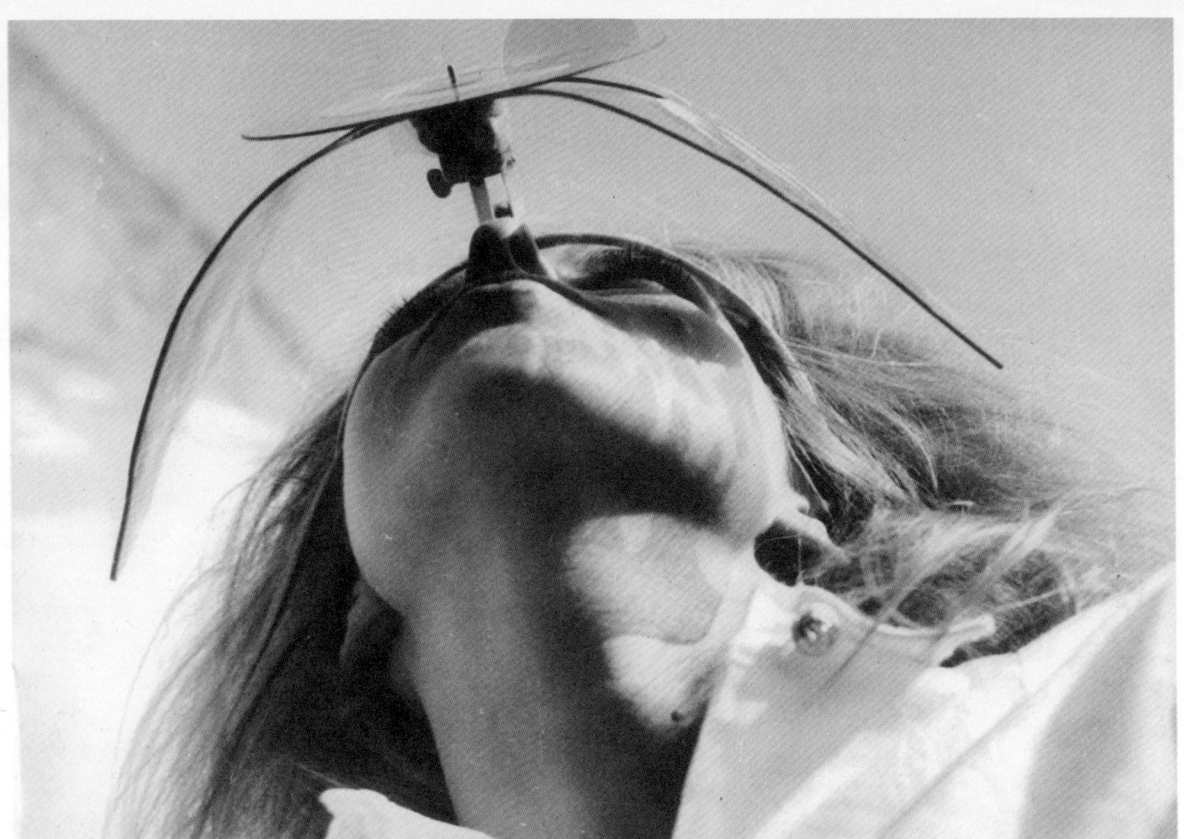

Drizzler, dividing the sky in moments, Haus-Rucker-Co, Laurids Ortner, Zamp Kelp, Klaus Pinter, Vienna, 1968

1968 Working as academic chairman, I deal with scientific research, designing and producing an annual catalog, and taking care of administrative procedures. To bring some variety to these duties, I begin preparing an excursion to the Netherlands and London. In May, a group of around fifteen participants in two VW buses sets off for Amsterdam. Götz Hagmüller participates as a further assistant of the institute. For the trip, he generously provides and drives his own minivan. The second bus, driven by me most of the time, is being borrowed from the university students. We travel through Heidelberg and Düsseldorf, where we visit the Dreischeibenhaus, a high-rise building that was then known as Phoenix-Rheinrohr A.G., and continue our journey towards Amsterdam. Upon arrival, we visit the van den Broeck and Bakema office. Jaap Bakema offers an overview of their work and recommends buildings that we should see. Among others, we study those of the Amsterdam School, including the "Het Ship" and the orphanage by Aldo van Eyck. We arrive in Rotterdam via Delft and Eindhoven to visit the Van Nelle factory by Leendert van der Vlugt, a building that enraptured Le Corbusier who, in 1932, called it "the most beautiful spectacle of the modern age."

The third *Environment Transformer*, *Drizzler*, works electromechanically. A motor causes a mounted plate, transparent at one end of its periphery, to rotate at the center in front of the field of view. The transparent spot on the plate fragments the field of view into a visual staccato, similar to a stroboscope, in which the environment is perceived for a split second before disappearing again.

The visual alienation effect of all three helmets is complemented by a controllable device that distorts the background noises in the surrounding space.

The *Environment Transformers* aimed at questioning ingrained reflexes and habits, while generating the potentials within the user's consciousness in a way that allowed a rethinking of the perspectives of the cultural landscape.

The *Environment Transformers* found their successors in today's virtual reality glasses. They accommodate the critical situation of dismal aspects found in the human spectrum of experiences by creating virtual havens together with computers and PlayStations. These devices, along with portable music devices, temporarily switch off the visual reality of everyday life and open viewpoints into unreal or even utopian spaces of experience. The modern Gullivers and Gullivas travel to a virtual Lilliput,

Nike of Linz, Haus-Rucker-Co, Laurids Ortner, Zamp Kelp, Manfred Ortner, Hauptplatz Linz, 1977

Flying Frame, salute to Charles and Ray Eames, Post-Haus-Rucker, Zamp Kelp, Berlin, 2018

Frame Building, view in direction of Aue, Haus-Rucker-Co, Laurids Ortner, Zamp Kelp, Manfred Ortner, documenta 6, Kassel, 1977

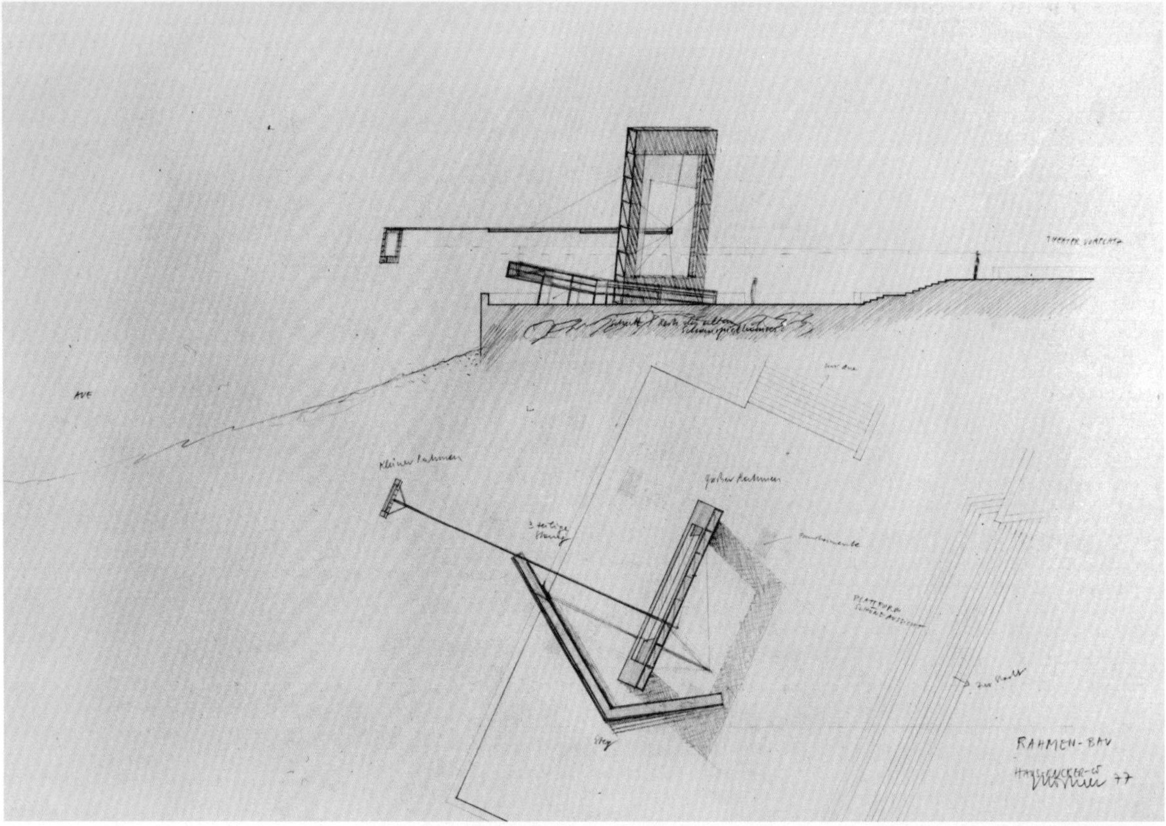

1968 One week later, we set course for Great Britain. We take the overnight ferry from Hoek van Holland to Harwich, whereupon we arrive early in the morning and I am immediately set to task with the obligatory left-hand driving as I dodge an incoming truck while leaving the ferry. In London, we go to see James Stirling, who mainly elaborates on his latest work, a library in Cambridge. While visiting the Architectural Association, we meet Peter Cook, who is clearly delighted by the reopening of the Triennale di Milano. The exhibition titled *Il Grande Numero* had been organized by students and artists and temporarily run. Our plans to visit Stonehenge are quickly scrapped after realizing how far away it is.

1968 In the summer, a letter from New York flutters into the studio. The Museum of Contemporary Crafts in Manhattan, right next to the Museum of Modern Art, is hosting an exhibition titled *Plastic as Plastic*. They ask for *Environment Transformer* and *Electric Skins* to be part of the exhibition, which we agree to. We confirm that we will also come to the opening and immediately begin to procure funds for the trip.

Frame Building elevation and plan (above), view from Aue, documenta 6, Kassel, 1977

where anxiety dreams and a sentimental feeling of joy may liaise closely.

In another work, the collage *Way to Lillyput*, the flow of images is depicted by landscape sceneries that are generated by one another to demonstrate and predict the fragmentation of perceptual processes—an effect that today's global society increasingly has to deal with.

Frame Building, side glance and view from Friedrichsplatz, documenta 6, Kassel, 1977

Way to Lillyput, collage with drawing and brass sticker, Haus-Rucker-Co, Zamp Kelp, Düsseldorf, 1975

Balloon for 2, photomontage
Ant Farm, 1968, Washington

1968 Jim Burns publishes the *Balloon for 2* in *Progressive Architecture*, an American architecture magazine. Three months later, we get a reaction from the West Coast and San Francisco. Ant Farm—a team similar to Haus-Rucker-Co, who will implement the *Cadillac Ranch* several years later—sends material on their current activities. They show the "Crash Festivals" in San Francisco and a photomontage of a gigantic *Balloon for 2* mounted on the dome of the United States Capitol, apparently having taken the photo from the magazine. Doug Michels sends a photo of himself wearing a hat, and Chip Lord adds a few bright sayings. When we inform Ant Farm about our visit to NYC in the fall, they too consider flying to the East Coast to see the exhibition.

Mindexpander 2

Millennium View, Post-Haus-Rucker, Zamp Kelp, 2000

1968 Soon after presenting the *Yellow Heart* in the foundation pit near the Schottenring, the young film director Hermann Jauck approaches us. He intends to make a colored 16mm film about our work. In order to obtain the means for production, Jauck submits an exposé at the Austrian Film Commission and Funds. He procures the needed film material, and the film is shot on a summer weekend in Wieselburg. The main actors are dressed casually in white and put on the first prototype of the *Environment Transformer* helmet, the *Flyhead*. Following the director's script, the two terranauts turn their gaze, and their helmets, to the *Yellow Heart*, walk in a half-circle around the object, and climb into the entrance zone that is composed of three consecutively arranged air-filled tires made of yellow PVC foil. Another sequence is a close-up of the helmeted heads, which, after a while, turn right to face the object. In the coming scenes, the couple advances to the center of the heart, take off their helmets and headphones, and relax on the pneumatic, soft platform inside. Extremely detailed shots of the object are taken both from the inside and outside, and then the film material runs out and the director has enough content for a five- to ten-minute-long movie. Diether S. Hoppe accompanies the event with a Super 8mm camera, also capturing photos of the illuminated object at night. The film is lost during screenings in the US—sadly, without an existing copy. In the fall, Hermann Jauck's movie is finished. Accompanied by music by the band Iron Butterfly, an explanatory text about the object and Elli Foerster's poetic description of experiencing the internal space, the movie is shown as the opening program at the Burg Kino cinema near the Opernring.

Twenty-five years after this collage, the *Millennium View* is created as a decentralized exhibit of the Expo 2000 in Hanover at the edge of a stone quarry in Schaumburg Land, Lower Saxony. A staircase made of stones from the quarry leads up and merges into a steel construction with a viewing platform, encompassed by a series of ten frames made of green glass arranged in a row.

At the top of the platform, visitors find a total view of the Schaumburger landscape and face the ten frames lined up one behind the other. *Millennium View* is untainted by mechanical or projective techniques of a prevailing perception. The ten frames made of glass metaphorically represent the fragmentation of contemporary perception. They portray a concept in which images create spaces, and thus generate new orders in the minds of individuals as they store visual phenomena.

A landmark of great tranquility, visible from afar, the structure lies in the flow of time and denotes the turn of the millennium. As a monument of perception, *Millennium View* provides a wide view to the north and south, as well as a view to the east and west, disrupted by glass frame lamellae.

The global community will have to adapt to the burgeoning of perceptual spaces and possibilities with which it is constantly confronted. The question is whether the diversity of impressions can be made manageable with new perceptual technology. Optimistically, we hope for a development similar to that of train journeys, where passengers have their first view from the wagon window blocked by curtains to counteract the anxiety generated by speed, before gradually grasping the thrilling experience of panoramic perception when traveling from one place to another.

ANNO 2222

Sylvia in

Empire State Building, extended by biolevels, Zamp Kelp, Berlin, 2018

the Dome

Fifty years ago, in 2172, the *Dome over Manhattan* was finally built. Buckminster Fuller's spectacular utopian idea was commissioned and implemented by the City of New York more than two centuries after it was first proposed. By now, every metropolis with a claim to offer a good quality of life had to create a spectacular hot spot in its urban fabric to keep up with worldwide competition. The *Dome* became an instant icon of New York City. Because of its attractiveness, the covered neighborhoods acted like a magnet for all visitors to the USA and it quickly became a place of longing for many Americans and many more world citizens. As a synthetic sanctuary, the enclosed space offers the possibility to simulate the climate of cities from other regions of the globe. In psychological terms, however, the most important phenomenon is the apparent extension of the permanent residents' life expectancy, which is achieved by shortening the time units within the Fuller cathedral. The *Dome* has its own accelerated calendar, to which visitors must adapt. Thus, the inhabitants perceive themselves as staying young longer and believe that they will live longer lives. The aspect of security is also essential. The dome structure makes it possible to seal off the entire area if necessary or to control the flow of people entering or leaving.

In 2222, Sylvia Scanner had fulfilled her dream of a perceived extended youth when she moved from Madison, Wisconsin to the *Dome* in New York and accepted a position as manager of internal communications at an ad agency. It took a while for her organism to adjust to the shortened rhythm of life and the peculiarities of this cityscape, but eventually the activities of her everyday life returned to normal. She lives in Chelsea, near the eponymous hotel that has been a local fixture since time gone by. Today, she finally wants to pay the new Empire State Building a visit and ride up to its viewing platform at an altitude of some 2000 feet, which offers visitors a panoramic view of the city and the inside of the dome. The original building, which was erected in 1930, had to be demolished in 2137 due to dilapidation. It was reincarnated in the form of a modified new building with a total height of 2300 feet. One of the reasons for the new height was a municipal

stipulation that each high-rise building must make twenty percent of its floor space available for utility gardens, which help to supply the residents with organic food.

After Sylvia has passed the electronic security gate to the lobby, she buys a first-class ticket at one of the available machines and takes one of the three-story elevators to the uppermost of the three viewing platforms. The elevator cabin is mainly filled with visitors to the cathedral. The tangle of foreign languages puts Sylvia in an atmosphere that might have surrounded the construction of the Tower of Babel. Lost in thought, she arrives at Panorama Platform Three. After the doors of the elevator cabin have opened, the throng inside the cabin dissipates. Everyone strives towards the light and the views from the platform. At first, Sylvia concentrates on the information panels that talk about the construction of the building and the dome. It says that Buckminster Fuller's design could only be technically realized after structural engineers found a way to design the upper sections of the structural mesh of the dome with carbon rods. Buoying up the load-bearing structure by means of helium-filled pillows inside the framework's panels that are made of a specially manufactured membrane also played a significant role.

In the end, however, Sylvia's excitement at finally being able to enjoy the magnificent view is so great that she pulls away from the information panels and steps up to the platform's balustrade. There are two views on offer. First, there is the view of the unfolding cityscape which is similar to that from the window of an airplane during the landing approach. Only much more open. The second view is immediately drawn toward the immense space created by the dome above the city. In contrast to the diffuse impression one gets from the street level, at an elevation of two thousand feet, the structure is clearly visible, especially from the southern side of the platform. One can clearly see the lattice shell and the helium-filled membrane pillows of the panels. Some of the pillows are black because the control of the day-night setting has gotten stuck. The nodal points of the

carbon rods are equipped with light sources that produce familiar constellations of the night sky. Looking northwest, Broadway and Times Square are easily recognizable due to their powerful dimensions that distinguish them from their surroundings. A few weeks ago, Sylvia was once again in this amusement district, which is especially popular with tourists. As a slightly claustrophobic personality, she avoided the crowds rolling down Broadway and chose to float above the action in the Peoplemover. While riding, she had availed herself of the Virtual Reality Adapter, which, to her eye, transformed the street's real course into a futuristic scenery. As she recalls this, she traces Broadway from its entrance to the *Dome* in the south all the way to the passage in the direction of Columbus Circle in the north. 53rd Street is bathed in yellow fog from Broadway to 5th Avenue, a reference to a current exhibition about the color yellow at the Museum of Modern Art.

Sylvia can hardly pull herself away from the urban spectacle in front of her and decides to stay on the platform until nightfall. To bridge the time until then, she has a drink at the bar and talks to some tourists from New Jersey about the different calendars inside and outside the *Dome*. While it is September 25, 2222 inside the *Dome*, the calendar of the outside world dates to April 3, 2215, which means that more than seven years of time difference have occurred since the *Dome*'s construction and the introduction of an accelerated time system inside of it. When Sylvia leaves the bar, dusk is slowly falling inside the *Dome* . The first helium-filled cushions of the outer shell lose their transparency and change color to a nocturnal blue-black. More and more of them switch, until finally the entire interior surface of the *Dome* turns midnight blue. Down below, the network of street lighting flares up and the representative office towers of global corporations begin to outdo each other with lighting effects. The hologram of an artificial moon appears above the Public Library at Bryant Park. Sylvia takes the elevator down and looks up again after leaving the entrance hall. Today, it is the constellation of the Great Bear that shines above in the cloudless night sky.

At the Table of the 21st Century

1968 The *Environment Transformer* and *Electricskins* are well-received in New York. During the opening of *Plastic as Plastic*, we wear *Flyhead*, *Viewatomizer*, and *Drizzler* for a while, quickly becoming the center of attention. During those three days, we meet Jim Burns from *Progressive Architecture*; John Margolies, who interviews us; Raimund Abraham, who invites us to a lecture at the Rhode Island School of Design; and Philip Johnson, who is rarely available for a chat due to his status in town. As we sit with him at his conference table, he asks in conversation why I work under the name Zamp and not Kelp, which is also a nice name after all. I explain to him that this is due to my involvement at the TU Wien, which should not be associated with the actions of Haus-Rucker-Co in the city's public space. This argument does not convince him, and he prompts me to seriously consider combining both names.

The 1964 film *Dr. Strangelove or: How I Learned to Stop Worrying and Love the Bomb* ridicules Cold-War-related tensions between the US and the Soviet Union. After a manic US general decides to single-handedly go through with the planned attack flights, he orders to cut off the radio communication between the US Air Force bomber squadron and the Pentagon's War Room, making it impossible for the pilots to receive further instructions. Meanwhile, crisis-management authorities gather around the United States President, played by Peter Sellers, at a large, ring-shaped table with an illuminated world map in the background. While their deliberations come to nothing, the US Army finds a solution and calls back the bombers in time. However, the radio equipment of Major T.J. "King" Kong, the pilot in control of the B-52 aircraft equipped with nuclear bombs, was damaged, leaving him unaware as he prepares to drop the weapons over Russian territory.

Stanley Kubrick created this film in 1963, a time when tensions between the East and West were high and the risk of a nuclear disaster was, in hindsight, often bigger than was perceived in everyday life. In this sense, Kubrick's film is not addressing the

Table of the 21st Century, ring with 40 chairs and central water basin, part of the exhibition *Natur nach Mass*, Colliery in Aalen, Zamp Kelp neo.studio, Regionale, 2004

risk that global societies were actually experiencing without some irony or cynicism, while working on a high level of intensity and using images that established themselves in everyone's minds for the long run. So much so that Ronald Reagan, during a visit to the Pentagon after his inauguration, apparently asked to see the War Room—despite it only existing in Kubrick's film.

The *Table of the 21st Century* was developed in the context of the *Nature to Measure!?* exhibition in Ahlen, a small town in the North Rhine-Westphalia region of Germany, which mainly owes its existence to the coal mining industry. Similar to the conference table in Kubrick's War Room, the *Table of the 21st Century* has a circular shape, but with forty chairs: nine more than in *Dr. Strangelove*. For a period of three months, the table was placed in the main machinery building of the decommissioned coal mine Zeche Westfalen I/II and served as the exhibition's central piece. In an ambience that signaled the notion of an eschaton, the table and all the other scenarios of the exhibition marked the beginning of a new evolutionary phase of society, in which the fundamental ecological positions of our understanding of the world would have to be rethought. At the time of the exhibition, the power of machines and pipelines from the past was still clearly perceptible and lent the halls an atmosphere whose intensity aurally superimposed the exhibition scenarios with a taste of the future. In this future, the elements space, time, and water were considered luxury goods, that we would have to treat with care.

Water was also the table's central element. Inside the dimmed main hall of the coal mine building, it appeared like an over-

1969 In spring, Haus-Rucker-Co is commissioned to design a fair stand for the Austrian Institute of Design, which is to be set up as an outdoor information booth at the Trade Fair of Vienna. The first draft is an oversized index finger made of tire named *Direction Pointer* that alternately expands, loses air, collapses, and inflates to its full size again. It does not appeal to the institute's president, so we begin to think about alternatives.

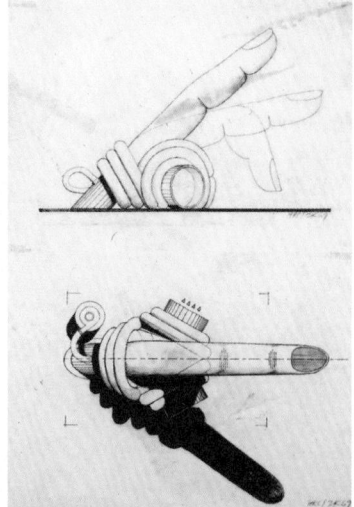

Direction Pointer

War Room, *Dr. Strangelove or: How I learned to Stop Worrying and Love the Bomb*, **Stanley Kubrick, 1964**

1969 In May, we present new projects, titled *Vanilla Future: Playroom for Erika Pluhar and André Mirifloor*, during a five-hour event inside the athletic sports center in Vienna's Schleifmühlgasse. Erika Pluhar and André Heller, who uses the pseudonym Mirifloor for this event, swing by for an hour and mainly play *Battleship* at the heart of the presented objects. Mirifloor, aka Heller, occasionally grabs the megaphone to shout, "To me, the best man of the space age is Pichler Walter."

sized jewel with a gigantic liquid gemstone of water at its midpoint, which in turn, was encompassed by a round table surface with a diameter of ten meters. Ten of the forty chairs were red. They were each assigned a red square on the tabletop. Each square was equipped with a radio control system for miniature yellow motorboats that could be navigated across the water surface. Next to the red squares were fifteen white and fifteen gray squares that informed interested visitors about the meaning of water as a life-giving element of the past, present, and future. The *Table of the 21st Century* thus appeared as a friendly hybrid at first, inviting the audience to participate. A second, deeper look at the bottom of the H_2O gemstone, however, revealed the model of a settlement, flooded and with no human life in sight.

Perhaps a vision of a disastrous development in the future, induced by ecological mismanagement. This is how the table obtained its metaphorical meaning. It became a warning sign for the onset of an era in which we would have to redesign the relations between society and living space.

On the other hand, the table function, analogous to that in Kubrick's film, provides the possibility to take a seat, get informed, follow one's play instinct by controlling the model boats, or talk both about and across the water. In the style of a round table, the history of an ecologically threatened world can be discussed here, and approaches to a new balanced solution can be found.

1969 This summer semester's project for the chair of Building Theory and Design is about the Vienna square Karlsplatz. The task is advertised as teamwork, and a group consisting of one female and four male students will join me for this project. They seem like a bright troop and begin dealing with the topic rather unorthodoxly. After several sketches of ideas in the style of comics, they decide for the utopian design of a racetrack. This track is conceptualized for "dragsters," a type of vehicle used mainly in the US for races in which paired cars drive straight at extremely high speeds. On the track, both contestants are meant to speed in two tubes from the Karlsplatz through the dome of St. Stephen's Cathedral. The tubes are supposed to start at the main road, Wiener Hauptstrasse, and lead through the Kämtnerstrasse to the St. Stephen's Cathedral, then penetrate the church's roof before coming to a stop in the direction of the Danube Canal. The so-called *Great Vienna Auto Expander* serves as the starting point at the Karlsplatz and resembles a gigantic pinball machine. Generally, the car as a means of transportation is this project's main focus and one of the significant themes is showcasing human machines as replacements for horses near historic equestrian monuments. The choice of location for the presentation, a garage at the square Am Hof, is not without risk. The creators also invite friends from the Harley Owners Group to bring their motorcycles in order to accentuate the fascination around motors and machines with engine noise. I accompany Karl Schwanzer as the highest evaluation authority. The creators explain the concept and individual drawings to him, and, at the end, he doesn't miss out on a ride on the backseat of a Harley through the first district's alleys. By and large, he will have enjoyed the presentation, which is actually an idea initiated by the group. However, he still demands improvements. In the meantime, the team has acquired the name Zünd-Up and is thinking of new provocative creations. They add pseudonyms to their names. Huber is called "Friedhof," which translates to cemetery; Pühringer is "Wampühr," or vampire; Mayer is the "Zünd-up-Mariedl," as in "Zünd-up-gal"; and Simböck calls himself "Spiegelei," the German word for fried egg.

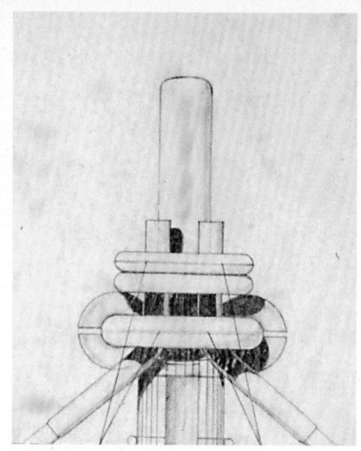

Design-Post

1969 Rudolf Zwirner thinks he can sell the *Yellow Heart* to one of the most important German collectors if we host an exhibition in his gallery on Albertusstrasse in Cologne. Yet another offer that we do not reject. Before that, however, we must finish the fair stand's design for the Austrian Institute of Design. The new project envisages a symmetrical figuration of pneumatic cylinders and rings, one inside another, reaching a height of around seven meters. This design seems more appealing and is approved and implemented.

Both the table in the War Room and that of the machine hall in the Zeche Westfalen I/II do not exist anymore. Now, they are only available in the form of two-dimensional documents. The formal and functional analogy of both situations from 1963 and 2004 is confronted with their different meanings. While the War Room table represents a nuclear threat posed to global society due to two rivalling superpowers and a government miscommunication, the *Table of the 21st Century* symbolizes an early warn-

Travelling Town 1, sketch, Zamp Kelp, 2018

ing for current bioecological issues worldwide, which in all probability will be significantly influenced by the element of water.

In a utopian urban planning study of the 1960s, architects Klaus Gartler and Helmut Rieder made the radical suggestion to flood the old quarter of their hometown Graz and to build a new city on top of the dam required for this purpose. This dam would be provided with energy from an integrated power plant. Considering the continual rise in sea levels, the urban planning provocation of those days could soon become a visionary idea, though surely under different circumstances. After all, a warming of the climate by around two degrees Celsius could lead to the melting of polar caps in the summer months, which would then cause the oceans to rise by more than seven meters. Thus, global warming would be a significant factor of the climate's development and, as a consequence, the living conditions on Earth. In a collage from 1964, Hans Hollein places an aircraft carrier into a wave of natural landscape and declares the giant ship to be a city. This was no surreal act, but a statement advocating a new understanding of cities, a declaration of war against the growing urban sprawl, and a statement promoting the compact compression of urban coherences.

Fifty years later, the urbanization of natural landscapes is progressing. Land reclamations that are currently being carried out by Holland, the United Arab Emirates, and Hong Kong through masses of earth shifting into the ocean are an unmistakable sign of the demand for living space by the growing world population. Naturally, colonizing the ocean's surfaces is an obvious perspective. Tendencies and plans for the utilization of the water surface are in the works worldwide. Gigantic aircraft carriers with their military duties serve as the first amphibious, mobile living and working places, each accommodating around 2,500 people, the size of a village or small town. Apart from the military equipment on these floating apparatuses with urban characteristics, it is the feature of a landing and departure site for airplanes as well as their mobility that provides them with an almost omnipresent mode of operation. In a way, this type of ship practically anticipates Ron Herron's Walking City. Even Kenzō Tange's proposed superstructure for Tokyo Bay, developed together with his students in 1960, points in the same direction. Based on the limited availability of building land on the Japanese island state, this project was used to examine the options of gaining urban space without reducing the ocean's surface. The idea was never implemented. Nevertheless, this proposal expanded the principle of building on solid ground to building above the surface of the ocean. The building measures for Tokyo Bay were planned as a permanent formation closely connected to the location's geography, in the style of modern

1969 In late summer, Ant Farm's "media nomad" Caroll Michels announces her planned visit and arrives soon after. We take her to Lake Neusiedl and rent a sailboat to cruise on the lake for two hours. These 120 minutes are enough for something beyond collegiality to develop between her and Klaus Pinter: a relationship forms between the two that, as time will tell, lasts longer. After three days, Caroll goes back on her Europe tour. We agree to stay in touch and focus on the next event. As the exhibition at Zwirner approaches, we start preparing for our transfer to the Rhineland. We decide to not only take part in the exhibition in Cologne, but to also move to the Cologne-Düsseldorf area permanently, where the cultural scene is big and exciting.

Travelling Town 2, photocollage, Zamp Kelp, 2018

1969 In Cologne, we stay at Gustl and Valerie Schultes's apartment, who are away traveling. Setting up the exhibition at Zwirner takes three days. In the meantime, artworks arrive at the gallery—among them, a photo of Mick Jagger in handcuffs sitting in the back of a police car. Gerhard Richter arrives as pale as death. Coming from Düsseldorf, he narrowly escaped an accident on the Autobahn. The *Yellow Heart* is clearly visible in the display window of the gallery's entrance in Cologne. Unfortunately, Zwirner is unable to sell the object to the collector. Instead, the broadcaster Westdeutscher Rundfunk Köln (WDR, West German Broadcasting Cologne) reports on the exhibition for Studio 45, a popular culture program. While the exhibition is running, we begin to make contacts. I visit Konrad Beckmann, the architect in Düsseldorf I had interned with in 1965. With the approaching second Cologne Art Fair from October 15 to 20, 1969, our Zwirner exhibition comes to an end. We are offered to display several objects and drafts at the Josef Haubrich Kunsthalle, the art hall where this year's Art Fair will take place. The *Yellow Heart* is placed below a ledge of the building, where Wolfgang Bauer, an author from Graz, reads poems from his book *Das stille Schilf* (Silent Reeds). Joseph Beuys presents a VW bus pulled by a team of sledges, which would later become famous under the title *The Pack*. HA Schult's girlfriend Elke Koska is present in a black-and-white, spotted cowhide jacket.

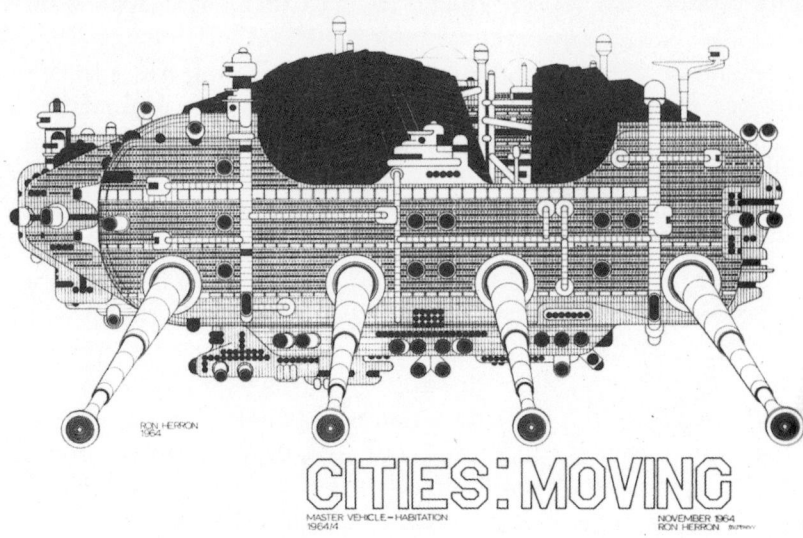

***Walking City*, Master Vehicle-Habitation, Ron Herron (Archigram), 1964**

stilt houses with foundations on the seabed. Today, the space-creating architectures of the modified road network in Tange's draft could be replaced with mobile urban housing and offers a similarity to cruise ships.

The current trends of floating architecture, such as vacation houseboats, differ from the 1960s concepts primarily due to their mobility. This means that these structures, with their characteristics of buildings on solid ground, are mobile; their location is changeable.

***A Plan for Tokyo*, Kenzō Tange, 1960**

The enormous hotel and entertainment steamers, which sail the seas in ever-increasing numbers, point towards the same direction. These ships already provide the option of buying apartments to live in as permanent residents of the sea, overlaid with the offer of a lasting cruise.

Finger Windows

The space-creating project of a major airport established on pontoons in the Thames Estuary hints at the possibility of developing swimming cities that could be maneuvered to a necessary location through their mobility. Similarly, a floating, functional, complex concrete pier was realized and produced on the Mediterranean Sea's southern coast, to be transported by tugboats to the port of Monte Carlo and serve as a berth for ships. These kinds of urban modules were made to combine and create complex urban formations and if needed, to be taken apart to establish new configurations elsewhere. These floating, swimming city modules could temporarily lead to population densification along certain sections of the seashore. Symbiotic relationships and synergies between urban structures onshore and those of the ocean are likely. The vast space beneath the sea surface with its potential of mineral resources has barely been accessed. It is true that, in addition to the strategic submarine technology and aquatic vehicles serving science and exploring the deepest parts of the ocean's floor, as well as the existing submarine housing complexes, such as exotic honeymoon locations, the establishment of an urban underwater world is still in its experimental phase, having started as oil and gas drilling rigs. Inhabiting the ocean's landscapes with humans or their avatars is imaginable, and modified experiences from exploring space may come in handy in this. After all, large rooms filled with water have and still are used by astronauts as training facilities for life and work in orbit.

The starting point for these submarine urbanizations could be offshore platforms and drill pipes, which can be used as a means of transportation for mechanical vehicles, humans, avatars, and other objects, in order to establish a functional link between the ocean's surface and its seabed. The settlement of urban modules around these drilling rigs with an entrance function would then only be a matter of time, with the goal of establishing bipolar cities, divided into above- and underwater cities. Empty oil deposits in the seabeds could be used for storing the CO_2 emissions generated in the city above. Alternatively, it could be examined whether empty cavities in which fossil fuel and gas had been stored could serve as a place of residence for humans, or whether that would create a human species, which, according to Jacques-Yves Cousteau's vision, could become sea dwellers through medical intervention or mutation.

The longing for nature prevalent throughout the 1970s appears nostalgic in these circumstances. More than fifty percent of the

1969 The most important encounter is with Alfred Schmeller, the newly appointed director of the Museum of the 20th Century in Vienna, and his wife Martha Jungwirth, who had seen our *Yellow Heart* at the Kunsthalle's entrance and appeared delighted to come across Austrian environmentalists in Cologne. Without thinking twice, Schmeller offers a proposal regarding his opening event and without thinking twice, we accept. Before that, however, we have to find, rent, and furnish a new residence, which we eventually manage to successfully do in Düsseldorf. We rent a house on Inselstrasse, across from the Hofgarten, the city's central park. The house has stood vacant for a long time, apparently because nobody had noticed its good qualities, but with our architect's eye, we appreciated exactly that. After moving in, we go through the phase in which we adapt the house to meet our needs. Simultaneously, we start with project work. Through Konrad Beckmann we meet Erika Kiffl, who introduces us to different ad agencies in town and arranges our first commission. In the Hofgarten, I occasionally watch Peter Handke play with his little daughter.

1969 We begin our draft for Schmeller's Museum of the 20th Century in Vienna, the building that had served as the Austrian Pavilion at the World's Fair in Brussels in 1958. Initial ideas deal with the material and technology of airborne constructions, a medium that we are now familiar with. Then it becomes clear that the participatory aspect must play an important role in order to create a contrast to typical art exhibitions where visitors view art passively. We want to break the classic, solemn *habitus* usually found in museums, and suggest moving the furniture that is still in our Vienna apartments into the museum and proceeding to live there for the duration of the exhibit. This is also why it would be titled *Haus-Rucker-Co LIVE*. In the center of the two-story main room, we conceptualize the *Giant Billiard* in the shape of a massive, white air mattress on which three shiny, white inflated balls lay, each with a diameter of three meters, and designed to create a sense of the dynamic on this object of interaction. On three sides surrounding the square, we position the three living rooms of Laurids, Zamp, and Pinter. Near the entrance, visitors come across the *Oxer*, a slanted passage designed as an obstacle to irritate the visitors' sense of balance. Between these conceptual arrangements are the objects we have created so far.

global population now lives in cities...and counting. In order to prevent the total urbanization of natural landscapes ashore, a shift to the ocean seems plausible. The social imbalance on Earth's mainland amplifies this development through a mass migration from areas of deprivation to highly developed civilizations in Europe, North America, and Australia, which can hardly be brought under control.

Lucius Burckhardt sees landscape as one entity composed of a society living on and within it. It is humans who are changing the concept of the landscape by, on the one hand, increasingly utilizing the available continental spaces, and migrating to socially attractive areas, and on the other, transforming the status of the landscape and way of life there. It seems that there is a similar effect in the relationship between humans and social quality, as in between cultural and natural landscapes. This longing for primal and natural spaces destroys these locations as soon as they are controlled by overflowing tourism. Therefore, one of the main tasks in examining the relationship between the global population and its landscapes is to strive for balance. Floating city modules could be produced in technologically advanced areas of the Earth's surface and then shipped to the coasts of countries in need of development to improve the quality of life. The fact that the relationship between humans, scenic surfaces, natural resources, and water is a fluid process in which destructive and constructive ambitions alternate becomes apparent through destroyed urban structures, such as the case of the Middle East. The tensions there are due to differing power interests developed during the World Wars, which are still relevant today. Exploring parts of the Earth's water surfaces and the regions underneath as living environments for humans may help to ease the tendencies of future overpopulation. The ability to provide drinking water will play a crucial role in this process.

Climate and Landscape

Giant Billiard, sketch

The human dream of having control over the climate, an essential requirement for life on Earth's surface, is presumably as old as mankind itself. Numerous archaeological traces of sacrificial altars worldwide are proof of that. When weather conditions would begin to compromise the harvest or a winter promised to be extremely cold, sacrifices were made to appease the gods.

Northern and Central Europe's inhabitants longing for the south of the continent is a historical phenomenon and an indication of the close connection between climate and landscape. Throughout Johann Joachim Winkelmann's journey to southern climates in 1760, he would close the curtains of his carriage window at the sight of the Saint-Gotthard Massif and preferred to wait for the harmonious landscape of Italy. In this respect, he anticipated the behavior of passengers travelling by train at the beginning of the Industrial Revolution.

Today we fight global warming, heat waves, and severe weather, knowing that our egoistic lifestyles are to blame. Buckminster Fuller was one of the first to conceptualize large-scale projects for controlled climate conditions. Based on his geodesic constructions, he and architect Shoji Sadao developed a concept for the *Dome over Manhattan* around 1960. Plans for a geodetic

1969 After we finish the concept and everything is noted in drawings and descriptions, we drive to Vienna to present our ideas. Alfred Schmeller is amused and, in my opinion, sold. Presumably, he is convinced by the approach of an exhibition that stands out against the classic, museological standards and instead works interactively. After we receive a written confirmation from the museum, in which we are officially commissioned to realize our project, we can start looking for supporters and sponsors. In Leverkusen, the company Bayer provides the white, bolstered material available by the meter for the *Giant Billiard*'s air cushion, provided that the material and source is visibly marked during the exhibition. We bring the material to a company in the Burgenland, which agrees to produce and deliver the air cushion for a reasonable price. The *Oxer* is made in the museum's carpentry workshop.

Protected Farmhouse, collage+drawing, Haus-Rucker-Co, Zamp Kelp, Düsseldorf, 1970

Growing Up in Chicago

Above the Chicago skyline, the John Hancock Center looms a hundred stories high, a splendid monument, or a damned sore thumb—depending on who's talking. Critics claim the building is too tall—at 1,107 feet, only 143 short of New York's proud but aged Empire State Building—and that it spoils Chicago's skyline. Others say it gives the skyline a needed emphasis. Similar buildings—and controversies—are high-rising across the nation, making passé the notion that one has to visit New York to see skyscrapers.

Protected Skyscraper, drawing on print, Haus-Rucker-Co, Zamp Kelp, Düsseldorf, 1971

Dome Over Manhattan, Richard Buckminster Fuller and Shoji Sadao, 1960

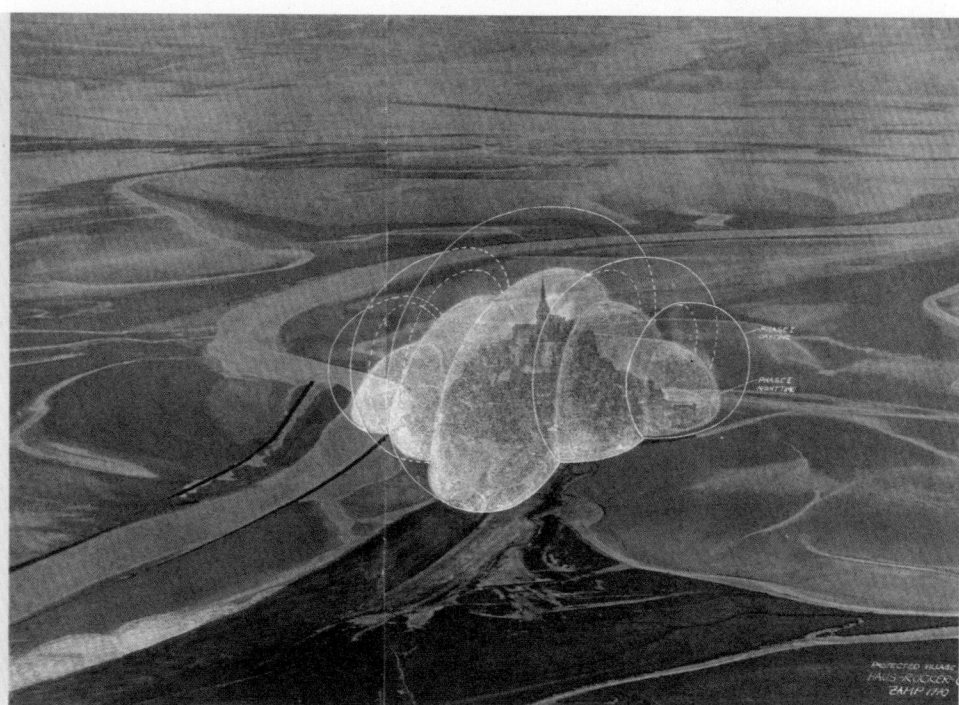

Protected Village, Mont St. Michel under a cover with both day and night positions, Haus-Rucker-Co, Zamp Kelp, Düsseldorf, 1970

CLIMATE AND LANDSCAPE

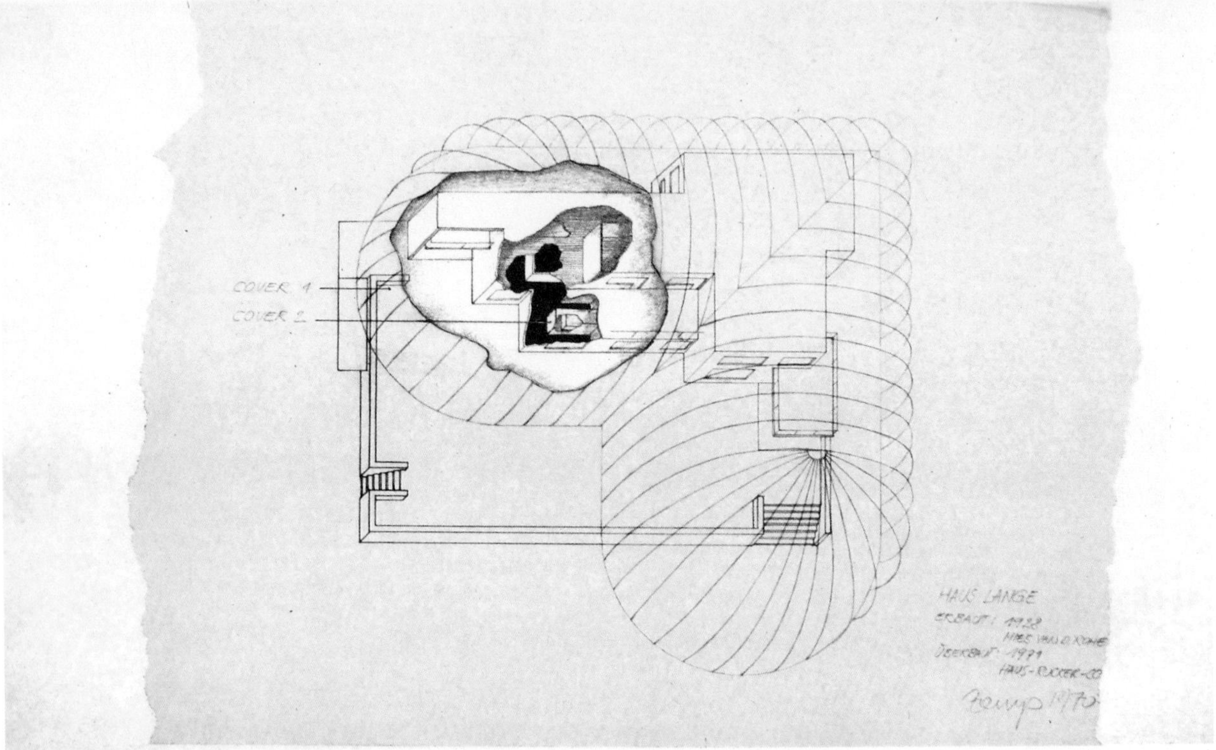

Haus Lange, built 1928 by Ludwig Mies van der Rohe, superimposed by Haus-Rucker-Co, 1971

COVER-Survival in a Polluted Environment, indoor view, Haus-Rucker-Co, Laurids Ortner, Zamp Kelp, Klaus Pinter, Krefeld, 1971

CLIMATE AND LANDSCAPE

COVER-Survival in a Polluted Environment, Museum Haus Lange, X-ray view, Haus-Rucker-Co, Laurids Ortner, Zamp Kelp, Klaus Pinter, Krefeld, 1971

1970 Mid-February, the exhibition is finally ready. On the entrance's left-hand side, visitors find Laurids's room; opposite is Klaus Pinter, lying in his bed during the press conference. Diametrically from the entrance, i.e., on the other side of the *Giant Billiard*, I have made myself at home. The *Yellow Heart* is displayed in the corner to its left, and across the room on the right, the Pavilion of the Austrian Institute of Design is installed. Above each living area, the names of Laurids, Zamp, and Pinter are emblazoned in huge white letters on transparent foil.

1970 We send images to Paul Smith, director of the Museum of Contemporary Crafts in New York. We add countless reports from the press. After a while, the Museum of Contemporary Crafts sends us the confirmation to display the exhibition from Vienna in May of the same year. At the beginning of April, a container filled with the exhibition items is shipped to New York. The same company that produced the *Giant Billiard* donates a second mattress, whose dimensions correspond to those of the New York museum. The first white square is intended for an event in front of the museum. At the opening, we offer the guests an edible model of the museum building for them to taste and enjoy. Still, the main attraction is undoubtedly the *Giant Billiard* on the street in front of the museum, where it is presented for two evenings. At first, passersby gather along the four sides of the mysterious white, square cushion spread out on 53rd Street. They are obviously waiting to see what might happen next. As soon as an animator demonstrates what to do on the mattress, everyone waiting catches on to the idea and throws themselves onto the heaving air mattress to enjoy the sensation of experiencing previously unfamiliar combinations of movement. James Lee Byars, the artist who likes working with golden surfaces, is also standing on the edge of the *Giant Billiard* in a group. He is dressed in white, and wears a black hat and a black cloth covering his mouth, which he takes off after a while.

dome with a diameter of 3 kilometers and a height of 1.6 kilometers were developed on the basis of a special structure system whose inner climate could be controlled. Central Park remained excluded, though its small side touched the dome's foundation tangentially.

The exhibition *COVER — Survival in a Polluted Environment* took up the subject of urban exclusion from existing urban landscapes and cultural contexts of Fuller's concept, mentioned above, as one aspect of its subtext. The former mansion was built in 1928 for the director of a silk weaving mill in Krefeld by the German architecture icon Ludwig Mies van der Rohe and was transformed into an experimental space for art in the mid-1960s. At the beginning of 1971, Haus-Rucker-Co temporarily

***COVER*, air-inflated hall with tree shadows on translucent skin, Haus Lange, Krefeld, 1971**

covered the brick building with an air dome made of white, translucent fabric. This separated the building from its environment. A spatial drama was created between the brick stone façade of the mansion and the translucent skin of the air hall, ornamented with the shadows of surrounding trees in the sunlight. The dystopia of an introverted living situation as a syn-

Rooftop Garden, corner of Broadway and Broome Street, silkscreen, Haus-Rucker-Co, Zamp Kelp, Klaus Pinter, New York, 1971

Palmtree Island, Manhattan, Triborough Bridge, collage, Haus-Rucker-Co, Zamp Kelp, New York, 1971

Four Seasons Hotel, Manhattan, Times Square, silkscreen, Haus-Rucker-Co, Zamp Kelp, New York, 1971

Fresh Air Reserve, Broadway Bridge, silkscreen, Haus-Rucker-Co, Zamp Kelp, New York, 1971

1970 Word has spread in Düsseldorf about our activities in New York and Jürgen Harten, director of the Kunsthalle Düsseldorf, wants to display *Giant Billiard* on the occasion of one of his "Betweens," brief interludes between the big exhibitions. The question of financing arises, which seems to be solvable through contacts from advertising. The company Henkel agrees to fund the event on the condition that the three yet-to-be-produced giant billiard balls be marked with blue letters advertising Henkel's detergent Weisser Riese. Some artists protest, seeing it as the intrusion of commercial factors in the art zone, but eventually the interactive object is installed in the art building's great hall and once again becomes an attractive, interactive element for visitors.

thetic, climate-controlled reserve was produced assuming that environmental pollution had considerably worsened and was threatening the health of society. An assumption which, as has been said before, was not a reality at the time of the exhibition but had nonetheless been put up for discussion as a perspective for possible future developments, thereby creating awareness. The intensity of the fabricated situation was enhanced by the snow and the associated cold. In the white of the winter surroundings, Mies van der Rohe's house had disappeared behind the white shell. On the inside, the warm air from the air-pressure-generating fan and the upstream heating gave the garden an impression of spring—an impression that began to germinate. These activities of the natural landscape elements in the hall room were supported by acoustic simulations of natural sounds, such as wind, rain, or chirping birds. This created a scenery heavy with artificiality, which prompted the majority of visitors to contemplate the isolationist perspective of future development in an urban context.

The exhibition *COVER* inspired us to project the subject of synthetic reserves in urban contexts. Which city could have been more suitable for these reflections than New York? The city,

Climate 3 Sleeping, collage+drawing, Haus-Rucker-Co, Zamp Kelp, Düsseldorf, 1970

106   **CLIMATE AND LANDSCAPE**

with its high density and the resulting climate issues, was an ideal field to develop ideas for improving its citizens' quality of life. In 1971, a series of collages with synthetic reserves was created, the so-called live cells embedded in the metropolis's architecture, which offered the conceptual perspective of improving life in the city and defining spaces that were eligible for it. The Rooftop Garden, a forward-oriented vision of a climatic reserve on the flat roof of the 491 Broadway building in Soho, pursued the visionary aspect of the rooftop landscape's active vitalization and cultivation. The ideas back then are currently, forty-five years later, being turned into a reality roof by roof.

1970 Communicating through various phone calls, we show our interest in having an exhibition at the Kaiser Wilhelm Museum or Museum Haus Lange in Krefeld. Paul Wember, head of both institutes, informs us after a fairly long time that we are welcome to work out a proposal for Haus Lange. Mies van der Rohe built this house in 1928 as a villa for a silk mill director and has been used as an experimental museum since 1965. The first thought that comes to mind is to cover the house with an air-supported dome and to then thematize the subject of living with a critical outlook on the future. With the title *Cover – Survival in a Polluted Environment*, Laurids and I work out a scenario in which the isolation of living situations compared to the social environment is addressed in dystopian terms, considering the increasing pollution of terrestrial habitats. Once the meeting with Paul Wember is set, I drive to the Haus Lange on Thursday, November 5 to pitch our ideas. Wember has no issues with implementing the concept short term. Together we walk around the house and I point out that a Japanese Cherry Tree will probably have to be uprooted to make space for the air dome, which is not an issue for him either. We end our first meeting both convinced that this concept will be presented in the coming year, 1971, in the form of an exhibition. Which it did.

Matterhorn, scene painting with mobile mountain peak, Haus-Rucker-Co, Manfred Ortner, Brunswick, 1974

CLIMATE AND LANDSCAPE

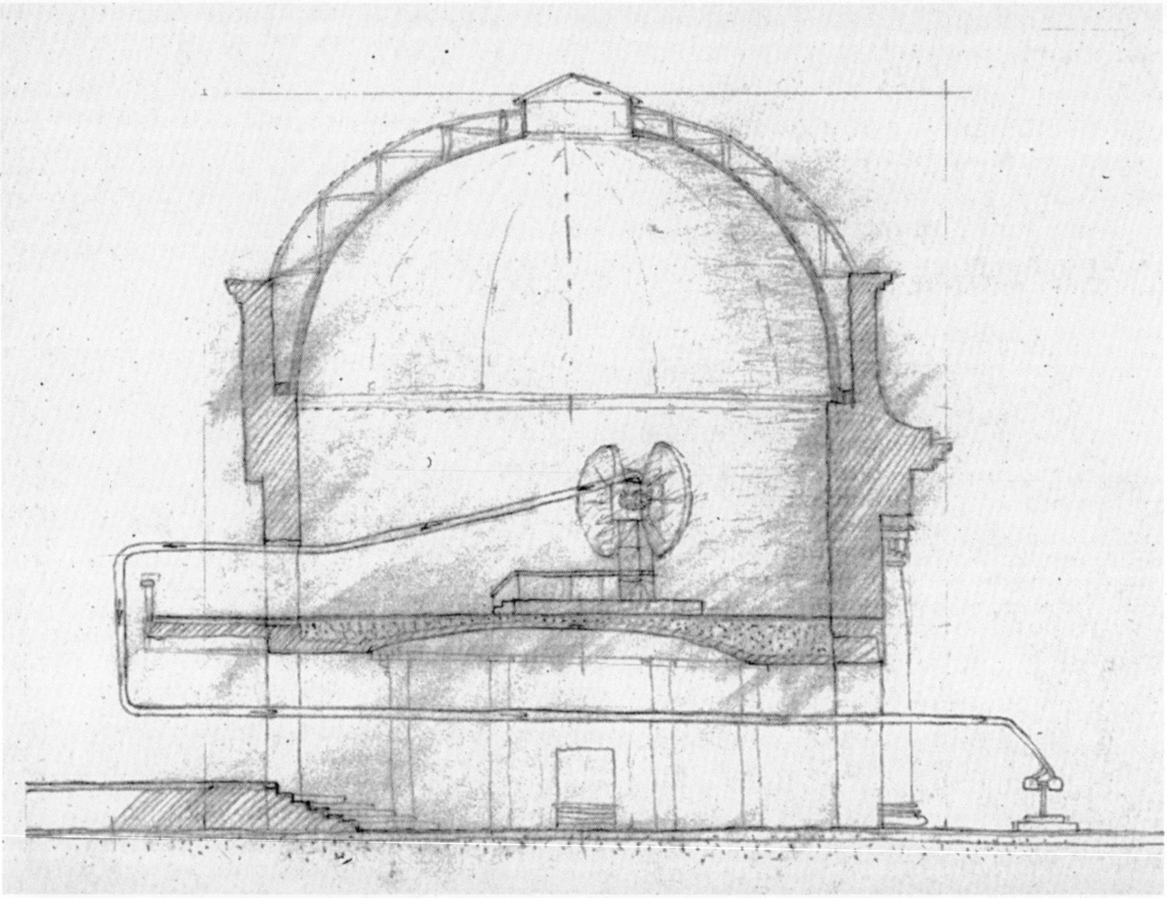

Green Lung, Kunsthalle Hamburg, Haus-Rucker-Co, Laurids Ortner, Zamp Kelp, Manfred Ortner, Hamburg, 1973

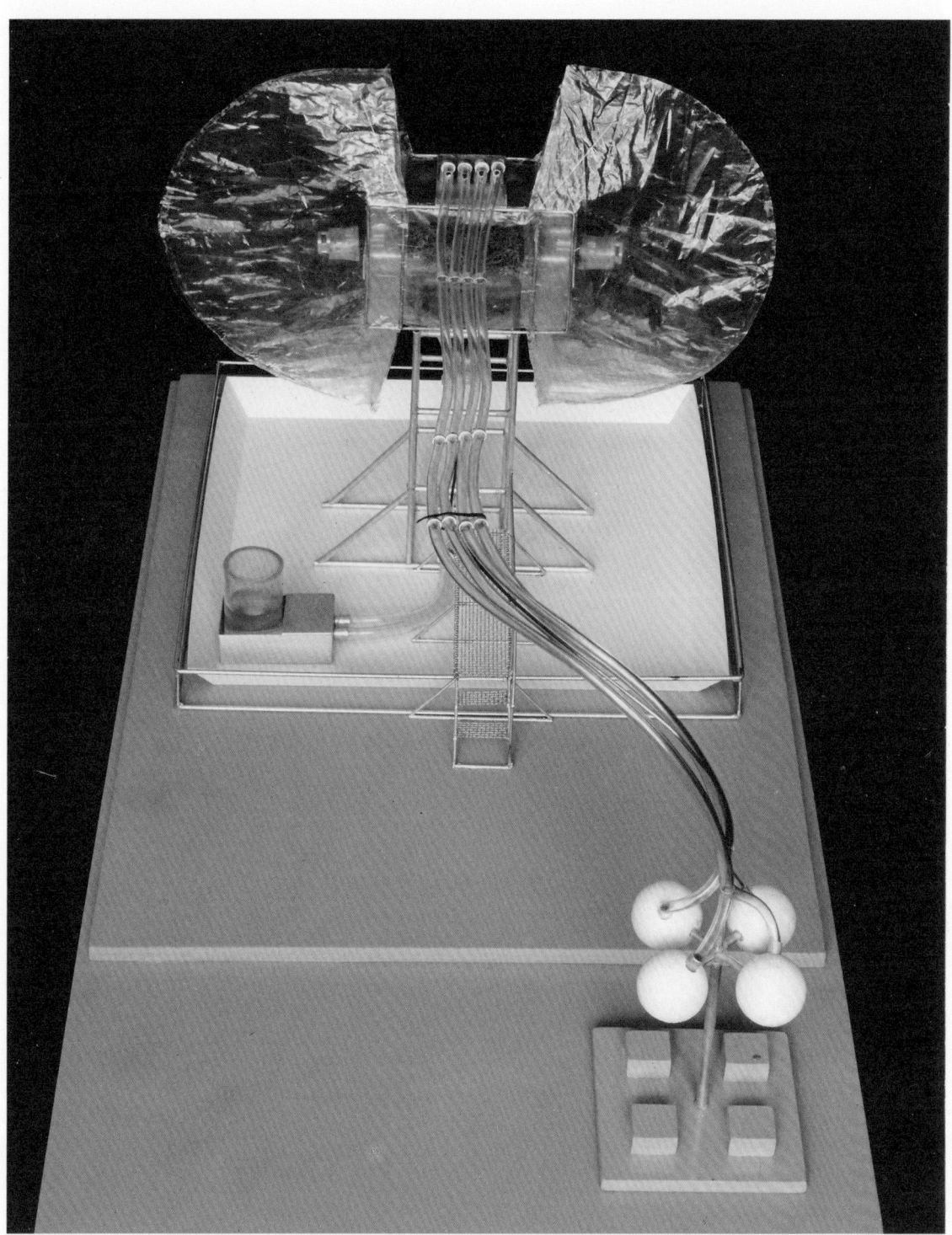

Green Lung, model, Haus-Rucker-Co, Düsseldorf, 1973

Green Lung, Haus-Rucker-Co, Laurids Ortner, Zamp Kelp, Manfred Ortner, show opening, Hamburg, 1973

Oxygen Service Station, outdoor object *Green Lung*, Haus-Rucker-Co, Laurids Ortner, Zamp Kelp, Manfred Ortner, Kunsthalle Hamburg, 1973

Oasis No 7, view on Friedrichsplatz, Haus-Rucker-Co, Laurids Ortner, Zamp Kelp, Manfred Ortner, Klaus Pinter, documenta 5, Kassel, 1972

Oasis No 7, mounted at Fridericianum, documenta 5, Kassel, 1972

Fridericianum with *Oasis No 7* and banner by Ben Vautier, documenta 5, Kassel, 1972

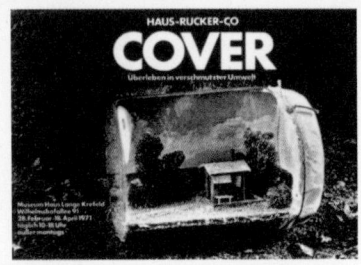

Exhibition poster for COVER

1971 We win over the company Wülfing und Hauck near Kassel to loan and set up the angular air dome. This requires a down payment of eighty thousand deutschmark, which Paul Wember advances from his private funds at first as time is of the essence. In order to balance out the different levels around the museum for the air hall, we recruit engineers from the German Armed Force to use sandbag barricades and create an even ground. On Saturday, February 27, about four months after the first meeting, the exhibition *Cover – Survival in a Polluted Environment* opens at 7 p.m. The Haus Lange is swallowed up in the temporarily limited surroundings of the air dome. Inside, the clinker façade and the hall's white skin struggle for optic superiority. The intensity of the overall situation is especially impressive, feeding off the contrast between these two conditions. Coupled with residential objects, which further illustrate the theme of isolation inside a house, this creates an intentionally oppressive perspective of possible future living conditions for visitors to the exhibition. The exhibition closes on April 18th of the same year, having been—in terms of visitor figures and media feedback—a total success. I prepare my departure for New York.

The collage *Palmtree Island* planned the translocation of a palm tree island, including its local climate, into the city traffic on the Triborough Bridge, called Robert F. Kennedy Bridge today, at its Manhattan bridgehead. The conceptual considerations on the subject of "synthetic reserves" and nature in the city eventually manifested in 1972 at the documenta 5 in Kassel, with the realization of *Oasis No 7* on the façade of the Fridericianum at the city's central square Friedrichsplatz. An additional airborne dome construction was created for the duration of the exhibition, which contrasted the classical elements of the Frederician façade and, as a synthetic reserve, presented the prospect of a climate-controlled development of urban formations. At the same time, the artificiality of the two palm trees made of synthetic material and metal in the center of the spheric ambience created a critical perspective on the longing for nature experienced by city dwellers. It also demanded that the existing urban spaces—both with their positive and negative moments—can be accepted as a living environment.

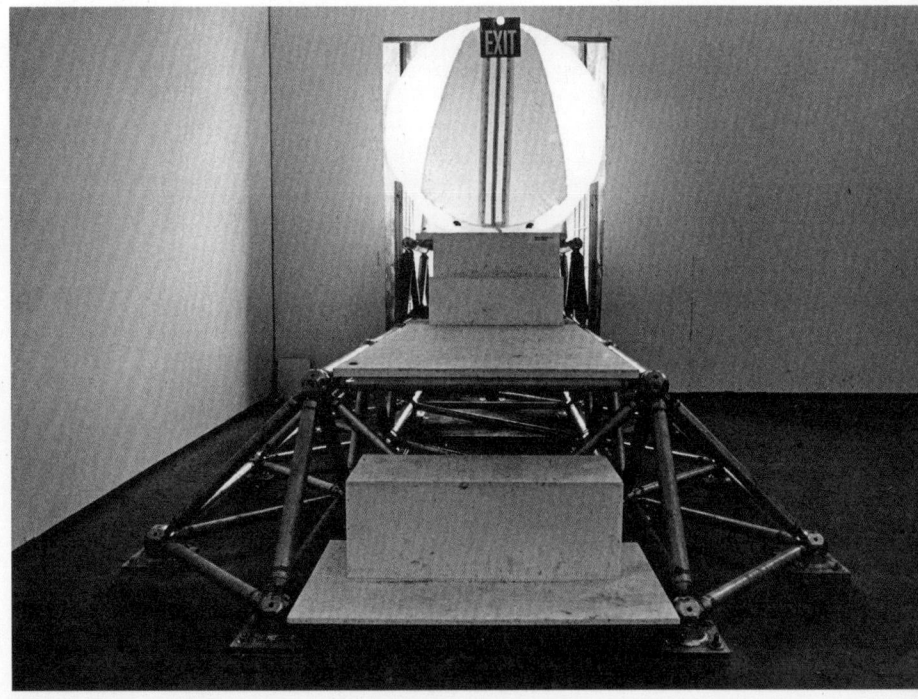

***Oasis No 7**, sluice indoor view, documenta 5, Kassel 1972*

IN THE YEAR 2172

Balthazar

Big Piano, Haus-Rucker-Co, in Newton's Kenotaph by Étienne-Louis Boullée, Illustration by Zamp Kelp, 2016

Plays the Piano

In the 22nd century, in the year 2172, a historical project is to be realized for the documenta 45 exhibition in Kassel, in addition to other contemporary designs. The choice has fallen on *Big Piano* by Haus-Rucker-Co—developed for documenta 5 in 1972. Just like two hundred years ago, procurement of the funds for the project's realization was the main difficulty. In the end, a company that develops virtual reality games offers to finance the project. The technical implementation of the scaffolding design with stairs that

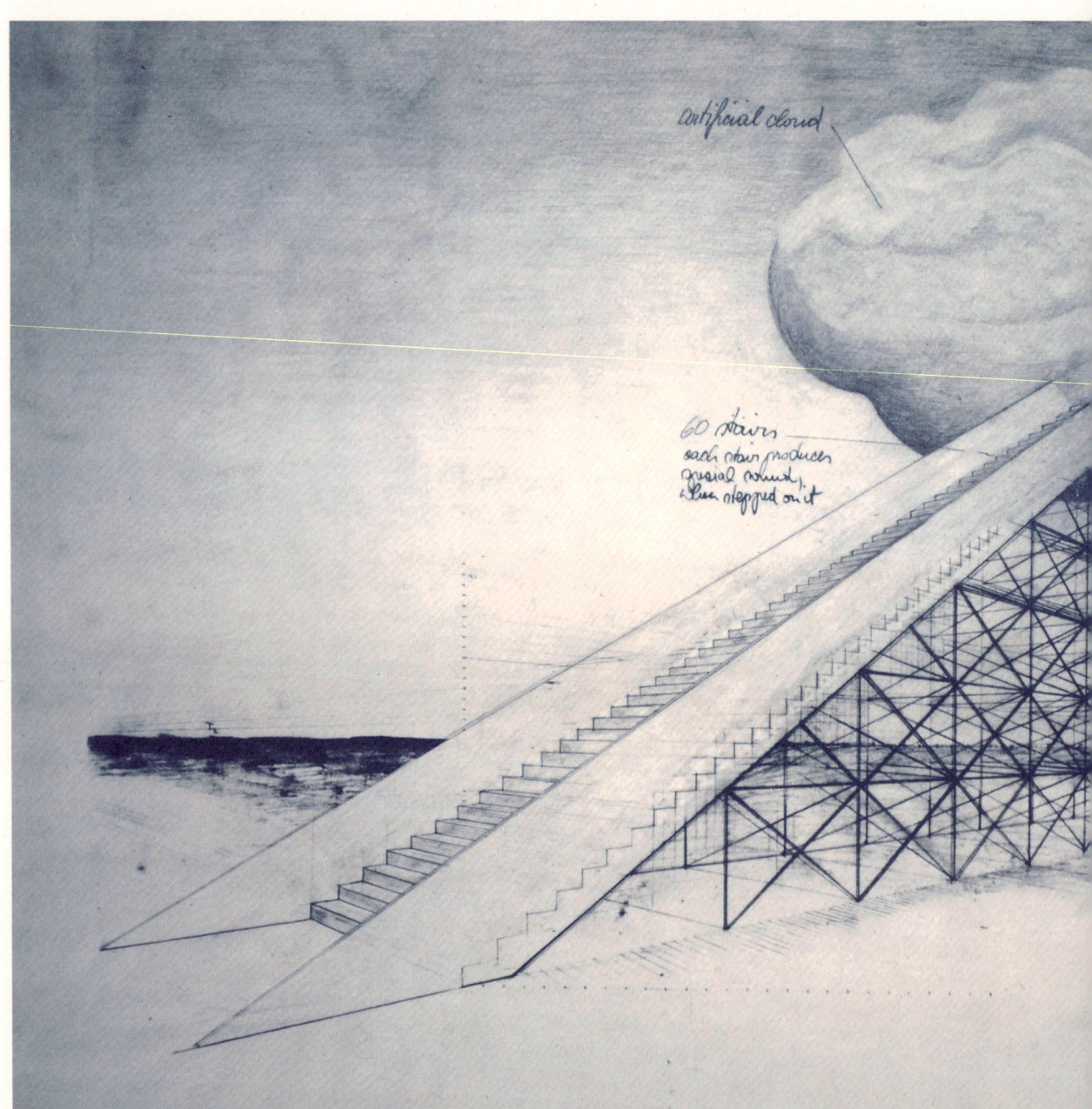

Big Piano, urban musical instrument, project for documenta 5, Haus-Rucker-Co, Zamp Kelp, New York, 1971

make sounds as you step on them goes smoothly. Only the creation of the cloud of water vapors runs into problems at first. Thankfully, a solution is found in time when a participating engineer discovers the documentation of the Swiss national exhibition Expo 2002, which describes the artificial creation of a fog bank. Thus, shortly before the opening of documenta 45 and with a delay of two hundred years, the *Big Piano* finally stands on Friedrichsplatz, where it should have been installed in 1972.

Balthazar, an architecture student at the city's university, has been following the construction on Friedrichsplatz over the past few months and, after the show's opening, is now one of the first in the queue to climb the stairs to the platform inside the temporarily formed cloud. As he approaches the location of the object, he notices a yellow office container on which the word "instructions" can be read in bold, white letters. He enters the container to learn how to interact with the object. The instructor explains with professional friend-

Big Piano, model, Post-Haus-Rucker, Zamp Kelp, Berlin, 2014

liness that there is more to it than just experiencing the *Big Piano* here on Friedrichsplatz. With the help of virtual reality adapters, the staircase structure can be overlaid with three alternative spatial constellations. From these alternatives,

Balthazar chooses Newton's Cenotaph, an unrealized concept by Étienne-Louis Boullée from 1784. He knows this to be a spherical volume with a diameter of five hundred feet and jumps at the opportunity to experience that intriguing space—if only in virtual reality.

On handing over the appropriate adapter, the instructor directs him to the starting point, directly in front of a fifteen-foot moving walkway that's right before the staircase. Balthazar puts on the headset and steps onto the walkway. Before him, he sees a platform towered over by the colossal scale of the Cenotaph, just like Boullée's drawings, but in realistic 3D. Balthazar begins to walk towards the opening in the sphere. There is an air of familiarity about the whole thing, as if he has seen this building before.

Although a light breeze is blowing from the west, the poplar trees surrounding the structure on different levels appear strangely rigid. Finally, he reaches the entrance and follows a dark tunnel into the interior. Arriving at the hollow sphere's base, Balthazar has to adapt his vision to the dim light. At first, he can only see the illuminated steps of the *Big Piano* in front of him. Little by little, he grasps the enormous dimensions of the hollow sphere in which he is standing. With his right foot, he steps onto the lowest step of the stairs, whereupon a powerful organ chime booms out and is reflected in multiple echoes from different points of the sphere's curvature. After a few moments, he begins to walk up the steps. In doing so, he creates a sequence of tones forming a melody he somehow recognizes but cannot quite place. After a few steps, he pauses, walks back down a few steps, and then immediately goes up again. He repeats this process several times during his ascent to the platform, creating a variation of the given melody. Upon reaching the platform, he looks around for orientation. First, he looks up and recognizes the simulation of the stars and the moon in the form of perforations in the upper half of the sphere, through which the exterior daylight enters the interior. At the opening for the moon, naturally the largest, he can tell how this effect of a night sky comes about particularly well. Then he lowers his gaze and notices that the *Big Piano* seems to float in the sphere. The sarcophagus for Newton is located directly under the piano. As he looks down, he feels a slight dizziness, so he looks up again. He claps his hands and shouts to test the echo. After a while, he notices how each echo comes flying back in the form of a bird. This prompts him to animate the spherical space with fluttering birds by clapping a kind of applause for several minutes.

This interactive scenery comes to an end with a soft hissing sound coming from the *Big Piano*'s scaffolding. A cloud of water forms in the platform's area, blurring his view. Suddenly, Balthazar hears an older voice explaining Newton's Laws of Motion, according to which masses attract each other, and how these omnipresent forces of attraction between the stars and planets are an elementary prerequisite for the universe's existence in its present form. The fog around the platform lingers for a considerable time before it slowly dissipates. Suddenly he feels raindrops on his clothes and face. He wonders how the rain could penetrate through the small star-shaped openings in the dome. A matter-of-fact voice sounds from the headset, asking him to press the button on the right earpiece, otherwise the device will switch off automatically.

Balthazar does not press the button and removes the adapter. He finds himself in the middle of Friedrichsplatz, which opens up to the Aue park and is bordered by the documenta hall and the *Rahmenbau* sculpture. Despite the considerable rain that he already felt back on the virtually perceived cenotaph, he remains on the platform for some time before walking down the thirty-six black and fifty-two white steps again. In doing so, he plays descending scales, which are counterpointed by the notes produced by the next visitor climbing up.

Aura, Network, Node

In the history of Western culture, there is hardly a myth as pervasive as the Tower of Babel and the punishment of humanity's sacrilegious attempt to draw closer to God. Only after the turn of the 19th to the 20th century did researchers discover that the Tower of Babel had actually existed. In the form of a temple tower approximately 91.5 meters tall, it was a ziggurat called Etemenanki, which translates to "house of the founding stone of heaven and earth." The tower was erected around 480 BC by Nebuchadnezzar II and was rendered unusable by the Persian general and king Xerxes, who had the central stairs of the ziggurat torn down. The now-inaccessible building lost its image as the Babylonian's cultural symbol of power and began to decay. Alexander the Great then wanted to rebuild the temple tower and, in preparation for his plan, initiated the removal of the ruin's existing parts. His death in 323 BC prevented the reconstruction and the tower, apart from its foundation, which was around 1900, was lost. In the time between the disappearance of the temple ruins and the discovery of its foundations, specula-

1971 Klaus Pinter and Caroll Michels have rented a loft together on the corner of Broadway and Broome Street in SoHo and asked if I could come to New York for a while to help set up their studio. The Island Air aircraft takes off in Brussels around noon one day in April. Pinter and Caroll welcome me in the arrival hall. Alexander Heinrici, our screen printer from Vienna, lives in part of the loft with his girlfriend and has joined them. The loft is on the twelfth floor of a former commercial building on Broadway and is great in terms of size and location. From its windows, you can see both the Hudson and the East River, as well as their bridges. Little Italy is just across Broadway, and Canal Street is three blocks down. In SoHo, on West Broadway, branches of all the major galleries are opening. Our first activity together is designing a silkscreen poster with an edition of 125 copies, which we use to announce the opening of our studio. The accompanying poster shows the junction of Broadway and Broome Street with the house number 491, where our loft is located. We develop *Rooftop Garden/Planet of Vienna*—a spectacular pneumatic roof construction and annex of the building as a synthetic reserve, which we use to set a programmatic focus for the goals that the New York office will pursue in the seven years of its existence: the cultivation and socialization of the city's roofscapes through space-creating and shaping vitalizing offers. What follows is a period full of optimism and, to some extent, overconfidence. I remember a risky "stroll" across the cornice sill of the twelfth floor high above Broadway to the corner at its end and to the firewall fitted with windows, and then, without experiencing the slightest wave of panic, returning to the open window and feeling the safe floor inside the loft again. I have no explanation whatsoever for why I did that. Perhaps it was the euphoria of the newcomer who was seduced by the city's urban energy.

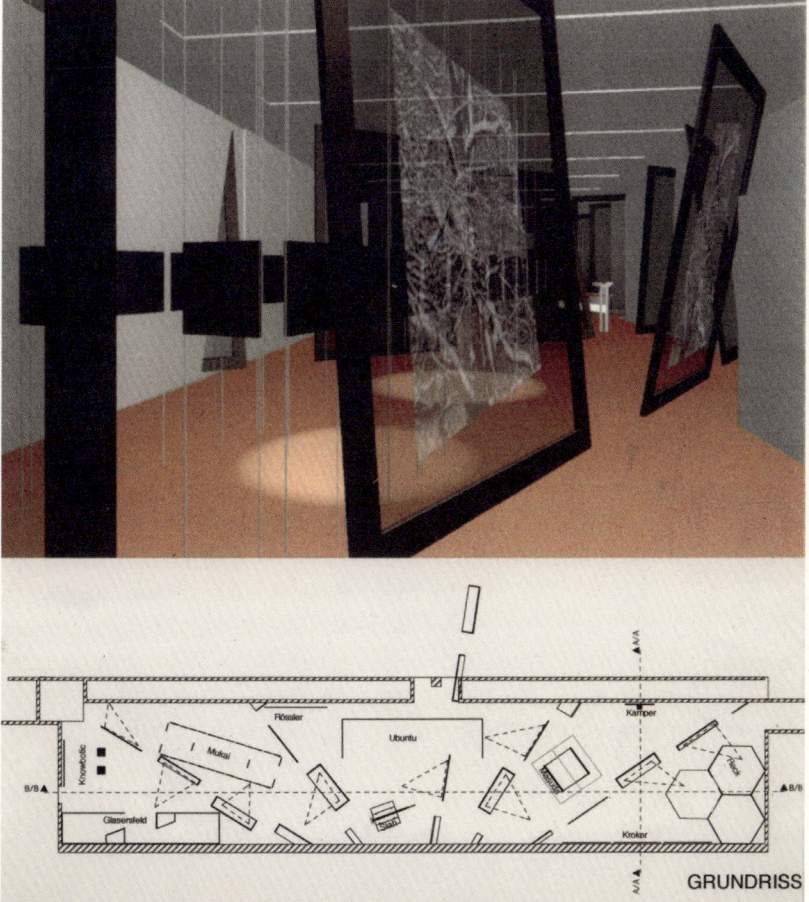

Today is Tomorrow, Exhibition, Bundeskunsthalle Bonn, space study and plan, Zamp Kelp, Düsseldorf, 1999

1971 In New York, we meet the up-and-coming photographer Tom Jones, not to be confused with the British singer of course. He has just changed his profession from carpenter to photographer and agrees to take black-and-white photos of Broadway for our planned silkscreen series. For the time being, Alexander Heinrici is still staying at the Haus-Rucker-Loft, while also having his silkscreen workshop in our shared workspace. In the middle, we have placed our *Battleship* from the 1970 Museum of Contemporary Crafts exhibition. One day, Raimund Abraham swings by and brings a book about the latest findings on the Tower of Babel. According to the book, the tower was actually the "Zikkurat Etemenanki" and a Babylonian sanctuary during its existence. I am impressed by a drawing of the ziggurat with the central staircase that Nebuchadnezzar demolished in order to take the Babylonians' faith away from them. With these stairs in mind, the project *Giant Gamut* is created: a freestanding steel framework and staircase with steps that produce various sounds when walked on. It is from this concept that the *Big Piano* emerges, a variant whose end point—a viewing platform—is temporarily veiled by an artificial cloud of water vapor. When Harald Szeemann, head of the documenta 5, announces his visit over the phone and eventually arrives at the studio with Christoph Amann, we propose turning *Big Piano* into a reality on the Friedrichsplatz in Kassel. The compositions that the visitors created would be omnipresent in the city center through the use of speakers. Szeemann seems interested but tells us that Haus-Rucker-Co in Düsseldorf are working on a proposal as well.

tions about the Tower of Babel's existence were upheld by the biblical story: a tale that developed as an auratic element from the existence of a real building and has survived until today.

The story of the Tower of Babel as a message from the past is a precursor of myths that are built around consumer goods, houses, cities, and people, or are self-produced in the age of information transfer. In all the categories listed, the profile and quality of the personal or object-oriented myth become important prerequisites for their presence in the communicative space of society.

Today is Tomorrow, view into the exhibition space, Bonn, 1999

The network as an apparatus has accompanied the evolution of humanity since the beginning of its time. Its principles are applied diversely in communicative fields as well as in collecting goods of all kinds. The sea of information offers virtually anything, and the way we can reach the content relevant to us becomes the central question of survival. Networks channel the supply; they create points of connection; they transfer data. Networks make space disappear. An intercontinental telephone call through a phone company's network reduces the distance between the colloquists. Networks set the stage for space. A letter from Europe overseas creates distance and objectivity while developing a multilayered relationship between sender and recipient, which is already the postal network's basis. Networks in their original sense are representational. They are of an ambivalent nature. On the one hand, they consist of material in the form of ropes, threads, or cables. On the other hand, they are shaped by intermediate spaces. Their appearance is always accompanied by drama; after all, they pose a threat to all those beings that are unable to slip through their interstices. The technology of the network production has not only developed in the field of information transfer. Through production processes, traditional networks are also becoming increasingly diverse and refined in terms of features and applicability. This makes them

1971 In autumn, on behalf of the City Art Festival in Houston, Texas, we produce *Food City 2*. The hosts provide us with a tuned model of a Japanese car brand, whose exhaust system occasionally backfires and produces an audible bang with each time. So, when I get in the car and hurtle around the corner of a block of houses, I lay off of the gas and wait for the backfire to bang before stepping on it again. This is when Klaus Pinter and I suddenly hear the wailing of a police siren. After checking the rearview mirror and seeing red-and-blue flashing lights, I park the car on the side of the road and get out. A cop approaches me and asks, "What did you throw out of the window?" Apparently, he interpreted our vehicle's backfire as an explosive charge that we threw onto someone's front lawn. After we explain to him that we are guests of the Art Festival, he calms down, but not without checking our bags for weed and other illegal substances. At last, he sends us off with the question, "Do you know what American jails look like?"—which we do not really understand since we had just proven our innocence. During the presentation of *Food City 2*, we meet Doug Michels and Chip Lord of Ant Farm. As we are still processing our encounter with the police, this meeting is only very short-lived.

Today is Tomorrow, view into the exhibition space, Bonn, 1999

AURA, NETWORK, NODE

Today is Tomorrow, view into the exhibition space, Bonn, 1999

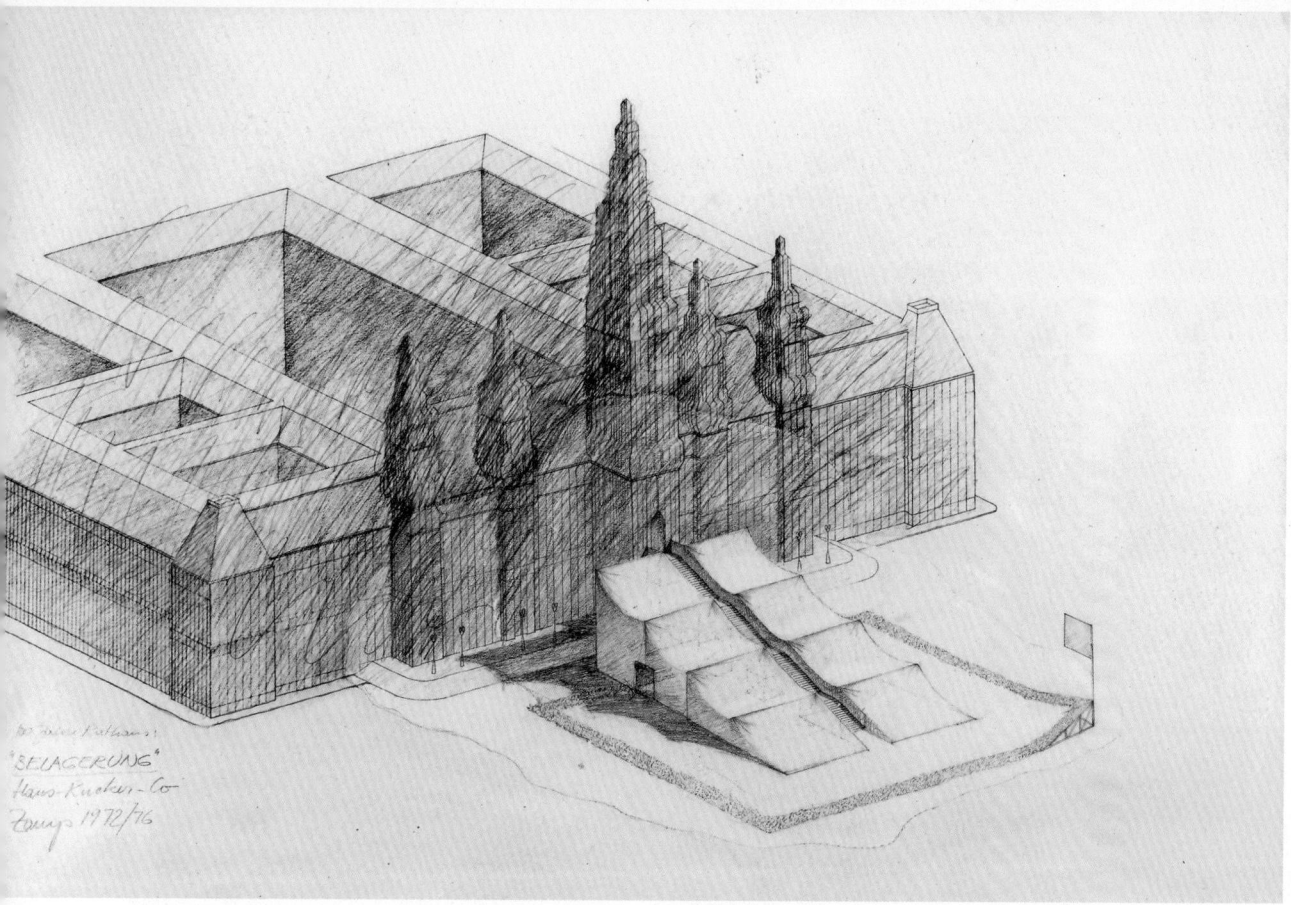

Siege, concept for a centennial for City Hall of Vienna, Haus-Rucker-Co, Zamp Kelp, Düsseldorf, 1972/76

ideal carriers for informative projections of all kinds. When projected onto networks, information becomes visible, though perceiving the space in the background throughout the network remains an option.

The stretched net surfaces in the exhibition *Today is Tomorrow* use light to project era-shaping visual documents that contribute to the evolution of humanity and science. These documents are aurally pushed between the visitors, the exhibits, and scenarios of the exhibition. In an exemplary way, the exhibition shows how complex the positions of networks are and how involved their effects can be in areas of perception. In many ways, they serve as mediators between the objective world and nonmaterial scenarios of a projective virtual information space. Like anglers, we collect goods and information with our nets for surviving in the representational as well as the virtual sphere of our living environment. Whether we collect seafood, catch butterflies, or surf the internet, it is our various nets and filters that help us make the invisible visible, separate the necessary from the superfluous, or build relationships interactively. The economy and the economic network, respectively, transforms information into money. Money is one of the keys in procuring tangible and virtual products. Monetary systems as networks are

1971 After returning from Houston, we create a scenario titled *Piece of Nature* for the Austrian Economic Chamber's ski show at the New York Coliseum at Columbus Circle. We get into serious trouble with the local trade union bosses for working as artists without a trade license.

1971 One day, an art broker from San Francisco stops by the studio. She seems impressed by our work and suggests the option to have an exhibition in her museum. Hence, I fly to San Francisco in mid-November to discuss further details. When talking to the institute's director, I favor the implementation of the *Big Piano*, before he asks me whether I am aware of the fact that San Francisco's everyday life is closely confronted with an enduring danger of earthquakes. He illustrates the potential catastrophe's effect on the *Big Piano* so dramatically that I envision a jumble of humans and steel tubes outside of the museum, accentuated by uncontrollable synthesizer sounds. I take a flight back to New York and am in the studio in time for Thanksgiving.

1972 In February, we talk to a journalist from *New York Magazine*, who suggests that we develop ideas for an event celebrating the one-hundred-year anniversary of Central Park. Obviously, we want to create an interactive and edible city model again. This time, however, it should relate directly to the place where it is presented. The suggestion to make an edible model of Central Park is well received by *NY Magazine*, and the necessary funds for its realization will be made available on April 30th.

predestined for the task to mediate between objective and virtual areas of perceptual space.

The concept of "knots," or rather "nodes," from the economy of the internet is—we can all agree—a transformation from the real, objective world of traditional net manufacturing. Today, knots and nodes are less representative of the process of tying threads to form a net. Instead, they stand for the convergence and concentration of news threads that lead to a superimposition of information at the switching points of globally acting webs. Perhaps, society's latent issues with orientation are based on the lack of significance on the World Wide Web. Perhaps it is necessary to represent the virtual node of information through meaningful representationalism in the concrete world. Such tools of transition between development stages, similar to the whip holder from the era of horse-drawn carriages to the first motor-driven carrosseries of the 19th century, have always been an assuring gesture from the past for a society that first had to get used to these new circumstances. Now that the projective aspect of our perceptual offer is in a phase of constant expansion, "nodes of meaning" from the objective world raise awareness and generate orientation. Thus, they become sanctuaries of perception, like *The Lightning Field* by Walter De Maria, or the astronomical buildings of Jaipur. The *Millennium View* is designed as a cult site of perception too. The staircase structure made from the residual stone quarry pieces transitions into a steel framework at its top. People visiting the platform stand in

Fiction, stair to Babel, Zamp Kelp, Berlin, 2018

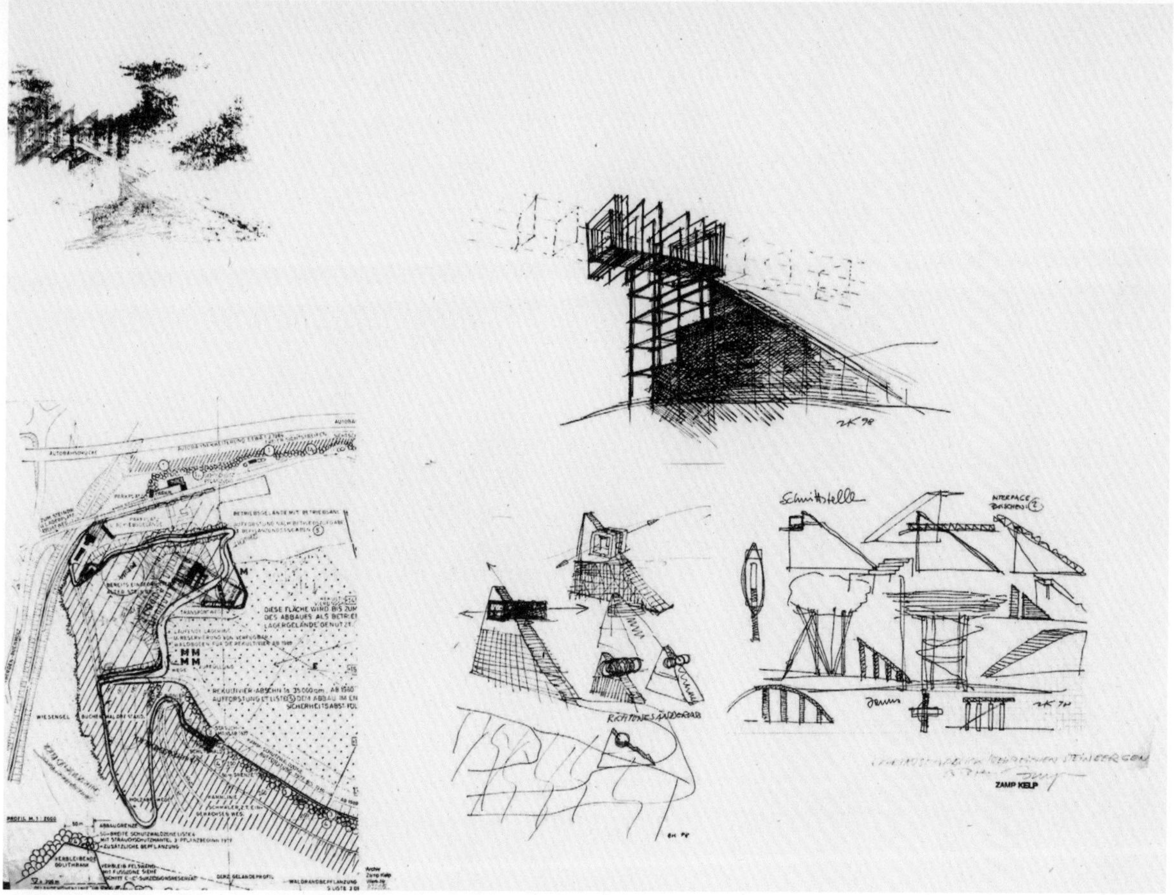

Millennium View, sketch-grouping, Zamp Kelp, Düsseldorf, 1996/97

Millennium View, peripheral project Expo 2000, Steinbergen, sketch, Zamp Kelp, 2000

Millennium View, Expo 2000, Steinbergen, realization + fictitious addition, Zamp Kelp, 2000/2015

Millennium View, observation deck, 10 frames out of green glass, Zamp Kelp, Steinbergen, 2000

Edible Architecture, Central Park

1972 The Central Park event takes place on a Sunday in front of the park's so-called mall, at an open, half-domed space where choirs or musicians usually play, filling the area with their sound. *Edible Architecture*, the edible model of the park, is installed on a table and it does not take long until a remarkable number of park visitors gather around. We are wearing shirts that say "Urban Cook." Thanks to the large number of interested people, the edible park disappears in no time, leaving only an empty plate with a few still-recognizable contours of the model.

1972 Back in Düsseldorf, *Oasis No 7* has been prepared to the extent that we can begin working on the Fridericianum's façade for the documenta 5, more precisely installing the pneumatic construction to the fifth window on the right of the portico.

a space formed by ten green glass frames that metaphorically represent our perception's fragmentation while also superimposing the view of the landscape. The upper end of the stairs as a historical element carries symbols that reflect the current state of our media-influenced viewing habits and reminds us of the stairs at the ziggurat Etemenanki, torn down as instructed by Xerxes to take away the faith of Babylonians. The only difference is that this symbol of a new perception replaces the cult space of an archaic faith. The *Millennium View* thus defines itself as the statement of a new religiosity, namely one of information. The Gods of information, so it seems, are hiding behind the mysteries of a virtual world. Should we draw too close to them, they will not confuse our language, but rather, the order of our images.

Fluxus and the World of Provisional Architecture

1972 Wrapped in the flair of its temporary internationality, Kassel is a different city during the documenta period. Harald Szeemann's *Questioning Reality — Pictorial worlds today* will be the most important exhibition in this series. We meet Panamarenko, the Belgian sculptor who set up his *Aero Modeller* in the same room of the Fridericianum, from which we mounted *Oasis No 7*—a pneumatic ball with a diameter of seven meters and a steel pipe construction to the floor of the room. He tells us that his fragile zeppelin could really fly. He doesn't, however, tell us how high or how far. He also inspects the *Oasis No 7*'s interior and appears to enjoy the atmosphere as well as the view through the two artificial palm trees through the transparent ball shell over the Friedrichsplatz. Francois and Linde Burkhardt had written about our exhibition *Cover — Survival in a Polluted Environment* in the current documenta catalog. They too, along with many other cultural insiders, show up to visit and photograph the oasis. On the morning of the opening, Ben Vautier is trying to sleep on a cot in Joseph Beuy's office and in front of the guests of the vernissage. James Lee Byars is standing on the Frederician tympanum's roof and shouts names toward the entrance through a megaphone. Sometimes he drops a red thread and communicates with the person who catches it.

1972 The Vienna City Hall is celebrating its centenary. We design an event structure in the form of a staircase that leads directly into a room on one of the upper floors of the city hall's central tower. We do this based on the assumption that the mayor's office is located there and that this way, citizens could talk directly to the head of the city, bypassing bureaucratic obstacles. Together with Alfred Schmeller we bring the concept to the city administration; however, there is not enough time for the idea's implementation.

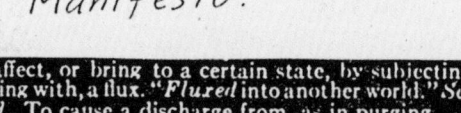

Fluxus, manifesto of George Maciunas, Festum Fluxorum Fluxus, February 1963

Fluxus, a global artists collective founded by George Maciunas around 1960, represented flow and transience. It considered itself to be a counter position to the classical art establishment and it was not the work that stood in the foreground, but the idea. The goal was not an individual's artistic product, but the processes and results that arose from communication or the attempt to provoke communication. Fluxus was designed beyond the art scene as a factor that wanted to influence social structures and their associated living spaces: Geoffrey

Hendricks's *Cloud City* from 1967, for example, puts the notion of urbanizing clouds up for discussion. In the year 1972, Ben Vautier wrote "Kunst ist überflüssig" (Art is Superfluous) in white letters on a black banner and attached it, in celebration of the documenta 5, to the roof balustrade of the Fridericanum museum in Kassel, directly above the entrance's tympanum. In her project *Parts of a Body House*, Carolee Schneemann limited her works to describing rooms, scenarios, and possible functions taking place there, refraining from using any kind of visualization. Dieter Roth's sculpture *Schokoladenmeer*, which translates to chocolate ocean, integrated the aspects of change and decay into the artwork through the utilization of organic and decaying material, such as sour milk, cheese, and excrement.

Urban landscapes have a certain dullness about them. They only change slowly, especially in comparison to human life, which today lasts an average of eighty years. Mistakes in the city structure can be corrected through considerable efforts alone, as construction measures are the result of complex processes that, once completed and visibly stable, have to gain the trust of their users first. Provisional structures—or, in other words, interventions of temporary character within urban space—are just like Fluxus ambassadors of transience. Their tasks are versatile. In Berlin, for example, new buildings individually implemented at the Leipziger Platz were fitted with tar-

1973 Haus-Rucker-Co is spending its fourth year in the house on Inselstrasse 32 in Düsseldorf. The owner, who used to live on the first floor, has passed away and the house is up for sale. Eventually, an investment company buys the house and commissions Haus-Rucker-Co to design the new building. "The Drawer House" receives its name from the balconies that pull out from its façade and eventually, after a fuss about the preservation of historical monuments, gets approved. At the end of the year, Haus-Rucker-Co moves its office across the Rhine to Oberkassel in the Glücksburger Strasse. The new location, a house built around 1900, has similar qualities to the one on Inselstrasse, which would soon be replaced. While the atmosphere on Inselstrasse, with the Hofgarten park opposite of it, offers representative but hardly communicative elements, the house on Glücksburger Strasse has a counterpart of same-sized buildings. The small-town vibes of Oberkassel offer a myriad of creative possibilities, such as the Muggel, a café and bar that I visit, often twice a day.

Provisional Mix-Up, collage + coloring pencil, Haus-Rucker-Co, Zamp Kelp, Düsseldorf, 1977

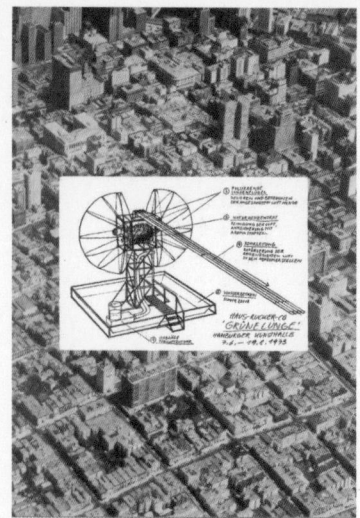

Green Lung folder

1973 In June, Werner Hofmann, the Hamburger Kunsthalle's director, shows our exhibition *Green Lung — Superseded Paradise*. During the set-up, I can observe the highly concentrated actor from the Viennese Burgtheater, Helmut Lohner, as he rehearses a role for a play at one of the theaters in the area. The object *Green Lung* is divided into a "breathing station" in the outer room, which is connected to the main object in the rotunda on the second floor by a hose system. In the accompanying brochure, Werner Hofmann writes: "To destroy the veil of a beautiful illusion, to lift the cosmetic varnish ... that is one of the ways in which artists can do something for society today. This can create forth an object such as the *Green Lung*. Denunciation is combined here to an ironic apparatus that provides a demonstrative purpose without bowing down to it. The *Green Lung*'s sacral gesture of showing off has to be understood; it demonstrates how artificial the ritual is that is sold to us as good air. When we step under the helmet, it should take our breath away. Anyone who flippantly criticizes society will mistrust this formalization. But critical intelligence is expressed perfectly in the fact that there is a clever, formal encryption. That is the difference between this hybrid pseudo-altar and the aesthetics of artificial flowers."

paulins that possessed façade motives forming the spatial octagon of the square. This design of the square, evocative of a Potemkin village, required complex scaffolding constructions in the background, to which the tarps with mock façades were fixed, thus making the prospective impression of the square tangible. In a way, an urban space of the future was projected onto the present.

Whenever house façades on the roadside are renovated, the necessary scaffolding is often covered with tarpaulins that bear an image of the original hidden behind them to somewhat ease the resulting irritation in the streetscape. In this case, it is a constellation of three elements. First, there is the house façade, including the stable properties of the building behind it. Then the scaffold, temporarily connected to the building, which makes the renovation even possible. As a last step, the tarp with the imprinted new façade is attached to the scaffolding construction in order to conceal the mess. In this case, the architect's second task is, according to Adolf Loos, to form a static combination of the building and provisional scaffolding, bearing the prospective façade. Creating the image for the print would consequently be the architect's "first task," provided there is an architect for such a measure. If that is not the case, a photographer could take their place.

The contribution of an architect is not always necessary in the process of constructing temporary measures that generate space and purpose within urban environments. The successful medium in this context is the container as a diversely applicable spatial unit. As a modular, standardized entity, it was mainly used in transportation at first. Throughout several developments, functional modifications, such as temporary offices, mobile research facilities, or exhibition and living spaces, were created to satisfy a momentary demand. As a model kit that allows multilayered buildings, this principle is utilized in various fields in locations today.

For the 1982 documenta urbana in Kassel, Haus-Rucker-Co developed the *Search-Field* for a project of the University of Kassel: an urban building study for a temporary, interactive container structure with the purpose of research and exchange. One important element was the country archive, which we defined back then as follows:

> The archive consists of a central, around eighty-meter-long and four-story-tall development structure, on which around sixty containers can be stacked in a way that allows for each one of them to be accessed individually. Each of the containers arranged here, from specific and distant countries, holds descriptive material about the characteristics and current state of those countries. The information and moods conveyed here cannot be stored

on computers. The interior of the containers uses various objects and the resulting informative constellations to display the present reality of the countries they come from. According to the currently addressed problem areas, the archive has to be constantly updated. This means that only containers of countries that are affected by the momentarily relevant topics discussed in the *Search-Field* are archived. Once the work for one issue is completed, the involved containers provided with developed solutions are returned to their starting point. This creates space for containers from other countries and the processing of their problems.

The study's aspects of transportation and exchange of objectivity and information found an analogy with utopian features in the story about a transport container filled with sneakers of all sorts and sizes that fell from a gigantic freighter on its way

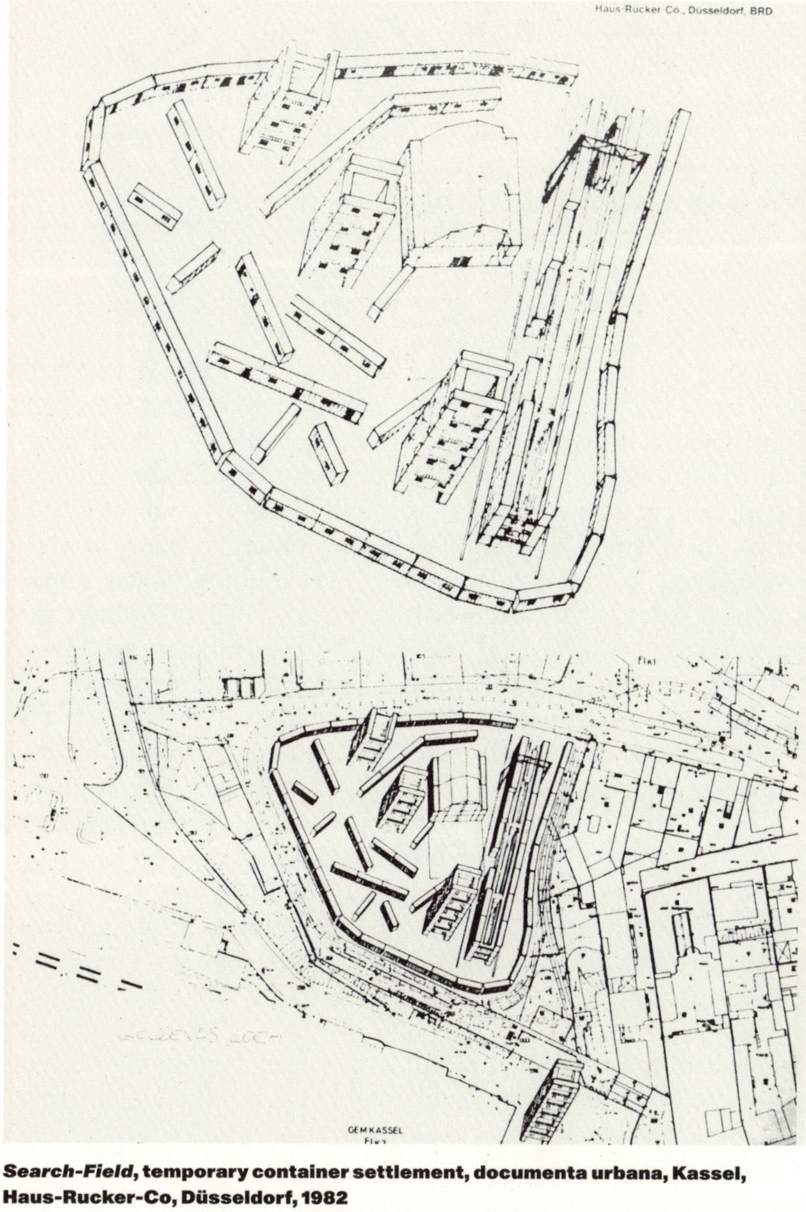

Bosch booth at IFMA (International Bicycle and Motor Fair)

1974 We conceptualize a fair stand for Bosch at the IFMA Trade Show in Cologne, a "Rippled Grassland with Luminary Rod" for the exterior spaces of the federal ministries of Justice and Science in Bonn-Bad Godesberg, and for the pedestrian zones in Linz, Austria, and Nuremberg. After intense considerations, the Bosch fair stand gets the green light. The detail of an oversized, helmeted motorcyclist holding on to his handlebars with two oversized gloves promises to stand out between the other exhibition stands. It would create the desired attention for Bosch, a company that is a primary supplier to the motorcycle and automotive industry. As we also agreed to oversee the production and assembly of the object, we commission a sculptress experienced in these tasks and procedures. After a while, it becomes clear that the load of work is at risk of exceeding the artist's capacities. With the help of my girlfriend Lilly and the contacts she has at the theater in Oberhausen, the executive team can be strengthened in order to make a timely completion possible. Still, it will be very tight, though the whole team works through the nights. Only two hours before the deadline, the scenario is finished.

Search-Field, temporary container settlement, documenta urbana, Kassel, Haus-Rucker-Co, Düsseldorf, 1982

1975 The highlight of the year is a collaboration with Karl Schwanzer. In Düsseldorf and Cologne, new buildings for the North Rhine-Westphalia art collection and the Wallraf-Richartz Museum have been tendered. Schwanzer wants to participate in both competitions, so he drives to the Rhineland to visit each location and discuss the modalities of a collaboration. Cologne will be handled by Laurids, and I will concentrate on developing the draft for Düsseldorf in Munich. In the middle of my editing process, I receive a call notifying me that Karl Schwanzer has passed away. I can barely believe the news, but it quickly becomes an unchangeable fact. Both projects do well in the contest but aren't able to advance to the top as winning works.

1975 In autumn of that year, I finally complete the collage *Way to Lillyput*. It consists of landscapes that are stretched over steel frames and emerge from one another. I give these drawings to Lilly for Christmas in 1975 with best wishes for 1976.

across the ocean and sank. In the process, it surrendered its cargo to the ocean's waves and undertow. Years after the event, hikers would still find sports shoes washed ashore on various coasts, though they were marked by their journey across the water. Only a few of the finders knew of the incident long ago and made the connection between the shell-studded shoe they found and the transport container lying on the bottom of the sea in the vastness of that water's salty mass.

On the mainland, in the field of built urbanity, containers are a medium in the game between demand and supply. They meet the dynamic requirements of the economy and the spatial needs in society's social and cultural fabric. Their tasks are manageable, limited in time, and have a beginning and an end.

In this sense, they belong to the cosmos of provisional arrangements and are related to the prototype of the provisional space: the tent. In the current era of nomads, the tent has gained importance as a flexibly applicable space that goes beyond its use as camping utensil. For many who are or had been part of the mass migration to Europe due to war or hardship, the tent is the only remaining refuge they can take with them. After reaching their destination, many migrants first spend their time in arranged tent settlements until the formalities regarding their residence in the European Union are resolved. The associated shapes of the tents do not offer sufficient sojourn quality, which frequently leads to social issues between their occupants.

Standing in contrast to this, the luxurious tent city Mina, in the vicinity of Mecca, Saudi Arabia, can accommodate several million Hajjis. The white, textile fabric, the arrangement of the individual tents, and its surface area of around twenty square kilometers are reminiscent of single-family home neighborhoods in Western culture. The high standard of these tents is emphasized by fire resistance, air conditioning, water supply, and electricity, which each unit is provided with. The fact that these cities are only available for the Hajj pilgrimage has an elitist effect. The question remains unanswered whether the tent city is provisional, thereby existing for a limited time, or whether it was planned and implemented as a permanent setup without any time limit set for its existence. In this case, the principle "trial and error" was a provisional part of a large, real long-term study that will not lead to a foreseeable result.

Within the cosmos of temporary constructions, "trial and error" is part of conceptual installations with experimental features in public space.

The claim of "provisional architecture" is to counteract the normality of urban conditions and open spaces with installations in order to create thought-provoking impulses for a different per-

Walking School, interactive provisional at Graben, Haus-Rucker-Co, Vienna, 1971/72

spective of cities. In the projects by Haus-Rucker-Co, the utilization of these interventions is an essential aspect of these concepts. The pneumatic constructions and objects from the 1960s were realized using similar ideas. The main difference to architectonic provisional solutions lies in their vulnerability. Even when unsupervised, these architectures are contrastingly robust and have to withstand the aggressions of passersby as much as possible. The *Walking School* from 1971, an installation of a linear structure composed of various surfaces on the Graben, a famous street in Vienna, did not withstand such aggressions. It was supposed to make urbanites more aware of the act of walking but was taken down after a few days. All that remained were comments in the daily newspapers, photographic documents, and the memory of the event. The aforementioned *Frame Building* at the 1977 documenta 6 in Kassel still stands today, although it was initially planned only for the duration of the exhibition. The object was never exposed to aggression, but if necessary, its sponsor, a financial institution, would arrange and pay for renovations. The frame construction had not been vandalized, either during the exhibition or afterwards. Only on the occasion of the documenta 7 in 1982 was the main frame provided with a makeshift scaffolding, probably to clarify that the object was not part of the current exhibition.

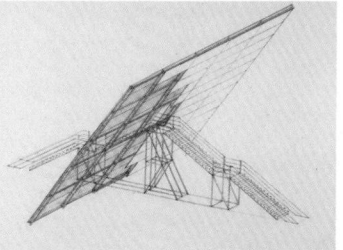

Inclined Plane

1976 We participate in countless exhibitions, such as *Erholungsraum Stadt* (the city as recreational space) in the Munich Lenbachhaus. Haus-Rucker-Co designs the entrance in the form of a drawing of a provisional street situation, enlarged on canvas and crossed by a staircase construction that's cut in the fabric. The exhibition moves to Vienna and Zurich. In the same year, Haus-Rucker-Co, Coop Himmelblau, Missing Link, and Zünd-Up participate in "Supersommer," an event near the Vienna Naschmarkt. We design the entrance *Inclined Plane*, the first realization of "provisional architecture," is a radical, abstract object in the urban space and simultaneously, it exists as a partition and gateway to the event room behind it.

The never-realized *Big Piano*, along with *Oasis No 7*, was the second installation by Haus-Rucker-Co that was proposed for the central square Friedrichsplatz in Kassel at the documenta 5. The project has been in a planning stage since 1972 and all that is left today are drawings, a model, and written descriptions. In a way, it remains in a preliminary phase of its possible existence as a provisional arrangement, even though its temporary presence in an open urban space would probably be stimulating. The staircase construction, with its musically programmable steps, meets two requirements of provisional architecture: its usability and the possibility to produce sound sequences either

1976 In the late summer, Uta Brandes and Michael Erloff from *Zweitschrift* visit the Haus-Rucker-Co office on Glücksburger Strasse in Düsseldorf. We sit on the terrace overlooking the green interior of the house block and drink, in addition to coffee, alcoholic beverages. As the *Zweitschrift 3* will be a magazine about architecture, the two publishers offer to elaborate on our team's intentions in an article.

1977 In May, Lilly and I move to an apartment with a panoramic view on the outskirts of town in the Gallberg. That same year, we visit New York for the first time in five years. I have been friends with Chris Britz, an artist with Austrian roots, since I began at Haus-Rucker-Co New York a decade ago. He bought a loft on Worth Street in SoHo with enough space to accommodate guests. We also visit Caroll Michels at 491 Broadway and I am able to repair the *Environment Transformer, Flyhead,* and bring it to Arthur Drexler at MoMA's Department of Architecture. We take impressive walks on the Westside Highway, which, freed from cars, creates a fascinating new urban space for flâneurs, street art, joggers, and events of all kinds.

Wall with Stair, urban space divider, drawing, Haus-Rucker-Co, Zamp Kelp, 1979

Westside Highway, 1977

individually or in a group, which are then broadcast to the surrounding area for other people to hear. The steam cloud generated in temporal intervals around the platform at the top end of the stairs adds visual significance to the object and momentarily obscures the view from the platform of the musical instrument's surroundings.

Music in public and urban spaces is a flowing, timely limited phenomenon in the cosmos of provisional structures. Music transforms spatial conditions for the duration of its presence. Music is invisible and has a euphorigenic, aggressive, and anxious effect. Music resonates from instruments, often in combination with mobile stage sceneries that serve as the backdrop for band concerts, an orchestra, or opera performance; they accompany the musical product with optical and dramatic effects. Music as atmospheric nomadism can appear anywhere. Music is powerful. This fact dawned on me at a rock concert in the Berlin Olympiastadion at the end of the fifth encore when the audience, wild with happiness, demanded further encores and the stadium announcer ineffectively suggested that the show was really over. Shortly thereafter, the floodlights came on and Richard Wagner's "Ride of the Valkyries" was blasted from the stadium speakers. This shocked the audience and everyone, while refraining from physical protest, went home somewhat disenchanted.

Provisional architecture, a lubricant in functional and creative processes within the urban landscape, takes on conceptional ideas from Fluxus and forms the haptic link between a world of objects and the volatility of a dematerialized, digital world.

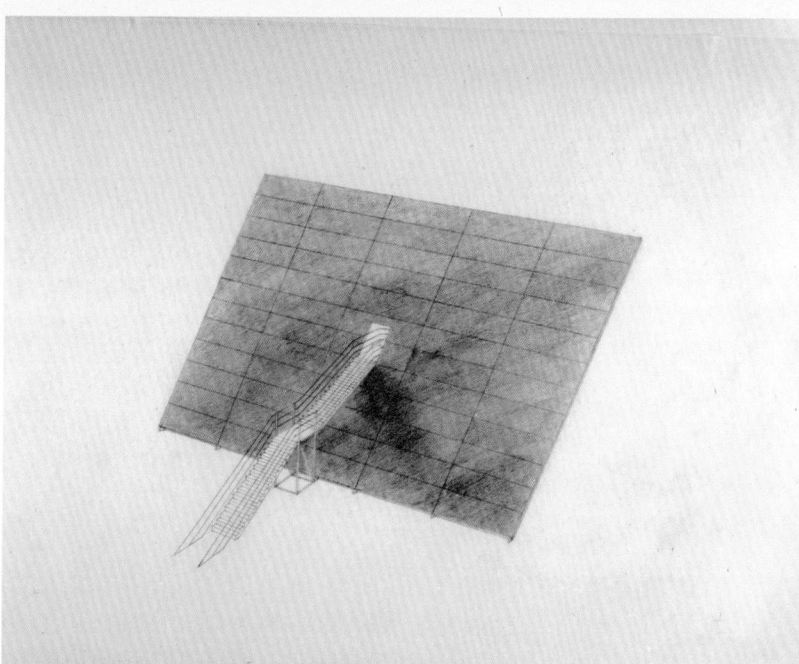

Inclined Plane, drawing, Haus-Rucker-Co, Laurids Ortner, 1976

1977 The documenta is back in Kassel. At documenta 6, supervised by Manfred Schneckenburger, outdoor sculptures play a decisive role. Haus-Rucker-Co's first proposal is a black cube hovering above rope constructions, which, referring to the portico of the Fridericianum, is supposed to wander around on the square it is installed on. The idea is not met with a positive response. Eventually, the *Frame Building* at Schöne Aussicht zur Aue, a terrace overlooking the meadow and park, is implemented. We are in great company. After Christo and Jeanne-Claude had presented an eighty-meter-high tower of "packed air" for the documenta 4, Walter De Maria dug *The Vertical Earth Kilometer*—a brass rod—one thousand meters into the ground of the Friedrichsplatz, which is still visible as a yellow dot on the square's surface, evocative of a lost coin. Richard Serra's *Terminal* had also taken up a position on the Friedrichsplatz and formed the beginning of a three-way constellation of the drilling tower for De Maria and the Frame Building near the meadow as a spatial finish, thus dominating the square.

Inclined Plane, entrance object for Supersommer at Naschmarkt (back side), Haus-Rucker-Co, Laurids Ortner, Zamp Kelp, Manfred Ortner, Vienna, 1976

FLUXUS AND THE WORLD OF PROVISIONAL ARCHITECTURE

Inclined Plane, entrance object for Supersommer at Naschmarkt, Haus-Rucker-Co, Laurids Ortner, Zamp Kelp, Manfred Ortner, Vienna, 1976

Art and Society

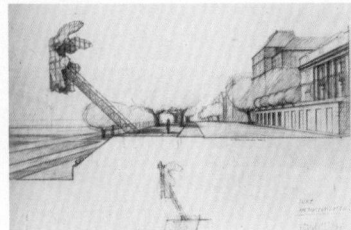

Nike of Frankfurt

1977 Meanwhile, the 1977 exhibition *Forum Metall* in Linz is a media sensation. Haus-Rucker-Co contributes *Nike*, which is mounted on the right-hand bridgehead building from the National Socialist era as a symbol of the victory of culture and democracy over dictatorship. This is a theme that, in conjunction with the emblematic sculpture, leads to heated discussions in the media. Bernhard Luiginbühl has contributed an atlas on loan and Günther Uecker, a table with oversized nails pointing threateningly downwards from its surface. The complete works can be viewed along the Danube's banks while taking the

Throughout the history of evolution, uncertainty is the driving force that stimulates humanity to permanently develop its living conditions. This requires an abundance of time, which only became available once humans were no longer exclusively occupied with hunting and gathering food. It was at this time that the development of art as a product of man began. The ability to create artistically grew into a suggestive network of innovation and curiosity, one in which art became the medium that accompanies society as a contemplative enrichment for the spectrum of their perception. Art as a universe of possibilities uses the existing, still increasing abundance of time in two ways. First, through the use of its protagonists—the artists—whose work challenges the uncertainty of time. Second, by those groups of society that spend their superfluous time dealing with art products. The increasing abundance of time and the associated rise in the demand for opportunities to view art account for the growing spatial network of art exhibitions. Art buildings are places of tardiness and contemplation in which uncertainty is thematized by use of art worlds beyond profane mundanity as well as the contemplation of current and historical conditions of society.

Haus-Rucker-Co, Zamp Kelp, Klaus Pinter, Laurids Ortner (from left) in front of Gallery Zwirner, Cologne, Albertusstrasse, 1969

In 1994, the federal art hall Bundeskunsthalle in Bonn hosted the symposium *Art in Architecture*, for which Steidl published a volume with the same title as part of the Forum series. My contribution dealt with the topic "Bulwark and Temporary Construction—A Projection on the Possible Functional Polarization of Art Museum and Art Exhibition Hall." This also involved the juxtaposition of the Art and Exhibition Hall of the Federal Republic of Germany in Bonn, with its clear institution as an art hall, and the Kunstmuseum Bonn, with its functional mix of collections and exhibition spaces. Over the years, I have made many practical experiences that have shaped my opinion on both alternatives.

The Kunsthalle of Mainz, a building created purely for exhibitions, was built in the former customs port on the Rhine from 2004 to 2007. The boiler house, which formerly served the operation of cranes at the port, was used for the building. The clinker brick house from the turn of the 19th century received a new entrance building, including an entrance hall between the large exhibition spaces in place of the obsolete chimney and a cafeteria in the former engine house. Three small rooms, arranged one above the other and accessible via an elevator and a staircase, provided the new building with a tower-like feature. The main characteristics included a cover of green glass with a vertical inclination of seven degrees that stood out against the existing clinker façade. The slope of the two narrow sides created an intentional and noticeable irritation of the sense of balance in many visitors, especially in the stairwell and elevator systems, which were also inclined. The vertigo experienced in three-kilometer walk. *Nike* will remain here for two years and then, in accordance with the mayor's promise and to the dismay of many Linz inhabitants, will be taken down.

1977 Hamburg tenders the competition for the Rathausmarkt, in which Haus-Rucker-Co participated with the cooperation of Thomas Jaenisch. The first ideas are based on the assumptions that the arcades on the Kleine Alster river, including its pier, define the quality of the overall situation at the Rathausmarkt, leading to the alignment of the square's surface and the façade of the arcades. This, and the suggestion to lift the square's space towards the Mönckebergstrasse using a ramp with a three-percent incline, turns the square away from the town hall and instead strengthens its connection to the ambience of the Kleine Alster. On top of the sloping square surface, a mobile canopy encourages active use of the space. Bus stops and commercial spaces are planned at the end of the marketplace on Mönckenbergstrasse but are not visible from the square itself.

***Kunsthalle Mainz**, surface studies of the inclined tower, sketches, Zamp Kelp, 2005*

ART AND SOCIETY

1977 Peter Cook founds the Art Net in London, a gallery presenting themed exhibitions on progressive positions in architecture. In the fall, I travel to London to take part in the opening of the exhibition *Haus-Rucker-Co/Provisional Architecture*. I also give a lecture at the Architectural Association School of Architecture and elaborate on our latest work, which is apparently so impressive that the audience is completely befuddled and leaves the hall without any applause. During the Art Net exhibit's opening, I ask Cedric Price for his verdict on the pieces of work, to which he replies, "Well, some of them are nice, but we should talk."

1978 For West Berlin, we create the draft *Green Table* at the Schlüterdreieck, the triangle between Schlüterstrasse and the Kurfürstendamm. It is a kidney-shaped table with a surface made of water and sixteen stationary chairs and benches around it. The work is liked by the selection committee, but not realized.

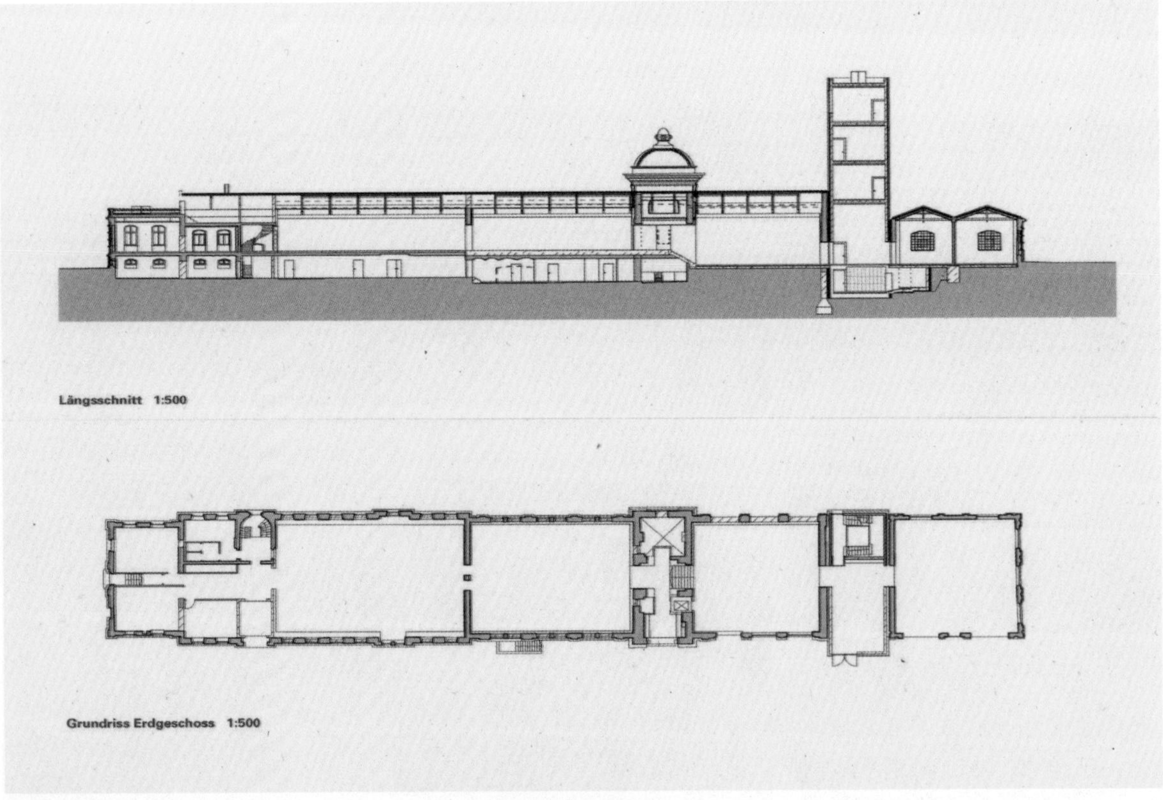

Kunsthalle Mainz, section and plan, Zamp Kelp neo.studio, 2006

ART AND SOCIETY

Kunsthalle Mainz, outdoor view and indoor exhibition space, Zamp Kelp neo.studio, Mainz, 2007

Giant Billiard model

1978 Liselotte Ungers opens the exhibition *Haus-Rucker-Co/Drafts and Models* at her studio gallery on Belvedere Strasse in Cologne. Heinrich Klotz, designated director of the German Architecture Museum in Frankfurt, buys the *Giant Billiard* model straight from the exhibition.

1978 We start our draft for the bank "Oberbank" in Wels, a project ending in 1980 with the realization of the building. One important element of the overall concept is the autonomy of the façade and the building structure.

the slanting rooms of the staircase expressed a certain message to exhibition visitors: art produces parallel worlds that take us into spheres where we can contemplate societal or individual conflicts. The new feature takes the form of a slanting tower, visible from the outside and continued on the clinker building's interior. The exhibition rooms were to be understood as white boxes, which contrapuntally faced the historical outer appearance of the boiler house and created various forms of artificial illumination in order to emphasize the boxes' adaptability.

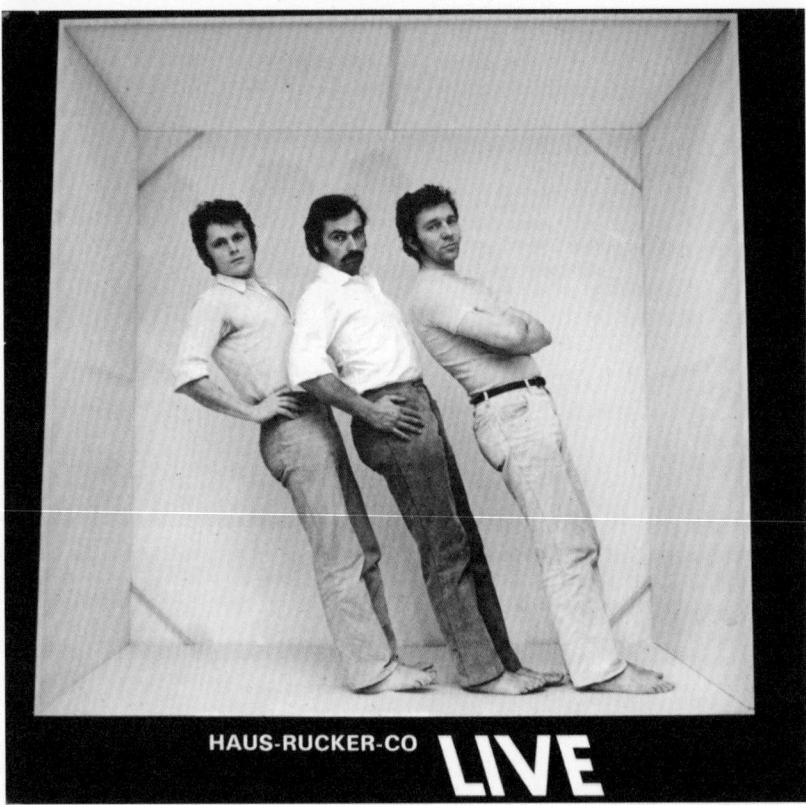

Haus-Rucker-Co LIVE, front page, catalog folder, Museum des 20. Jahrhunderts, Vienna, 1970

On the other hand, the 20er Haus—today's mumok—in Vienna was a hybrid of an art museum with permanent collections and an art exhibition hall with changing, limited works. In 1969, Haus-Rucker-Co were invited by the then-director Alfred Schmeller to exhibit there. To put our personal opinion in a nutshell, we considered art museums to be cemeteries where the history of painting and sculpture could be preserved and stored. We saw them as conservational institutions, big shots of retrospection and safekeeping; they were establishments diametrically critical of our ambitions and activities. The topic was not about the statics of history, but the dynamics of the moment. Upon realizing this conflict situation, we decided on a program that contrasted museums, and with all of our existing and new objects for the exhibition Haus-Rucker-Co LIVE, moved to live there in 1970. The central object placed in the middle of the four

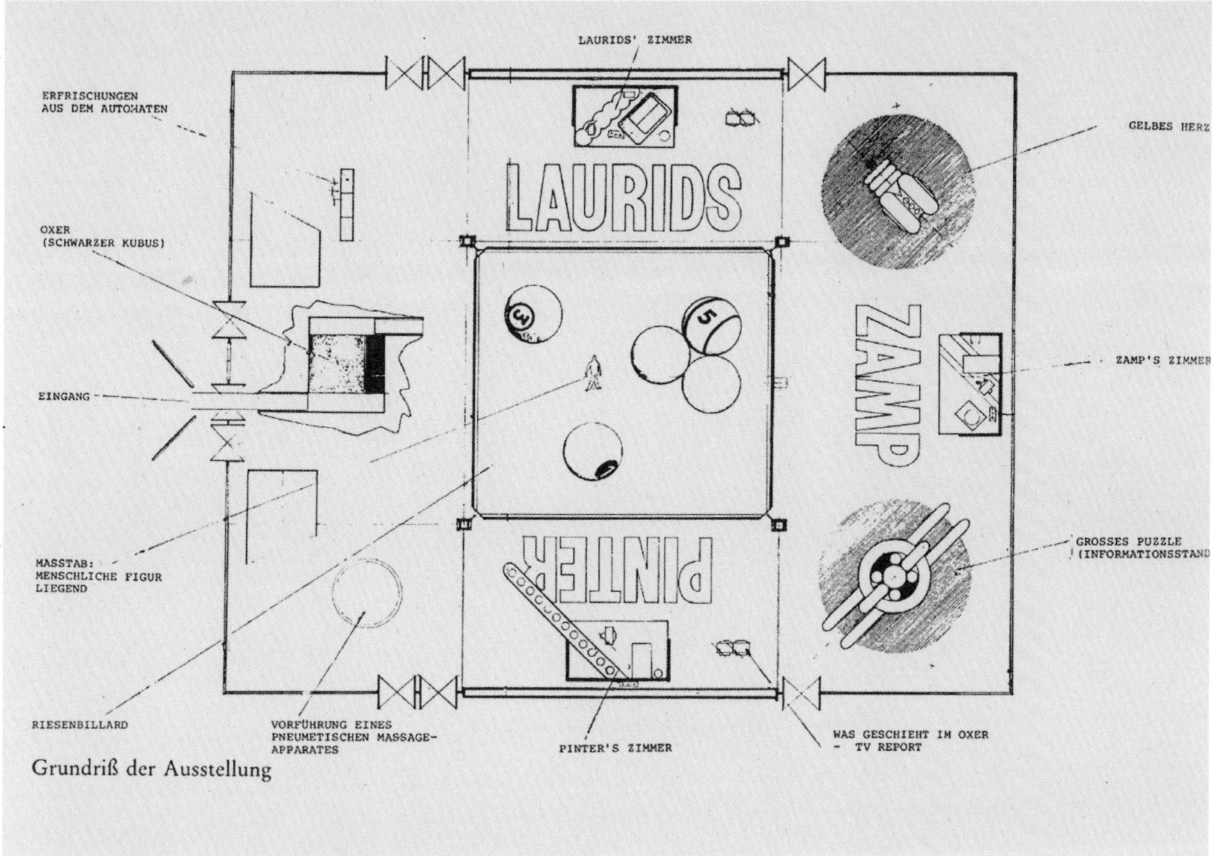

***Haus-Rucker-Co LIVE*,** exhibition plan, Düsseldorf, 1969
Laurids Ortner, Zamp Kelp, Klaus Pinter in Zamp's living area, Museum des 20. Jahrhunderts, Vienna, 1970

Giant Billiard, central object of the exhibition Haus-Rucker-Co LIVE, Museum des 20. Jahrhunderts, Vienna, 1970

1978 Planning the *Pavilion of the Elements* requires something different than the much-too-elaborate lawn of waves for the outside areas of the Federal Ministries for Justice and Science in Bonn. Instead, we design chemical elements integrated in a spatial fragment made of weathering steel.

1979 Haus-Rucker-Co is awarded the Berlin Art Prize by the Academy of Arts. Stanislaus von Moos gives a laudatory speech. In Linz, Helmuth Gsöllpointner, Laurids Ortner, and Angela Hareiter prepare the Forum Design. Haus-Rucker-Co is tasked to design the temporary exhibition building along the Danube and the old rail bridge.

grave columns supporting the upper floor was the *Giant Billiard*. Apart from the three white balls with a diameter of three meters, it was particularly the 14 × 14-meter walkable, white air mattress that seemed to merge with the white exhibition space and lend the museum the character of a peculiar martial arts facility. Visitors gamboled around on top of the *Giant Billiard* as if they were on a snow-covered meadow. The effects of gravity as a an essential force for gaining a sense of balance was challenged; in its place, the exhibition offered new, liberating ways of movement for the users. The mattress was the central attraction: the visitors interacting with it, the surrounding objects such as *Mindexpander 1* and *2, Yellow Heart, Battleship, Roomscraper*, and *Design Post* for the Austrian Institute of Design, as well as the living room furniture of the three Haus-Rucker-Co members, created a permanent source of unrest during the museum's operating hours.

In a time when information is becoming increasingly addictive, the demand for varied diversity in the art field is also growing. Many renowned museums have changing exhibitions that seem more important in the stream of information than the *gravitas* of their collections in the background. Most art halls with func-

Giant Billiard, installed at 53rd Street, in front of the Museum of Contemporary Crafts, New York, 1970

ART AND SOCIETY

Giant Billiard, exhibition Haus-Rucker-Co LIVE, Museum des 20. Jahrhunderts, Vienna, 1970

Photomontage, *Giant Billiard* at 51st Street, New York, Manhattan, 1970

tional features have characteristics that have yet to be realized in this form. The majority of them are labeled unrealizable and utopian; however, they are available as documented plans and models sitting in the drawers of architects, ready to influence and come to fruition. The *House for the Steirischer Herbst* at the city square of Fischplatz in Graz is one such case. The house is designed as a cone balancing on its tip, which enhances the square with its symbolic character and accommodates the administration and organization of the annual culture event. The shape of the building and its location on the banks of the Mur River make the Steirischer Herbst permanently present in the city beyond just the active time of the year. Upside-down cones are unique in that they are only able to hold their position

***Giant Billiard**, scenario out of the exhibition in Vienna*

while in a state of rotation. The fact that the cone belonging to the *House for Steirischer Herbst* does not spin accounts for a certain static magic that challenges the laws of gravity.

The competition design for the Center for Art and Media Technology (ZKM) in Karlsruhe was drafted in 1989 and inspired by the Vehicle Assembly Building on Cape Canaveral. With the metaphorical message that both art and media technology are two subjects with adventurous features, in no way inferior to those of space travel in terms of significance and impact on society, the location in connection to Karlsruhe's main station was an attractive specification of the tender. This would have significantly expanded the commuting area of the cultural house. Furthermore, the acting analogies to the National Aeronautics and Space Administration building and its assembly halls, just as tall, would have played a role, surrounded by service rooms and control functions. The Intention of the ZKM was to create points of contact between new and familiar cultural developments, as well as to make the many new advancements in the field of media technology more comprehensible through references to art. In the concept we presented at that time, space was once again turned into an experimental field for new dimensions of perception, whereby the fusion of media and artistic approaches was supposed to become a central task of the institution. The center's outer appearance in the urban environment would have been impossible to overlook due to its size, the volume of the buildings behind it, and the fact that it was composed of offset, net-shaped exterior walls. The interior concept was organized around a cubical room with a length of thirty-six meters, which could be opened to the East—similar to a stage. This room was equipped with lifting platforms, a rigging system, and other installations that allowed for a versatile and directorial use. It radiated the type of energy that would be required to bring about the intended fusion of art and media in spatial experiments.

The concept from 1989 was not realized. Twenty-five years later, more and more media elements are superimposed by concrete

1979 In the summer, I meet Heinrich Klotz for the first time while handing over the *Giant Billiard* at the construction site of the new Architecture Museum, next to the Main in Frankfurt. He tells me how surprised he is that we, Haus-Rucker, had left the beautiful city of Vienna unjustly. Once you have lived like a Viennese, you enter into a lifelong relationship with the city. Accordingly, Walter Pichler had also been torn between New York and Vienna, but had settled for the latter, knowing that his personal temperament would not be able to cope without Vienna's fertile soil, as he once said. Heinrich Klotz and I also discuss the circulating criticism against the development of Frankfurt, a city whose essence is being increasingly destroyed by the construction of high-rise buildings. Klotz elaborates on his view that Frankfurt is composed of two interwoven urban constellations: a historically flat city with regulated eaves heights and, rising from this formation, an energized high-rise city. I agree with him that this could be a model for European metropoles in the future, unlike the North American downtowns which consist of homogenous skyscraper architecture.

1979 The project for designing the central square Konstablerwache in Frankfurt is not realized. However, Haus-Rucker-Co wins two contests for Art in Architecture this year: one for designing the *Bowery Gates* at the residential complex Schlangenbaderstrasse in Berlin, and the other for a project advertising columns outside of a new school building on Melanchtonstrasse in Düsseldorf-Benrath. Both projects are made up of two stations that are connected through a speaking tube, and both are made a reality.

1979 In October, Lilly M. L. Koch and I fly back to New York. This time, mainly to get married. Prior to the trip, we have all our relevant documents translated, which turns out to be unnecessary as the registrar only demands our oath that the documents are "alright." We tie the knot in Chris Britz's loft. Eduard Schulz from Vienna and Caroll Michels are witnesses to the marriage. The Justice of Peace asks us whether it will be a one-ring or two-ring ceremony. We explain to him that it will be a "no-ring ceremony" that will also be celebrated that way.

Cape Canaveral, rocket assembling building, areal image

Rocket assembling hall, indoor view

sceneries in the theater sector, and it seems that planned fusions in the field of fine arts and media are likely to be realized there. As it looks, new perspectives appear through the evolutionary technologies of virtual reality. This creates opportunities to superimpose long-established scenarios with elements of virtual reality in order to arrive at new multidimensional phenomena of perception in which utopia and fiction can be illustrated in an immersive manner.

Forum Design

1980 Haus-Rucker-Co's most important project this year is the construction of an exhibition building, which will be erected as a provisional solution for the Forum Design in Linz. For Lilly Kelp and me, it is the birth of our son Christoph Friedrich Florian on March 14, 1980, just after midnight.

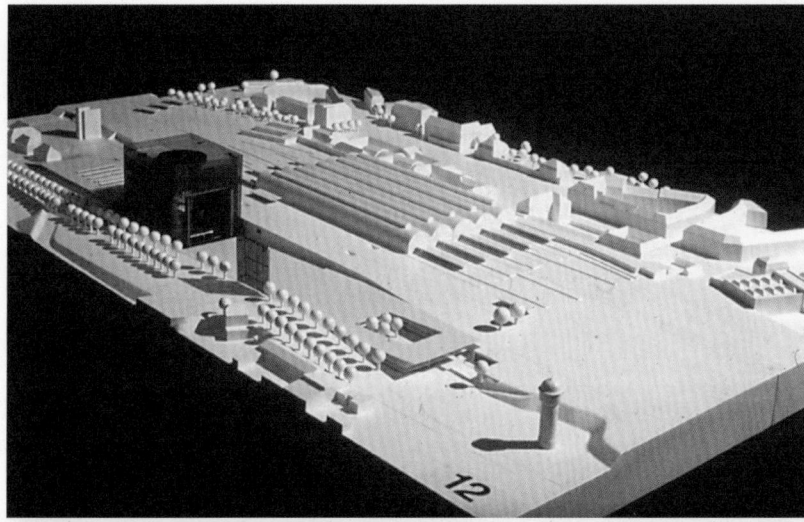

Center for Art and Media-Technology, near main station, Karlsruhe, Haus-Rucker-Co, Laurids Ortner, Zamp Kelp, Manfred Ortner with Julius Krauss, Barbara Bruder, Düsseldorf, 1989

Vanilla Future, event, Athletic Sports Hall, Schleifmühlgasse, Haus-Rucker-Co, Laurids Ortner, Zamp Kelp, Klaus Pinter, Vienna, 1969

1980 The city of Düsseldorf is launching a two-stage contest for the redesign of the Gustav-Gründgens-Platz. In collaboration with Thomas Jaenisch, we forgo most construction measures. As the main design element, we suggest a stage wagon that can move along a stretch of tracks that runs from the Goethe Museum on the corner of Jägerstrasse and Kaiserstrasse and the playhouse Düsseldorfer Schauspielhaus through the Schadowstrasse, where it ends in a pavilion that also serves as its garage. The stage wagon is allocated to the theater as an external element effective in the urban space and can be activated at any point on the rails. We are awarded with one of the first three prizes; however, the second stage of the contest no longer takes place.

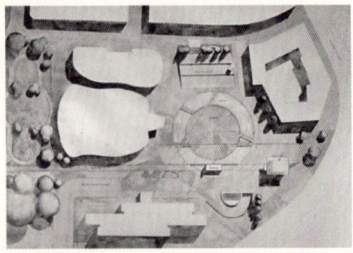

Gustav-Gründgens-Platz

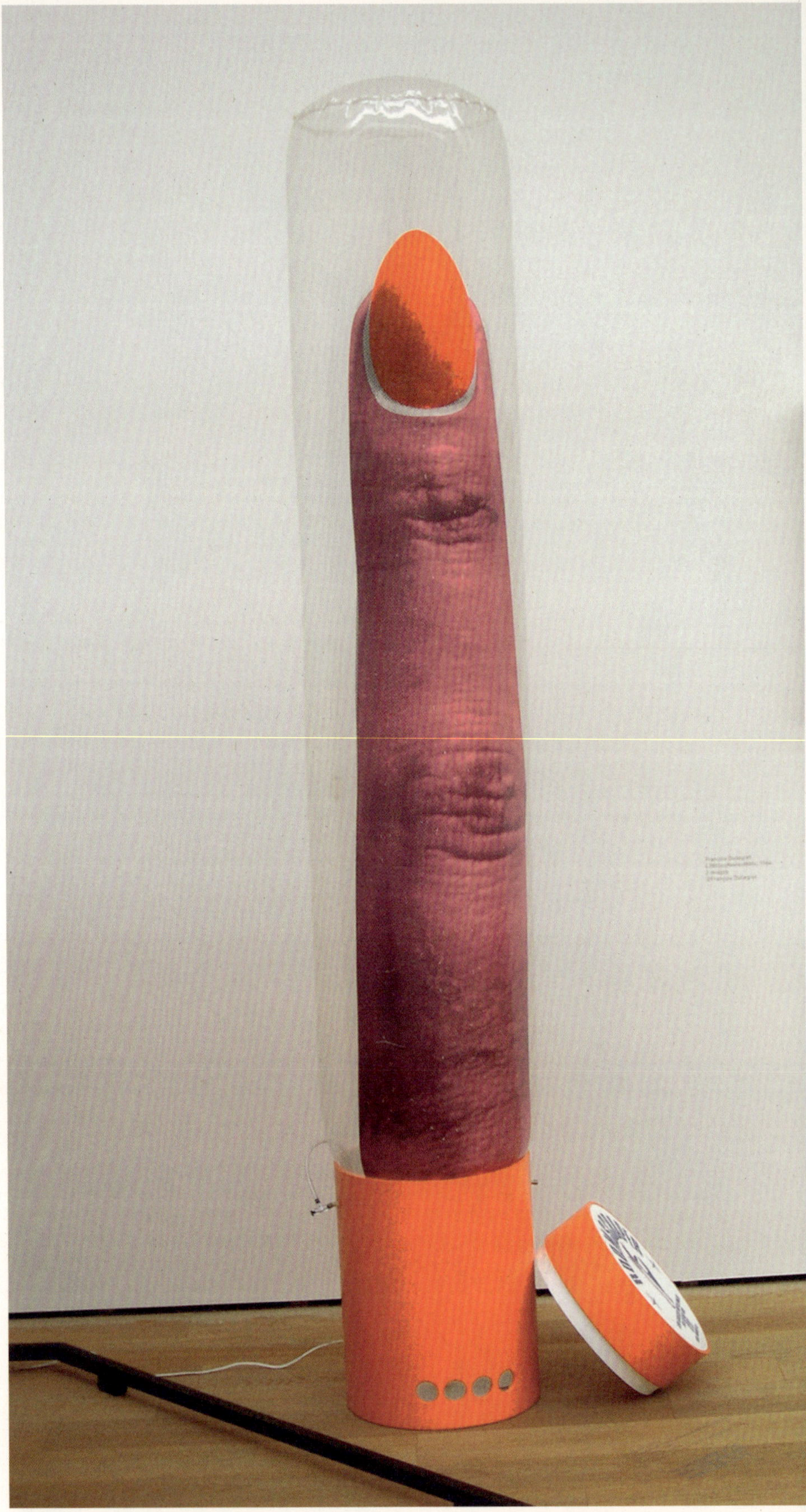

Roomscraper, air-supported cylinder out of PVC, finger silkscreen, base cardboard cylinder, inside white, outside red, Haus-Rucker, Laurids Ortner, Zamp Kelp, Klaus Pinter, Vienna, 1969

IN THE YEAR 2255

Carla and Carlo

at the Euracle

In 2255, the Conglomerate of Nations with their diverse interests in Europe has again become politically stable. However, the cultural-economic conflict between those rooting for growth-oriented, economic progressivity and the forces that strive for constant circular processes and conservatism persists among Europeans. Among the continent's citizens, this state of suspension between two opposite worldviews has led to a widespread culture of doubt that makes it increasingly difficult to make decisions. This trend has been reinforced by the fact that the dominance of a digital super-intelligence has resulted in an abstraction in the administration and perception of political processes that European citizens now have difficulties understanding. In response to this situation, Brussels has installed an institution for question-and-answer rituals based on the model of the ancient Greek Oracle of Delphi: the so-called Euracle of Mettmann near Düsseldorf. In the small town of Mettmann, there once was the site of the Neanderthal Museum for the History of Mankind, which opened in 1996 and operated for over two hundred years. The museum, designed as a concrete spiral of time, then stood empty for several decades, as the ever more perfect standards of three-dimensional projection techniques allowed the history of mankind to be accessed by anyone, anywhere, in countless variations, thus rendering the original function of the museum obsolete. The decision for the former museum building as the site for a European oracle was also determined by the building's design as a spiral volume with a metaphorical message. The fusion of computer-based processes with spatial components of a time-related architectural constellation for the reification of question-and-answer rituals that aim to eliminate doubt seemed particularly well suited here.

Carla and Carlo live in Teramo, the capital of the province of the same name in Abruzzo, about 100 miles from Rome. They have just finished their degrees in Communication Sciences and are about to decide whether to accept assistant positions at the local university or to travel to other parts of the world to share their acquired knowledge with the people living there. Although the climate in the Apennine

Mountains is constantly heating up, they are confronted with a choice between their love for the familiar scenery of their hometown, their attachment to friends, and the university's job offer on one hand, and the desire to change their personal situation on the other. After careful consideration, they decide to consult the Euracle on Mettmann, which is open to all Europeans, in order to obtain answers about perspectives for their future steps in life.

On a Friday, they board an automatic transport to L'Aquila and from there, they take the train on the historic railway line towards Roma Termini. They stay in the city for one night and then fly from Roma Ciampino airport to Düsseldorf. Upon arrival, they board a robocab and enter the destination of the Euracle in the Neander Valley into the control system. The transport robot sets off and reaches the oracle after a short drive. On site, they are a little surprised by the large number of people who are there to apply for an appointment. The wait times are considerable. Thus, the scenery is dominated by a hotel tower of impressive height, where those waiting to consult the oracle can stay. Carla and Carlo register for their Euracle consultation and receive a time slot in three days. After they have checked in at the hotel receptor by scanning their breath and physiognomies, they take the elevator to their room on the 27th floor. They spend the three days playing travel games, in which the hotel room becomes a multifunctional, audiovisual instrument that flies through time and playfully conveys information. On their third day in Neander Valley, it is finally their turn. Due to the large number of petitioners, the Euracle operates around the clock. Carla and Carlo have an appointment at midnight. As they approach the Euracle, its glass façade glows in the dark, giving the building a bright-green aura. At three minutes to midnight, Carla and Carlo enter the spiral-shaped interior of the former museum. Here, too, a scan of their facial features registers their identity and feeds the young couple's problem into the Euracle network. As they are waiting briefly, they discover that the winding room with its exposed concrete surfaces is completely empty and stands for itself as a spiral of space. At the same time, the hologram of a shimmering green-yellow sphere with a diameter of about seven feet appears in front of them. The sphere floats within the spiral and gives the impression that it is being propelled by a slight air current. A soft voice from inside the sphere chants the words "follow me!" After a while, Carlo and Carla notice that it is really two voices, and a little later, they realize that their own voices are emanating from the sphere. Carlo and Carla follow as the sphere moves along the gently rising ramp. At the first full turn, the sphere asks them about their problem, and they explain their doubt about the direction of their lives. The sphere chuckles kindly and speaks words of encouragement. Then it dances further up the ramp to disappear behind the next turn. It glides up the gradual incline with such speed that Carla and Carlo can hardly keep up. Behind the next bend, the sphere has holographically transformed into Albert Einstein, who briefly and succinctly elucidates the relativity of human existence to give the couple a liberating perspective of their situation. As Einstein's hologram dissolves, the yellow-green sphere reappears and chants again as it glides down the next few feet of the ramp. Carla and Carlo follow, approaching a zone of blue mist lit by a pale white glow, similar to the moon. Images of the countryside around Teramo appear. They are accompanied by the voice of Luciano Pavarotti singing the aria "Un di all'azzurro spazio" from the opera Andrea Chénier. At the same time, they notice an unknown aroma, which they initially find pleasant, though it confuses them. After taking a few breaths, Carlo and Carla do not recognize one another anymore. Horrified, Carla tries to escape the situation and starts running to keep the stranger at a distance. Charging after each other, their amnesia stops as suddenly as it appeared when the blue mist clears and they behold each other again. Relieved, they follow the advancing sphere as it moves up the spiral. Suddenly it stops and begins to rotate. The spiral volume fills with rhythmic clapping sounds. Not knowing this to be the piece *Clapping Music* by 20th-century composer Steve Reich, Carlo and Carla begin to move to the rhythm of the music and clap along. After the stress of the amnesia, this is a welcome positive diversion. Slowly the clapping sounds fade away and the green-yellow sphere glides on. Carla and Carlo arrive at the next turning point of the ramp. The sphere has stopped at the bend's apex and is within reach of the two. Finally, Carlo is tempted to touch the sphere's surface and finds no resistance. His hand dives into the projection of the hologram. The sphere gives off an aggravated, ominous squeak. Carlo pulls back his hand and the sphere changes color from yellow green to intense turquoise and swoops upwards along the central flight of stairs inside the ramp's open well, coming to a stop at the highest point where it illuminates its surroundings with more shades of green. Carla and Carlo stand abandoned on the ramp, on which appears a turquoise line made up of a directional, optical impulse accompanied by a synchronous acoustic throbbing sound that fades away in a rhythmical echo. The two follow the turquoise impulse on the ramp's floor further upwards. After about fifty steps, the line disappears and the throbbing sound changes to the pitch of a sonar ping. Carlo and Carla are now left alone in the upper part of the spiral volume. They still have to complete the last section of the path at the end of which the Euracle will give them the advice. In the silence of the situation, they pay closer attention to the room. The two-hundred-year-old exposed concrete radiates confidence and reminds them of the limestone caves of the Neander Valley that existed here before they fell victim to a quarry three hundred years ago. They still feel a slight tailwind and the impulses of the imaginary sonar reverberate through the room. The two notice a bottle emitting smoke, which begins to fill the ramp space. At the same time, the beginning of Stravinsky's "Rite of Spring" starts playing. As the ceiling and walls dissolve in the fog, a sparse plain with snow-covered mountains on its horizon emerges before Carlo's and Carla's eyes like a mirage. They listen to the imaginary sonar's impulses and see the snow disappearing as the white peaks turn gray. At the same time, parts of the plain are transformed into urban landscapes.

As the fog dissolves, the plain scenario also disappears. Before them lies once again the sober, winding space. As they walk around the last ramp bend, the turquoise-colored sphere they are now heading for floats in front of them. They reach a boundary line drawn in the ground, which indicates the transition of the spiral volume into its tangential endpoint and at the same time defines the space in which the questioners will receive the Euracle's answer. The sphere hovers behind this line and exits the building through the transparent window wall at the apex of the ramp as Carla and Carlo cross the line. It now floats outside the spiral volume that makes up the building. By circling around itself, it expands its volume and murmurs a message for the couple who gaze at the spherical phenomenon at the end of the ramp. Carlo and Carla spend some time in this "space of answers and advice" and listen to the sphere's murmur, which is incomprehensible to third parties. Then they take the lift down. On their way to the hotel, their ears are filled with music from archaic sounding string instruments. Carla turns to Carlo, mumbling one word only:

"zapadno."

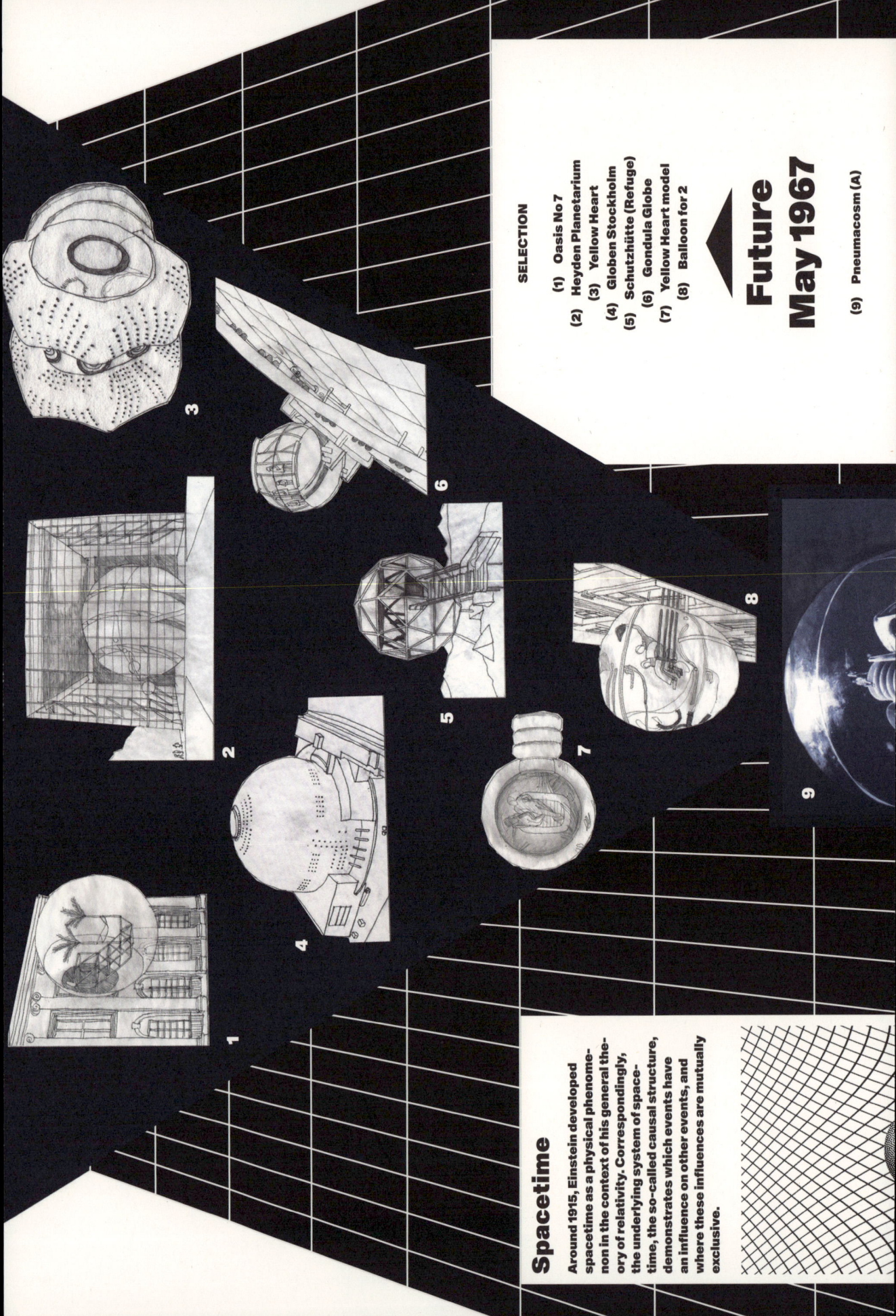

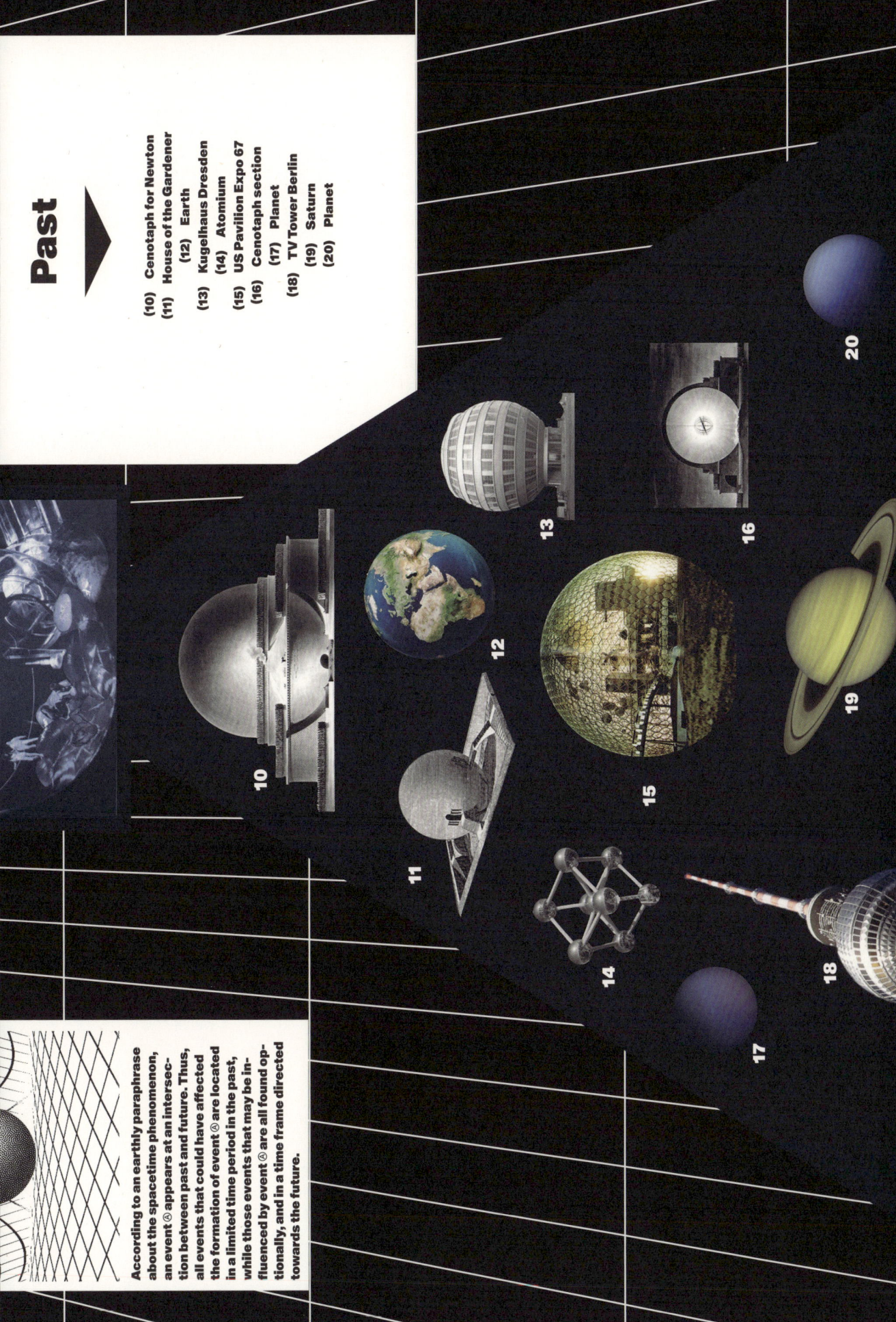

Past

- (10) Cenotaph for Newton
- (11) House of the Gardener
- (12) Earth
- (13) Kugelhaus Dresden
- (14) Atomium
- (15) US Pavilion Expo 67
- (16) Cenotaph section
- (17) Planet
- (18) TV Tower Berlin
- (19) Saturn
- (20) Planet

According to an earthly paraphrase about the spacetime phenomenon, an event Ⓐ appears at an intersection between past and future. Thus, all events that could have affected the formation of event Ⓐ are located in a limited time period in the past, while those events that may be influenced by event Ⓐ are all found optionally, and in a time frame directed towards the future.

Space-time

1980 Together with Karl-Heinz Schmitz, we develop a project for the contest as part of the program of the International Architecture Exhibition in Berlin for the area around the Rauchstrasse. The project *Geteilte Häuser* (separated houses) is comprised of four pairs of house elements and one house fragment. In each case, two buildings form parts of a complete imaginary building. The resulting gaps in between refer to the respective units and create an interrelated, flowing space with an adjustable, sojourn quality in its overall constellation.

1980 For the Venice biennial, Haus-Rucker-Co propose the project *Campanile*, a floating tower analogous to the bell tower on Saint Mark's Square. A tank filled with oil serves as the tower's foundation and with time, the oil will be absorbed by a flame, visible from afar, on top of the tower. This causes the tower to tip over into the Grand Canal at some point.

1981 For me, the year starts with a guest professorship at Cornell University in Ithaca, New York. Oswald Mathias Ungers has asked me to represent him there for some time. And so, I fly to New York's JFK Airport first, and then fly from La Guardia to Ithaca. The second airplane is small and every gust of wind becomes noticeable. From my seat, I can look out on the snowy landscape down below, which, the closer I get to my destination, the more it reminds me of James Fenimore Cooper's Leatherstocking Tales. Later, on campus and having left the bird's eye view, I notice that there is nothing left of the historical conflicts described in the book between natives, the British, and the French. Mathias Ungers has given his students an urban, Berlin-related topic as a task, a theme that is rapidly gaining momentum after its introductory phase. Inside the university library's archives, I am surprised to discover how extensive the plan and image material for Berlin is. I meet Simon Ungers off campus, who runs the office Ungers and Kiss with his partner Laszlo Kiss. Both would constantly debate whether to call the office Ungers and Kiss or Kiss and Ungers. As time went on, the problem was solved as both struck out on their own.

In the 1895 novella *The Time Machine* by H.G. Wells, the Time Traveler explains to his curious friends that the common view of a three-dimensional material world is wrong, and that time as a fourth dimension defines our existence. Without time, nothing would exist. No monuments, no provisional structures, no humanity. Marcel Proust's reflections in his book *In Search of Lost Time* (1923–1927) point in the same direction when he claims that places only exist in time due to their constant changing, dissolving, and melting. According to Proust, places remain in our minds solely as what they, at a certain point in time, had been. At the turn of the century, around 1915, Einstein also proved "spacetime" as a physical phenomenon in the context of his theory of relativity. Its structure, the so-called causal structure, includes the entirety of all assertions about which events may affect one another, and where influences are excluded. According to an earthly interpretation of the physical spacetime phenomenon, an event A develops at the intersection of past and future. The events that could have affected the development of event A all lie in a specific time frame in the past, while those events that may be influenced by event A are all located in a time period projected into the future.

Therefore, the present is to be understood as a place in our conscious mind from which we can look into the future and past: a point on the spectrum of our perception that accompanies us through time. A development model assumes that generations of society move through time in odd loops. This form of movement leads to a linear-cyclical perception of the world, giving people the impression of being confronted with periods of time that they have already experienced. The perception of these allegedly previously endured ages connects conscious memory with elements of the present and opens up perspectives for future developments. *The Neanderthal Museum of Human Evolution*, as a spatial spiral construction that is rooted in fundamental depth that tangentially points towards the unknown with its apex, manifests this model of perception as a built metaphor. This also corresponds to a linear model of perception of an individual looking from the past into the future, whereas the spiral-shaped exhibition space refers to the cyclical model composed of lived experiences.

In this respect, my take on the metaphor of *Neanderthal Museum* has changed over time. Though ten years ago, the transition from a secure developmental model of society to one shaped by uncertainty was epitomized by the museum building, it appears today as an object that problematizes the tension between the cyclical and the linear model of perception. However, the mere thematization of this tension is not enough. The metaphor of the *Neanderthal Museum* also paves the way to its dissolution. The cyclical model is motivated by supra-individual, historical observation and is symbolized here by the exhibition spiral. The lineal model, on the other hand, is driven by perspective and

Gänsemarkt, Hamburg

1981 Back in Düsseldorf, I accept the invitation of another guest professorship in the design department of the Berlin University of the Arts. Haus-Rucker-Co and Thomas Jaenisch participate in the peer review process for designing the Gänsemarkt, a public square in Hamburg. The main idea is to modify the existing Gotthold Ephraim Lessing Monument by placing the bronze statue next to the pedestal and by doing so, place it on ground level. This is supposed to take into account Lessing's dispute with the representatives of a then-prevailing lack of respect towards other world religions, which is addressed in Lessing's play *Nathan the Wise*.

***Tower with Bar*, Kant-Dreieck Berlin, hotel, office, and residential functions, competition entry, Haus-Rucker-Co, Laurids Ortner, Zamp Kelp, Manfred Ortner, Düsseldorf, 1985**

SPACE-TIME

Neanderthal Museum, sketch, competition project, Zamp Kelp, Düsseldorf, 1993/1995

1981 In the middle of the year, Haus-Rucker-Co opens an office in Berlin on Reichsstrasse near the square Theodor-Heuss-Platz. Heinrich Klotz wants to install *Nike* in front of the Architecture Museum in Frankfurt. At the same time, however, Düsseldorf's head of the department for culture would also like to install *Nike* on the banks of the traffic-free Rhine. With mixed feelings, Haus-Rucker-Co eventually opts for Frankfurt. Mostly because of its location near the Main directly in front of the Architecture Museum, which will open in 1984.

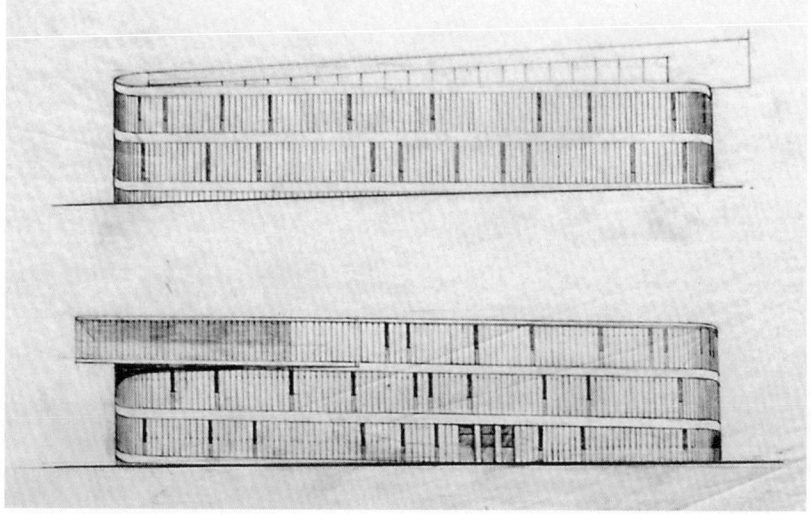

Sketches for design phase

individual consideration, which is symbolized by the transparent, and continues tangentially into the future of present individuals.

For the philosopher Vilém Flusser, only the present is important: the present in which the self is situated. The self is understood as a black hole, into which possibilities burst in order to realize themselves and become either present or remain a possibility. The end point of the spiral constructed as a tangent represents exactly that moment, the present, as Flusser understands it. It can serve the purpose of a café, displaying the

Neanderthal Museum, south-west elevation, bottom: north-east elevation
Blueprint planning: Zamp Kelp/Julius Krauss, Arno Brandlhuber, Düsseldorf, 1994
Detailed planning: Office Zamp Kelp, Düsseldorf, 1996

Neanderthal Museum, south-west elevation, Mettmann, 1996

Neanderthal Museum, empty exhibition spiral

With the Table Through the Wall

1981 On Saturday, September 26th, I celebrate my fortieth birthday one month late. The center of the party is the scenario that was developed for it, *With the Table Through the Wall*, installed between the gardens of the Glücksburger Strasse 18 and 16. Due to rain, guests only sit at the table temporarily, between rain showers, in order to get photographic documentation.

Exhibition spiral with exhibits, Mettmann, 1996

museum visitors who are present there, drinking coffee, as the part of the museography that embodies the Now. Guests of the exhibition in the café experience that moment—the presence of their being—as visitors at the end of their journey through the spiral of exhibitions about human history and can reflect on what they have just seen or contemplate the diverse possibilities of future developments while looking through the glass front. Thus, this building contains a permanent experimental setup in order to make the relationship between space and time visible.

Sisters of Imagination

The vanishing point in Leonardo da Vinci's *The Last Supper* is located on the right temple of the figure of Christ sitting in the center of the painting. This was found during the last restoration of the piece when the hole of a nail was discovered in that particular temple. As part of an auxiliary construction, the nail marked the vanishing point and held the strings in place while the artist worked on the spatial background of the scenery to create the basic outlines of the central perspective space. Using this technique, the projection of a three-dimensional space on a flat, two-dimensional plane was created on the north wall of the refectory in Milan's Dominican convent Santa Maria delle Grazie.

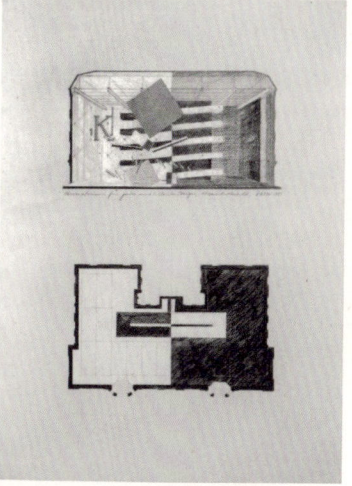

Observatory for Good and Bad Design

L'Ultima Cena (The Last Supper), Leonardo da Vinci, Milan, 1495–1498

While we can perceive two-dimensional images of spatial compositions with only one eye, we perceive the three-dimensional world with two. The view of the world from two perspectives is then first combined in the brain to form three-dimensional, stereoscopic images.

The projection of three-dimensional frames and spaces onto two-dimensional image planes reached its initial peak during the Renaissance. During this era, the close relationship between projection and perspective in different artistic fields became obvious. At the time, a "geometry of the imaginary" was created through painterly handicraft—with the help of grids stretched across frames through which the artists looked in order to transfer the real three-dimensional spaces behind them onto two-dimensional, uniformly spaced image planes. Through the invention of photography and film's moving images, the projective element has gained in importance and complexity com-

1981 As early as fall, we receive an invitation to participate in the exhibition *La Casa della Falsita*. The location for the planning is a house in Munich, Leopoldstrasse 87, home of the design furniture studio Focus. Our proposed *Observatory for Good and Bad Design* is radical. The house will be gutted to its outer walls and all windows will be bricked up. Its symmetry is offset by the contrasting colors of black and white. Seen from the Leopoldstrasse, the left section appears to be white with black blind windows, and the right part appears black with white blind windows. The resultant positive-negative surface ratio of the building halves continues inside. The interior can be accessed via a centrally located ramp-elevator construction, from which visitors can observe the *Good and Bad Design*, fixed to a floating net. This creates the impression of a thematically defined, self-contained design cosmos that is independent of the outside world and transforms over time, thus making the development of design graspable in its time-related actuality.

Façade Gallery

1981 Haus-Rucker-Co wins the contest for rebuilding the Wertheim store on the Kurfürstendamm in 1982 with the project *Façade Gallery*. As far as the concept goes, the house's façade is largely preserved and superimposed by five shop window elements, which are connected by an arched closure at the top. The basic conceptual idea of annually creating a new window display in relation to the city only works for the first few years after 1984. After that—perhaps for financial reasons—the idea is dismissed and instead, a permanent design is installed.

Projection of Signs, installation for Stammeskultur Unternehmenskultur, Symposium by Rat für Formgebung, Café Schirn, Zamp Kelp, Frankfurt, 1988

pared to the manually produced, perspectival documents of illustration and thought processes.

As the flood of information increases, the significance of the projective in various categories of perception and creativity grows.

In 1987, the installation *The Projection of the Signs* was created in celebration of a symposium regarding "corporate and tribal culture." Four signets of large companies were distributed in the room of the symposium on steles, casting their enlarged shadows onto a wall and illuminated by spotlights as a synonym for the projective principle with which visual information can become omnipresent.

Projecting information is not only evident on the surfaces of the respective hardware, but on all solid surfaces as well, including those of urban landscapes. Apart from the flow of information that leads from the source directly to our eyes and ears, there is also a flow in the opposite direction—namely when an idea created in our brain is made perceptible through projection techniques or spoken words. Thus, we differentiate between the projection as a message that is ubiquitously distributed and the projection of a one-dimensional creative deliberation that leaves the brain to be noticed by others in two- or three-dimensional form or through spoken word.

Balloon for 2, Bielefeld, 2009

1981 Haus-Rucker-Co wins the contest for the redesign of City Hall's peripherals in Bielefeld. The jury has honored and recommended the implementation of the proposal to cover the "Leinenweberstadt," literally translated to "linen weaver city," with a stone cloth that's weighted down by columns of leaves arranged at the side that form an identity and are reminiscent of the city's historical function. The project is our first contact established to Bielefeld, which ends once the work finishes in 1987 but comes back to life around thirty years later, with the installation of *Balloon for 2* at the Kunsthalle Bielefeld in the form of an exhibition about the year 1968.

This path from the creative thought process in our brains to the projected public document is also essential for the development and perception of utopias. After all, they do have a projective character as they bear no relation to reality. Therefore, they are dependent on content-related projections and projection techniques in order to not exist solely for their creators.

In 1516, Sir Thomas More described the island of Utopia as the place where a society with an ideal social structure lived, but whose very name foreshadowed the vague nature of its narrative. In doing so, More created the guideline of utopian novels. Utopia became a term for all invented, speculative, or idealistic contexts that are far from reality or that deal with contexts which seem unfeasible but usually have critical references to societal conditions. Utopian films and digital projections, with content of varying quality, are based on utopian narratives or self-written scripts. Along with Georges Méliès's screen adaptation of Jules Verne's *From the Earth to the Moon: A Direct Route*

Utopia, woodcut from Thomas More's novel *Utopia*

Boris Karloff in *Frankenstein*, 1931

in *97 Hours, 20 Minutes*, one of the first film adaptations in this field was *Frankenstein*, based on Mary Shelley's novel and directed by James Whale in 1931 with Boris Karloff in the leading role. *Blade Runner* from 1982, directed by Ridley Scott, or the *Matrix Trilogy* (1999–2003) by the Wachowskis, were prominent contributions to this genre, which can certainly be classified as cult.

To this day, Boris Karloff is the epitome of the monster sewn together from dead body parts and brought to life by Dr. Frankenstein and a lightning bolt. The movie *Blade Runner* examines the fate of replicants, who have a life expectancy of only about five years, in apocryphal urban scenery. In the *Matrix*, the central theme becomes the relationship between individuals and their avatars in an increasingly digital, hostile world. While the moving pictures usually draw their narrative foundation from

1983 The house on Glücksburger Strasse is up for sale and we move the atelier to the Kaiser-Wilhelm-Ring 1, right next to the Rhine. The main duties for our office this year include the concept for an arts center in the Deichtorhallen in Hamburg; participating in the first stage of the contest for the urban renewal of the Fasanenstrasse in Berlin with the design for a film academy at the high-rise building Kant-Dreieck; as well as an urban building report for the International Architecture Exhibition. Joseph Paul Kleihues, director of the International Building Exhibition Berlin (*Internationale Bauausstellung Berlin*), invites Haus-Rucker-Co, Nalbach+Nalbach, and Sartori/Kohlmeier to work on an urban building design for Block 7 on Schöneberger Strasse, opposite of the site of the former railway station Anhalter Bahnhof. During the following realization phase, we refrain from building the integrated daycare center and instead implement the edge of housing blocks along the Schöneberger Strasse and a single apartment building on Dessauer Strasse.

Headquarter in Ridley Scott's *Blade Runner*, 1982

SISTERS OF IMAGINATION

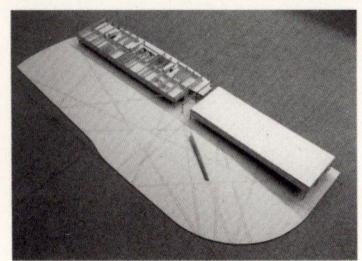

Bundeskunsthalle Bonn, competition model

1984 Götz Stöckmann introduces himself as graduate of the Architectural Association London with his final assignment, which was awarded as project of the year. In answer to our question of whether he would collaborate with us in the competition for the Bundeskunsthalle and the Art Museum in Bonn, he says yes. However, our concept, a slanting "museum ramp" sloping up from the Friedrich-Ebert-Allee with the museum buildings in the background, is not met with the jury's approval. As has happened plenty of times before, we are left only with plans and models for our archive.

novels, utopian projects in urban spaces were and still are created as a warning sign for critical developments or as optimistic contributions and suggestions for the perception and evolution of global cultural urban landscapes.

Accordingly, the contest entry for the BMW-Welt, a delivery and visitor center for Bayerische Motoren Werke AG (BMW) in Munich, was classified as a collection of thought-provoking utopian ideas by the jury and not admitted to the second stage of the contest.

The result did not leave me unencumbered as I had, after all, codrafted the contest project for the so-called *Vierzylinder* in Karl Schwanzer's office at the time. This was the main reason why a thematic focus of our contribution to the contest was laid on the interrelation between the existing *Vierzylinder* with the new BMW-Welt. A Ferris wheel was then conceptualized as the exotic feature of a functional building in order to attract worldwide attention. The overall constellation lived off of the contrast between the rationally arranged delivery center and the wheel construction, responsible for an attractive, popular touch. The wheel was designed as a circular steel framework with a diameter of ninety meters, which simultaneously provided a cover for the dynamic, rotating section of transport cabins. In an urban context, this ring was related to the *Vierzylinder*, the project realized at the beginning of the 1970s as an administration building. From certain angles, the circular body framed the

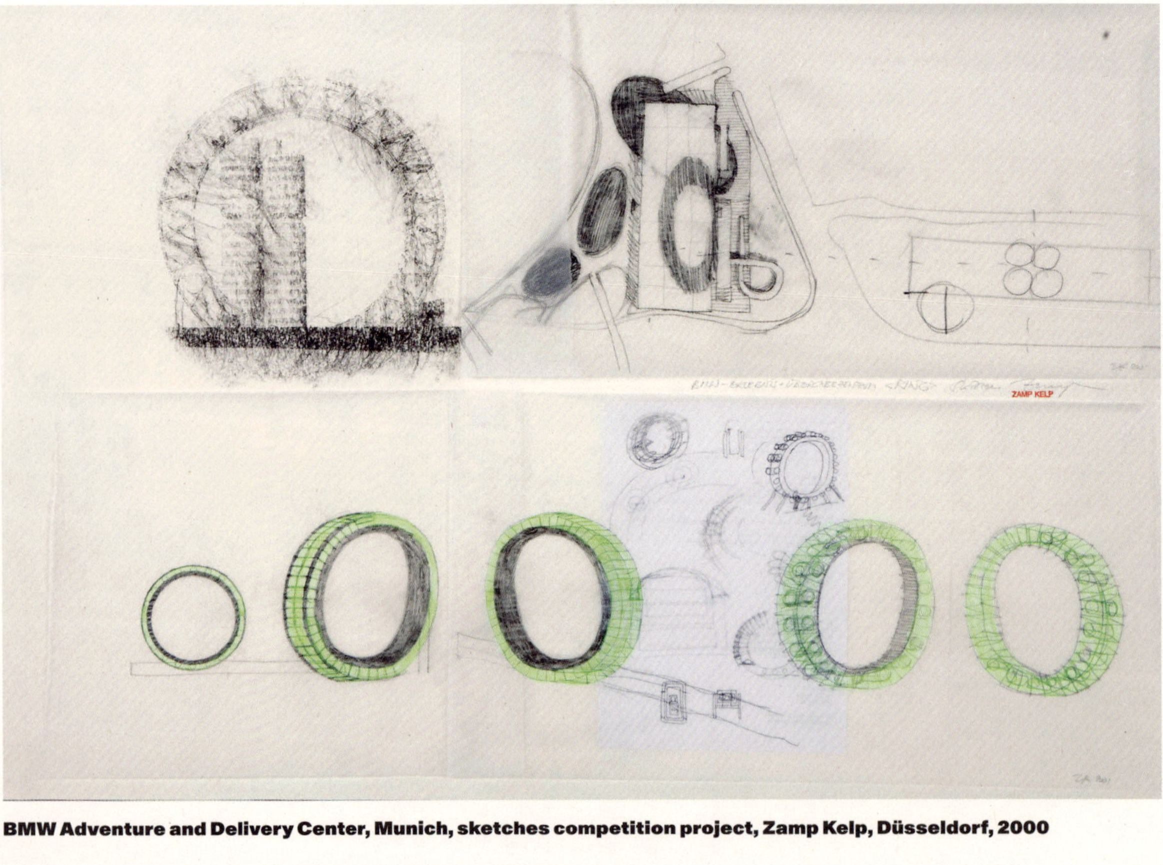

BMW Adventure and Delivery Center, Munich, sketches competition project, Zamp Kelp, Düsseldorf, 2000

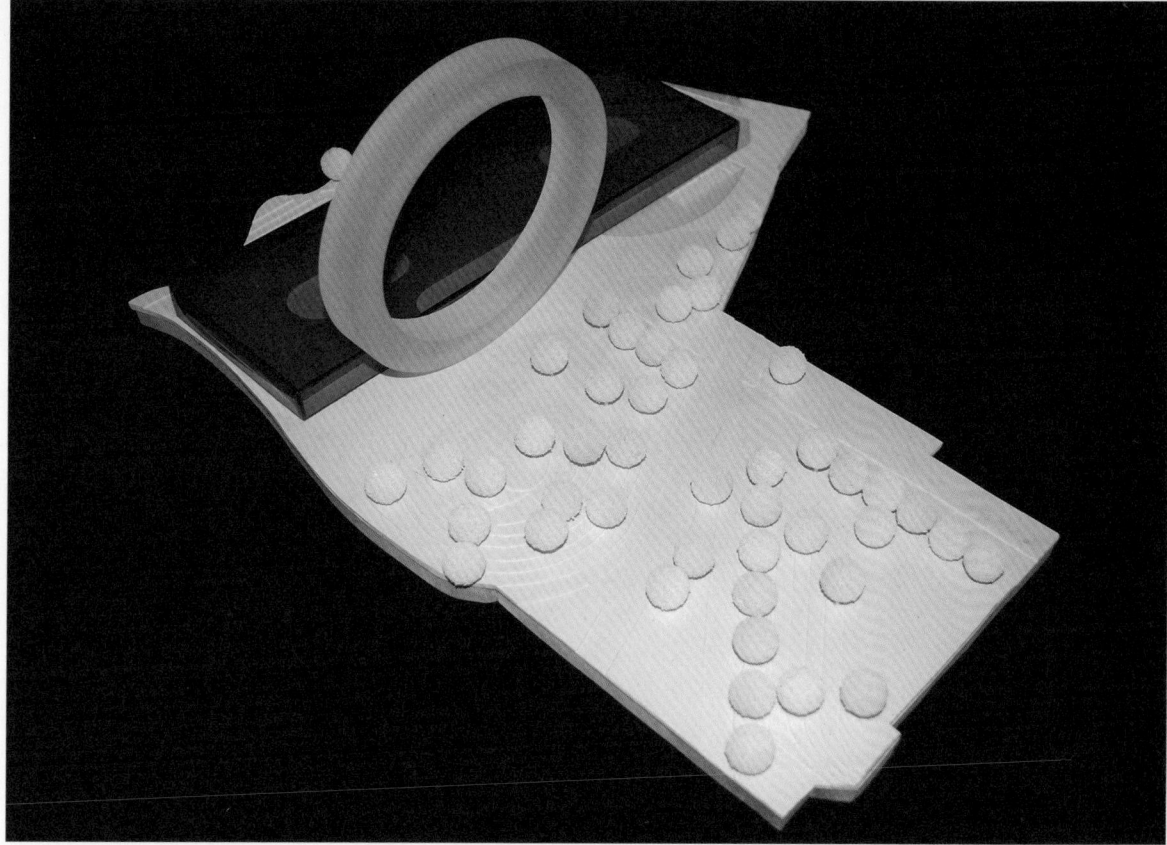

BMW Adventure- and Delivery Center, model fragment, Zamp Kelp, Andreas Hanke, Düsseldorf, 2000

four-cylinder building in a similar manner to what the Mandorla does for the car company's logo, so to speak. The Ferris wheel's function certainly offered popular features in terms of content, as visitors of the center would have been able to use it as well. The main purpose, however, was for the new car owners and their freshly acquired car or motorcycle to have a spectacular first experience together. As part of the planned, formal handover ritual, the new car and driver would have gone for a round in one of the passenger cabins to experience the view of the city and across the panorama to the Alps before reappearing together into the mundane again. Designed to be an element integrated into the city, the Ferris wheel, which could also be interpreted as a giant ball bearing, would have served as a monument and farewell to the fading, mechanistic era. At the same time, it was an original location intended to brighten the city's profile and the company worldwide.

1984 *The Tower in Neuss* is built. An object with a rustic outer surface of steel and wood that contrasts with the lavish, brass sheet inner cavity in the shape of a truncated cone, standing with a vertical axis reaching to the sky. The tower is formally reminiscent of the construction principles of Sardinian nuraghes, whose outer cylindrical shapes of layered stones create cone-shaped interior spaces which, open at the top, provide the option of a central fireplace.

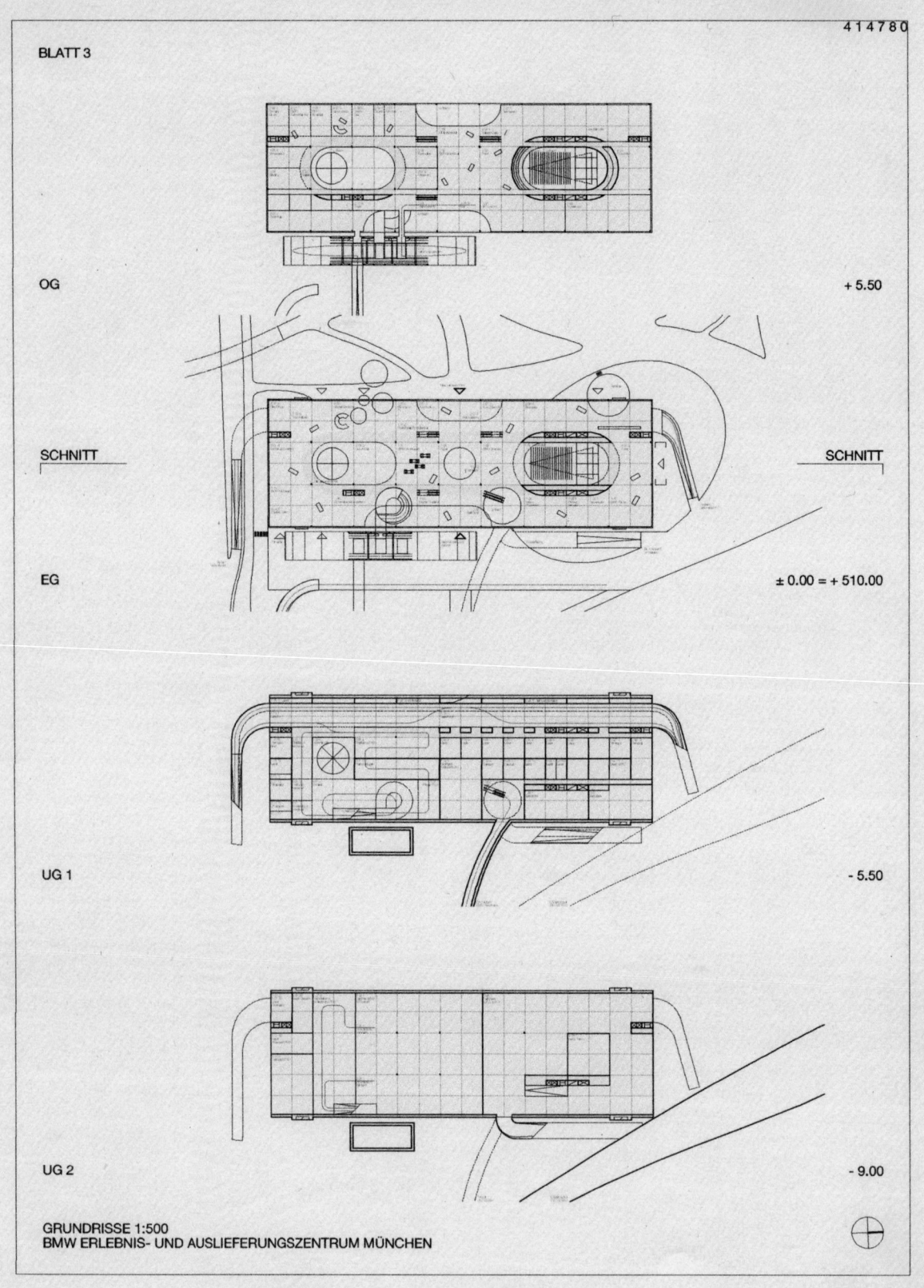

BMW Adventure and Delivery Center, Munich, plans, Düsseldorf, 2000

BMW Adventure and Delivery Center, Munich, animation, Düsseldorf, 2000

Hagia Sophia, Ronchamp, St. Elijah

Culture-Foundation, mass model

1984 In June, the German Architecture Museum opens in Frankfurt. Due to a protesting citizens' initiative from Sachsenhausen, *Nike* has not been installed. Haus-Rucker-Co is busy following an invitation by Francois Burckhardt to create an exhibition in the Neue Nationalgalerie in Berlin on a topic of our choice. With the title *Drei Grossstadtbauten (Three Buildings for a Metropolis)*, three situations in West Berlin are challenged and reflected upon. The radial drill plant in Reinickendorf keeps its outer appearance, but inside it is arranged for living and working purposes. The so-called Kulturstift in Neukölln provides for the establishment of an industrial production facility. This includes the former office buildings, in the construction of which the architect Otto Rudolf Salvisberg was involved and which, equipped with cultural ambition, make the coordination of social development processes their task. The proposal to build a film academy at the then-vacant Kant-Dreieck in Charlottenburg originates from the geography of its surroundings as well as the Delphi Cinema, which has always been a focal point in the Berlin International Film Festival's development. Establishing the film academy and a film museum here would permanently turn this area into a pivotal point for the event series. Each project is represented by four models in which mass, construction, surface, traffic, and materialized constellations of space are addressed.

In 1960, when I visited the Hagia Sophia during a trip to Istanbul, Turkey, I was immediately corrected by the guide on duty that the building was not in fact called Hagia Sophia, but Ayasofya. This was the Turkish name of the epochal basilica, with its dome of thirty-two meters in diameter, crowned by four pillars in the city center. While from the outside the four minarets gave the impression of a mosque, the atmosphere inside was dominated by at least six circular, black discs several meters in diameter with golden edges and large, golden Arabic lettering—the meaning of which was not revealed to me and had clearly been added later. The panels still hang in the basilica's interior today, an indication that the former Christian place of worship had been used as a mosque. Since Mustafa Kemal Atatürk founded the Turkish Republic, the property operated as a museum for contemporary history and was recently converted back into a mosque.

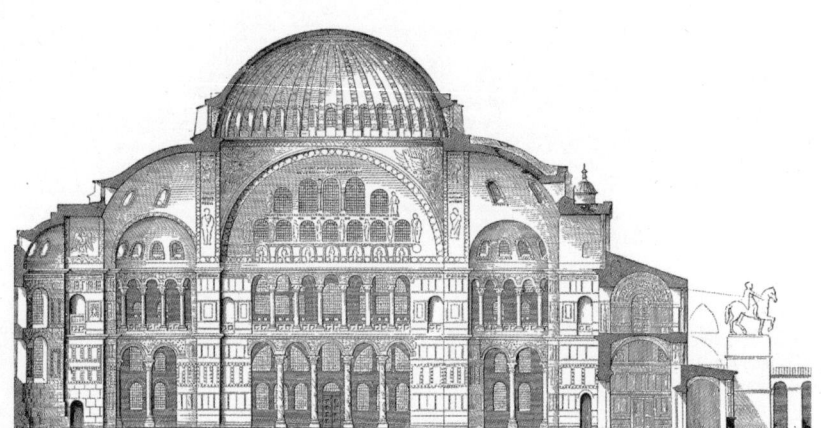

Hagia Sophia, reconstruction drawing, longitudinal section

I gradually began to understand the constructive system of this building, which, despite the monumental size of the interior space, created a division of niches and subspaces that exuded a certain intimacy. The building originated as a site for Greek Orthodox rituals around 537 AD and was rededicated as a mosque after the Ottomans stormed Constantinople in 1453. The house of prayer is considered one of the greatest masterpieces of architecture and in those years, would have given the faithful the impression of not being man-made, but a wonder created by supernatural forces. Their belief in the divine and trust in the supernatural was never burdened by earthly problems. In this context, the primal need humans have to strive for the manifestation of the impalpable is shown in the establishment of monumental buildings bound by gravity, such as the Hagia Sophia.

One building that stands in contrast is the chapel Notre-Dame du Haut by Le Corbusier in Ronchamp, which was built from 1950 to 1955 on a hill with historical legacy.

Even the Celts are said to have held rituals there, whereupon several Christian chapels were built. Le Corbusier planned and erected the chapel as an atheist and was apparently ready to carry out the job after a longer period of doubt. The draft replaces the usual monumentality of buildings such as these with a sculptural concept that sets itself apart from common urban structures and gives the building the kind of significance it deserves. It does so in a different way than through monumentality and size; rather, through formal and spatial extravagances, the draft provides faith with a modern framework. The curved, free shapes and roundings of the building particularly point to the changed positions that religions are confronted with. When looked at, the roof triggers associations with a boat, an arc, or ship, which may be interpreted as a hint or recommendation to further develop existing religious policies to meet with the increasing demand in flexibility and mobility.

The virtual changes to the church's outer appearance by photographer Xavier Delory move in the same direction. He projects the images Le Corbusier painted in Eileen Gray's villa E-1027 onto the walls of the building, thus changing the character of the house to that of paper. The process reminds me of the 1:50 scale model of the Notre-Dame du Haut that Manfred Ortner and I produced on the occasion of Le Corbusier's death in 1965. We initially had only photographed individual parts of the model. Then, once it was completed and photographed, we also

Tower at Kant-Dreieck, Berlin

1985 During the course of the peer review process for the *Tower at the Kant-Dreieck*, Haus-Rucker-Co proposes to theatrically stage the triangular building site across from the Kantstrasse with exotic oversized props. We envisage three elements: a tower for hotel, commercial, and residential purposes on a modified square ground plan; a rod around ninety meters tall leaning against it; and a golden, helmet-like entrance pavilion leading into an underground market. After the first stage, the draft ranks on par with Josef Paul Kleihues's project. For the second stage, we present a model on a scale of 1:100, which leads to significant logistical problems if everything is to be built for the respective presentations. Kleihues is much more flexible with his 1:200 model, because he is able to take it to the many (more) one-on-one interviews he has. Anyway, he is awarded the contract to realize the *Kant-Dreieck*. Haus-Rucker-Co receive the confirmation to build the house on Uhlandstrasse next to the S-Bahn.

Chapel of Notre Dame du Haut, Ronchamp

1985 In Munich, Mrs. and Mr. Haffner establish an architecture gallery and invite Haus-Rucker-Co to design the opening exhibition. The central theme is the presentation of a project for the design of the Marienhof in the city center. Connected to the U-Bahn station, the multilevel open-air stage at the middle of the square forms the creative and functional focus of the approach. The *Wolpertinger Tower*, named after the Bavarian chimera, is planned to be placed in a corner of the Marienhof as a satellite, so to speak. A museum facility in which the diverse manifestations of this Bavarian mythical creature could have been collected and viewed.

1985 In Bonn, the *Kunsthalle am August-Macke-Platz*, following the plans of Haus-Rucker-Co, is in its final phase. The plans envision a functional change from a floral hall to museum exhibition spaces for the Art Association Bonn.

1985 I am contributing an essay, "The Dynamics of Vacancy," to the art magazine *K*, founded by Michael Erlhoff and Lothar Romain. I write, among other things, "Within the cultural landscape as a residential situation of society, architecture corresponds to the furnishings of homely interiors. In terms of its character, architecture has always been static and immovable by architects for long periods of time, preferably built for eternity. Where are the elements of urban renewal after all, if the expansion element is no longer available? When referring to the entirety of cultural landscapes, a more flexible and adjustable society is a crucial factor. In this case, it is not the local scenery of landscape sections that changes, but rather the renewal of all-encompassing situations, the fluctuation of occupants or users and, by that, certain parts of society. On the other hand, creative potential lies in the vacancy of undeveloped properties. Perhaps, the dynamic of cities will be measured by the number of visible firewalls in the future. After all, before each firewall lies the potential of a vacant, undeveloped space. The number of firewalls thus suggests how much of an urban region is covered by wasteland, how transformable it is, how much untapped energy is at its deposal."

projected the slides of individual parts onto the white surfaces of the model's main body. This dissolved the shapes of the outer appearance and transformed the model of the building. We took photos of this process too.

In the same year, I developed my project for the church of Saint Elijah, the patron saint of aviators. Influenced by the recently completed model of the chapel in Ronchamp, which could be interpreted as an arc, it was thus a signal of a certain mobility and it set itself apart from the demand for the mass, stability, and size of classical cathedrals. It was precisely this sign of

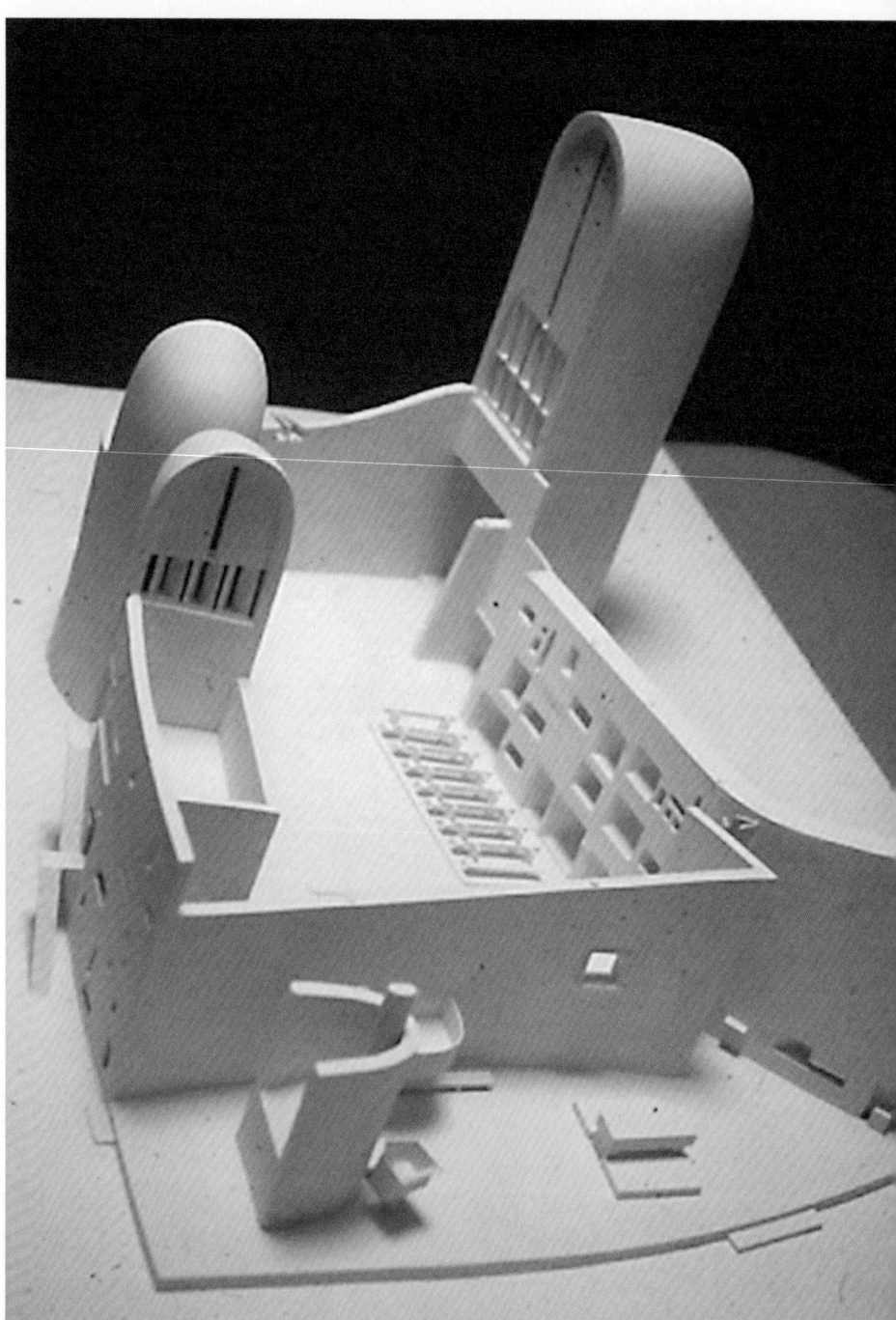

Model of Chapel Notre Dame du Haut de Ronchamp in scale 1:50, Zamp Kelp, Manfred Ortner, 1965

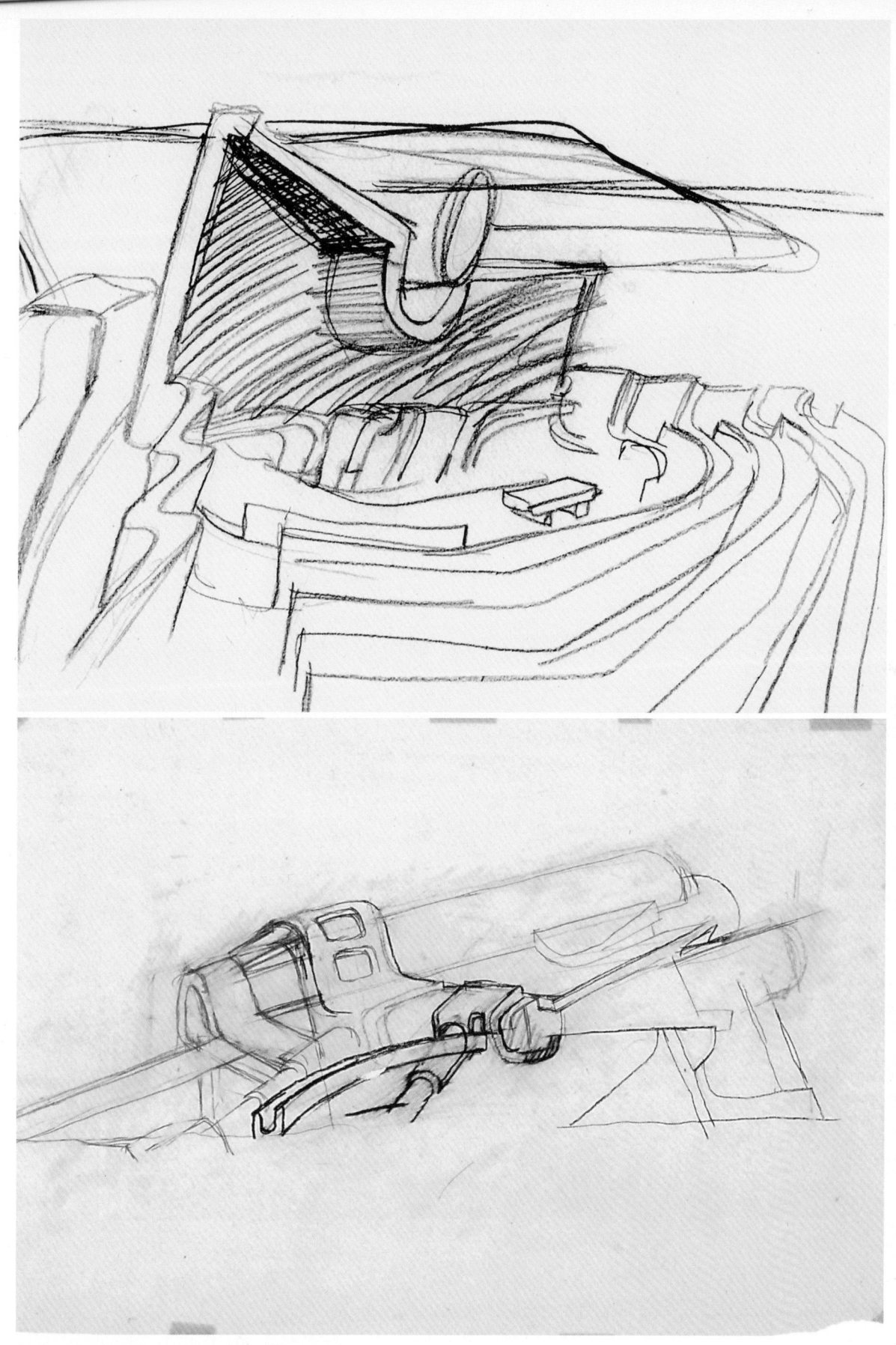

Church St. Elijah, sketches, Zamp Kelp, 1966

IKEA expanded

1985 As a Christmas gift for Chris Kelp, Heinz Baumüller turns my idea of expanding an IKEA crib into a two-story "play-and-sleep house."

1986 Some time ago, Götz Stöckmann, Gabi Seyfert, and Ottmar Hörl founded the group Formalhaut, a formation of architects and artists with the goal of developing and implementing conceptual strategies in urban spaces. In an article for their first catalog, *The Skin as Message*, I write, "Architecture will no longer have the task of demonstrating power. The media of the projected space takes care of that. In the presence of rapid change, architecture's claim for totality elapses. Simultaneously, new functions are looming on the horizon of perception. Making the spatiotemporal diversity of societal connections and divergences geographically readable will be one of their new tasks. A city becomes legible through its architectonic surfaces. This field offers the chance to react to processes in biological and projected spaces. In terms of content, the skin has detached itself from the architectural construction. It has become an independent, flexible medium within landscape spaces. The architectural surface serves as a base for the attempt to place the new and old parts of social living spaces into a new and integral relationship."

mobility, even if only presented as a message in an existing building, that fascinated me. As a result of these ideas, the draft of the Elijah Church developed as a hybrid between a house and an airplane, dissipating the vertical forces into the ground in one point and stabilized laterally by four telescopes.

Three years later, already as part of my work for Haus-Rucker-Co, I altered the function of this sacral building, which existed in drawings, and turned it into a night club by furnishing the interior with usable, pulsating, and pneumatic volumes. Thus, a content-related transformation took place from a church into a disco—analogous to the transformation of the Hagia Sophia from a church into a mosque in 1453.

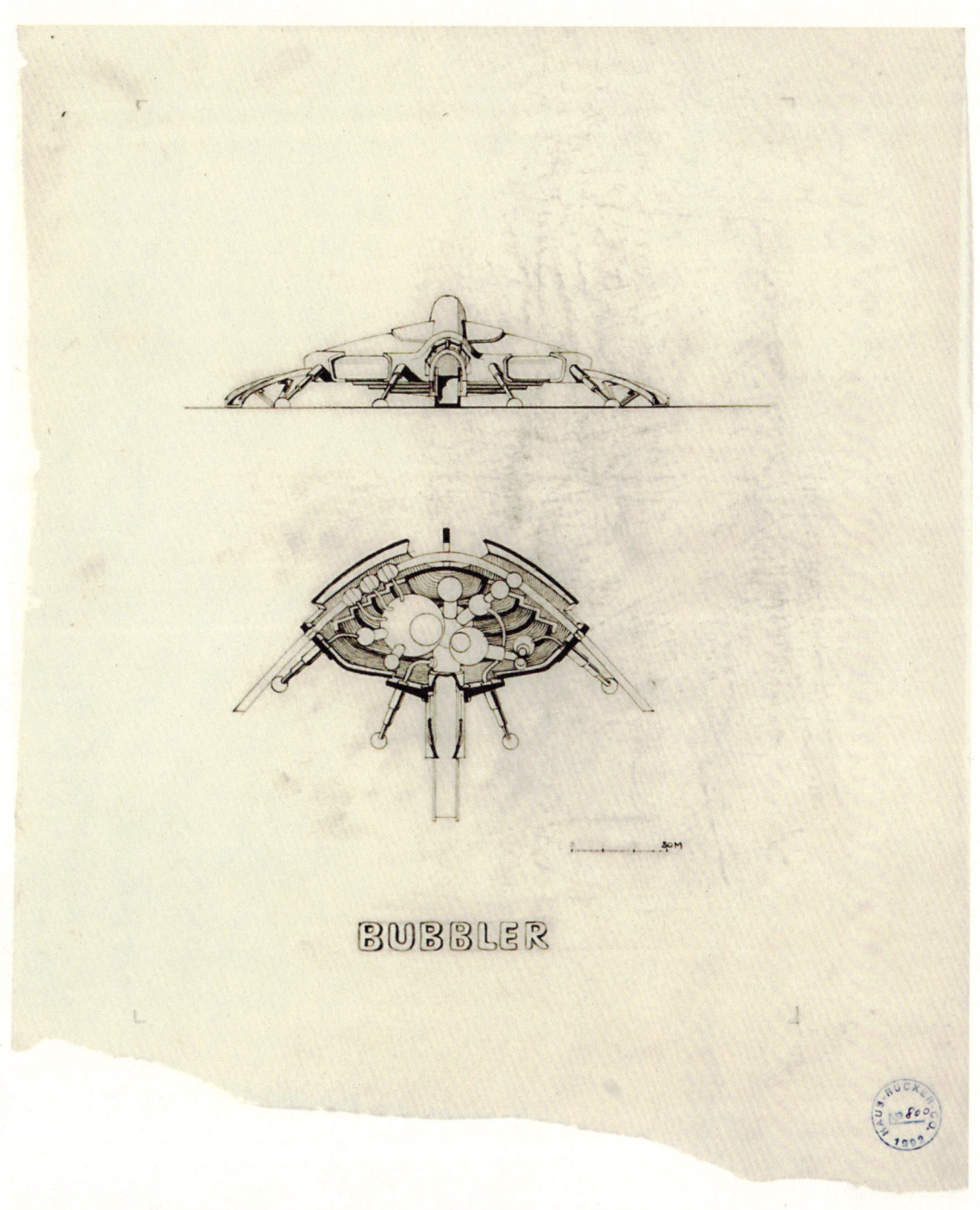

Bubbler, functional transformation of the Church St. Elijah into an event cathedral, ground view and elevation, Haus-Rucker-Co, Zamp Kelp, 1967

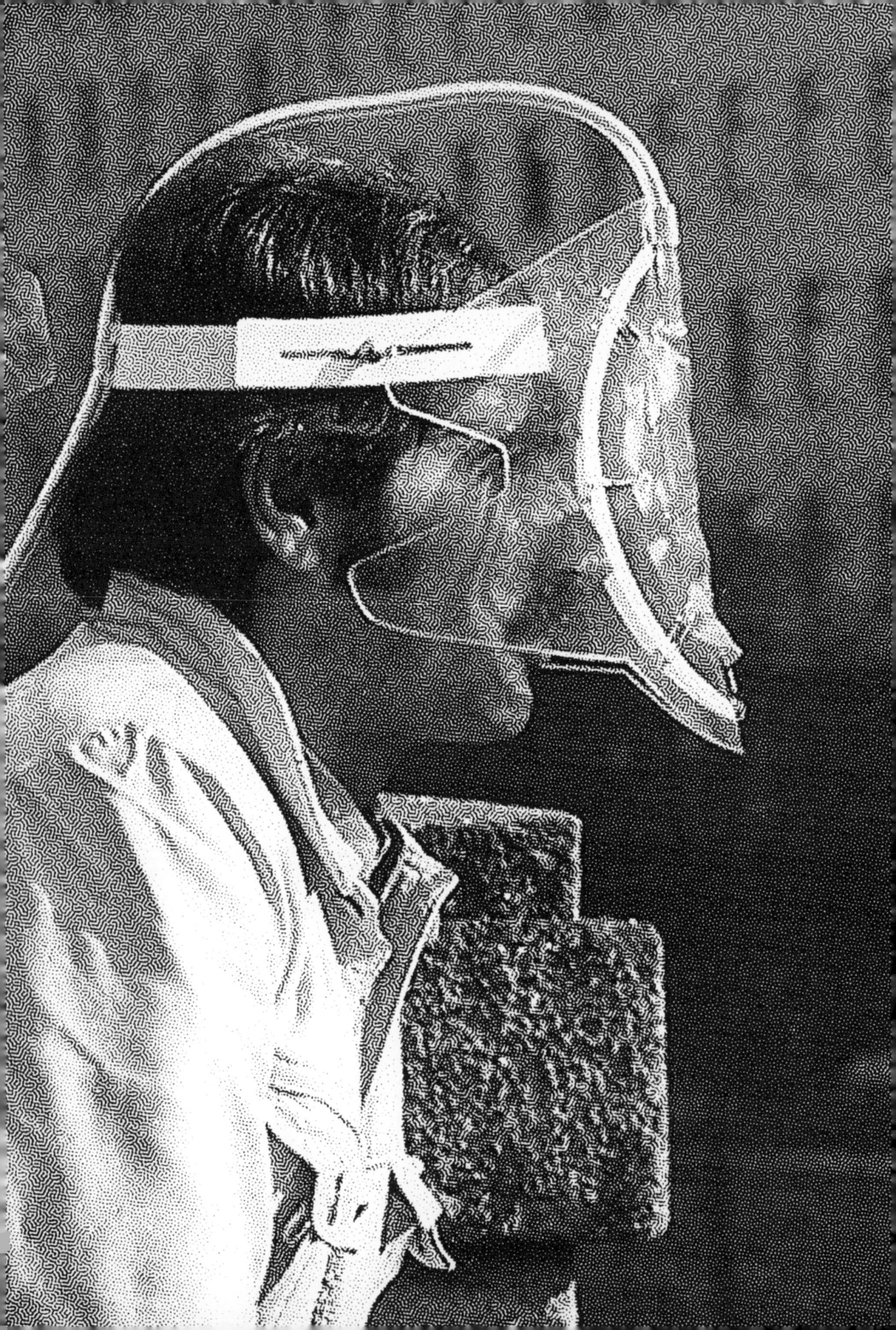

Ludwig Engel in conversation with Zamp Kelp

Ludwig Engel (LE) I was recently researching the year 1967, which is often described as a turning point. The hippie movement peaked that year in the "Summer of Love" in the USA, while it turned dark and brutal in Europe with students protesting everything, everywhere. Maybe we can start with that? You were a young man back then. Did you experience that sort of shift in Vienna?

Zamp Kelp (ZK) Well, I can't offer you any revolutionary tale that would really prove your point. But there was a noticeable hunger for change—even in Vienna. For me, personally, 1967 is of course important because Laurids Ortner, Klaus Pinter, and I founded Haus-Rucker-Co—a magical constellation with great momentum. We were following the doings of Superstudio and Archizoom in Italy and Utopie in France closely at that time and aspired to work in that direction. Vienna was less political than Florence or Paris. The younger generation was more interested in the creative and artistic aspects of life. The student protests in Vienna culminated in a demonstration in the university's auditorium. That was about it, if I recall correctly. Around the same time we presented *Yellow Heart* in the excavation pit for the new police headquarters on Ringstrasse. In *Time and Narrative*, Paul Ricœur says something along the lines of "time is nothing, if we don't tell it." That was our ambition: to create an update for architecture as the great narrator of human history. We had the feeling that architecture as it was practiced back then canonized an outdated idea of time, monument, and landscape. It felt like architecture had lost its ability to give orientation, to create identity. Instead it left us with a very diffuse feeling for heritage and homeland. Did we succeed in at least addressing that issue?

LE I think narrative structures—that also includes architecture as a representative of a specific epoch—have always shaped our understanding of time and space. Thus, architecture represents what we can see as heritage and what we can consider as home to an extensive part. But crucially you introduced three new dimensions: improvisation, temporality, and virtuality. These dimensions shape contemporary space much more than they did back then, when *Yellow Heart* was pulsating in the pit. But not

Stair-house

1986 Participating in the contest to design the Kurfürstendamm in Berlin is out of the question for Haus-Rucker-Co this year. The project concerns three creative focus points: the Olivaer Platz/Leibnizstrasse, the Lehnin Square, and the area around the Grohlmannstrasse. The most important feature will be the staircase on Leibnizstrasse. The design principle includes lifting the pavement up into a vertical position stabilized by a spatial steel construction that, fitted with glass, serves as an information center for the city and the bus stop for shuttles coming from Tegel Airport. In the outside area, the highest point of the structure takes on the role of a viewing platform for seeing the spatial depths of the Kurfürstendamm and the Leibnizstrasse. The platform can be accessed via a diagonally ascending staircase and a pathway leading over a waterfall. The stairs end in a triangular expanse of cascading water that corresponds to the upturned pavement's form. We receive the first prize for this part of the competition. However, the realization of the project peters out.

1987 There is an increasing number of signs foreshadowing the end to our work as a team. Responsibilities are divided and acquisitions are made individually from now on.

Fetish Cube

1987 Michael Erlhoff now heads the German Design Council in Frankfurt and asks whether I develop an object for a symposium titled *Object and Ritual* in order to create a scenic implementation of the theme. The result is a *Fetishcube* that can be visited in the event's periphery. The planned cube has a side length of 3 meters, 2.4 meters width, and a height of 3.5 meters. Black outside, white inside. At the center of one of the black exterior walls is an opening measuring approximately fifty by eighty centimeters that offers an insight into the white interior where everyday objects are arranged on an angled board around a television set in the middle. To mark the event, Erlhoff releases the booklet *Gold or Life*, which is published one year later. I wrote a comment about the object and say, among other things, "...the space is not accessible. A square opening in one of the room's walls offers a look inside. There is a television placed at the center of the back wall. The viewer's head, peeking through the opening, is reflected, bust-like in the glass of the grey projection surface. A coincidence or casual hint that even in the land of fetishes, representationalism will one day be displaced by the omnipresent fetish of information."

only has there been an increased feeling of time running faster, global processes have accelerated indeed. Buffering for example—the short latencies while a website or a video loads—today are incredibly short intervals, yet they seem excruciatingly slow to us. These accelerated processes within a given time frame—that's how the acceleration of time would be described correctly—lead to an immense fragmentation among the people who operate in parallel within the same time frame. To rethink the relationship between time and society we need to stop fighting acceleration and instead accept acceleration as the fundamental basis of our time. I think you did exactly that with your interventions. Later you substituted plastics and inflatables with stone, steel, and glass. It became less improvised, more monumental. Would you agree? I see less of your interventionist pragmatism in your later projects like *Neanderthal Museum* and *Millennium View*.

ZK *Neanderthal Museum* and *Millennium View* are works that carry all attributes of completed architectural building processes. There, you're right. But they still breath what you just coined interventionist pragmatism. At least in the message they carry. *Neanderthal Museum* is a spiral of time and thus questions the cyclical model of societal development with its galleries that submerge from the ground to the tangential high point. The spiral points into the open and the museum therefore is a synonym for society's uncertainty that we are confronted with in the digital age. *Millennium View* is a mark in a landscape in flux and symbolizes the transition between the 20th and the 21st century. It developed the theme of the staircase that we addressed with Haus-Rucker-Co—our unrealized project *Big Piano* without the artificial cloud at the top. *Millennium View* with its observation deck is also a metaphor for the fragmentation of our visual perception and can also be linked to *Rahmenbau*—a speculative instrument for field research we realized in the context of documenta 6. Both projects carry a critique of our perception of time and can therefore be again linked to our earlier works.

LE For example, the *Environment Transformers*. Their purpose was to fragment, to defamiliarize our visual perception in order to reinforce the user's awareness for the lived-in environment. Today's digital communication technology has indeed created an equivalent of your kaleidoscopic apparatuses: we're currently at a point where we don't know how this new perspective on the present will shape our understanding of it. Your transformers were—like many of your small-scale interventions—extremely visionary. Funnily enough, pictures of your transformers are still used widely today to illustrate the invisible aspects of digital processes. But there is no turning back now. The fragmentation of the perception of the world, as anticipated by you, is today's basic condition. LSD doesn't help us anymore. We need to accept that we are already deeply rooted in the digital infrastructure of our planet. Only then will we be able to cooperate on societal resonances, repair today's hyperfragmentation and continue our collective work on the Social Sculpture.

ZK That's Beuys, no? Also a bit of Niklas Luhmann, I reckon? In his systems theory he says, "society doesn't exist as the entirety of people anymore, but as communication." Peter Sloterdijk, on the other hand, has described the current state of Western society as an amalgam of egocentric individuals with limited bonding capacities, which brings him to the modern apartment as an atomic and egospheric form of living that can only be described as individualistic foam. Do you see any way to bridge that divide? To rewire society and the individual?

LE For me, Luhmann is relevant through his theory of societal resonances, which is quite central to my understanding of futurology, as the new that can only be recognized as something new when it reverberates within society. The possibility of thinking of society as a project of transformation is premised on the systemic belief that the message can already trigger change. Sloterdijk's claim in his Spheres project does resemble the sort of communication breakdown that he frames as the singularization and fragmentation of the individual in its own filter bubble. In both cases, human interaction is seen as the lubricant for building a society. Which brings me to the current condition of our cities' public spaces as places for debate. They appear to be in danger from two sides at the moment. Less and less public places are really public. Instead, they are controlled by particular house rules and guarded accordingly. And in the public spaces that are still available, technology leads to a quite passive coexistence. The only public interaction between strangers we see today are articulations of aggression after a supposed act of transgression. I actually hope in reality it's not as bad as I put it, but what do you think? But maybe that's nothing new at all. For example, your *Walking School*, intended as a

1987 Haus-Rucker-Co participates in documenta, the eighth edition, for the third time with the project The Ideal Museum, and Manfred Schneckenburger acts as director. This time numerous architects and designers are also invited. Andreas Brandolini presents his *German Living Room*, Hans Hollein showcases the draft for an energy museum in Essen, and Alessandro Mendini brings in the model of the Museo Universale.

1987 My essay "At the Table of the 20th Century" is published in the book *Design of the Future*, edited by Lucius Burckhardt IDZ Berlin. Burckhardt writes about Haus-Rucker-Co, "Günter Zamp Kelp works as member of the group Haus-Rucker-Co. Their designs are characterized by a distrust of conventional futures. In traditional planning, every solution to an issue quickly turns into a building design. Haus-Rucker-Co, despite their profession as architects, attempt to go the opposite way. They take a commissioned design and try to grasp the client's problem and solve it—perhaps not by a construction, but by using a strategy, method or even several methods, maybe a construction in connection to a new organization. This makes Haus-Rucker-Co advocates of a new behavior towards everyday problems and the requirements of the future."

1987 In December, the German Design Council hosts the symposium Corporate and Tribal Culture in the café of the exhibition venue Schirn Kunsthalle in Frankfurt. My contribution, *The Projection of Icons*, is supposed to, on the one hand, influence the room's atmosphere in which the event takes place and, on the other, convey the message that it is not the symbol of a business that acts representatively, but instead encompasses its repeated, awareness-raising projection into society's spaces. Essentially, the installation consists of three stands distributed throughout the room with logos mounted onto them that, illuminated by four spotlights, create enlarged shadows of the motives on the white walls.

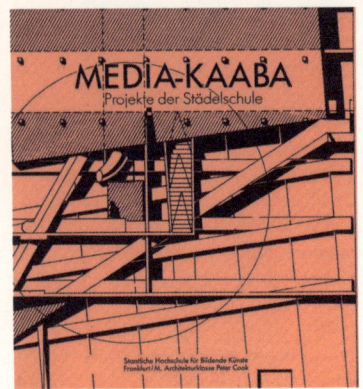

Catalog Media Caaba

1988 In the spring, I receive the invitation to oversee the architecture class at the Städelschule school in Frankfurt as a visiting professor for the summer semester. Because it mainly involves project work, I present the topic "Media Kaaba" to research possible interactions between architecture and media. The work with the students is carried out in cooperation with Götz Stöckmann from Formalhaut, an assistant to Peter Cook at the Städel Museum. I find it surprising that none of the students refer to the reduced form of the Kaaba in Mecca in their work, but rather claim that the dual topic leads to, architecturally, very complex results of notable expressiveness. In any case, the catalog of the students' work is still relevant today.

1988 I spend parts of my summer with Lilly and Chris Kelp at Lake Neusiedl. During this time, I am offered a professorship for Building Planning and Design at the Berlin University of the Arts (Universität der Künste Berlin, UdK) and am asked to begin the following winter semester. Until October, I am busy preparing the project and teaching content for this new task. The first assistants in my teaching field are Hubertus Duwensee and Jörg Hundertpfund.

tool to rethink the way we walk through public spaces, was instantly vandalized, wasn't it?

ZK Rejection might lead to an initial positive effect on communicative interaction. In fact, it is important to acknowledge the way that fear can stimulate the need for interpersonal relationships. Haus-Rucker-Co's first intervention in the public sphere was the installation *Balloon for 2*. Two people floated in a transparent bubble about ten meters above ground on Apollogasse and bonded during this collective yet risky experience. The *Walking School* may have been too didactic—not just the set-up but also the title. It somehow rubbed the promenaders of Vienna's inner city the wrong way. I don't really know why, but it triggered the most destructive instincts. The *Walking School* was vandalized in one of the first nights of its existence and [was] later removed by some official entity. *Oasis No 7*, which we produced for documenta 5, was also damaged with a nail on a long latch in the night before the opening. Anyway, I guess that's at least proof of some physical communicative interaction, as you have noted. Today we experience a shift in communication which becomes ever more closely tied to long distances, not least thanks to our smart phones. Physical togetherness in public spaces is almost exclusively limited to soccer matches, music festivals, and other staged events. Interpersonal relationships are brokered by a dating app. Communication options presented to us from the outside organize people's lives today. Well, when I talk like that, I always ask myself how much of my ideas of the future are based on the past and not the present. I read this interesting sentence in Robert Menasse's *Die Hauptstadt* (*The Capital*)—in English, not translated in the German original text: "The past forms the future, without regard to life." What do you think? Or does the future inform the future differently?

LE I'm not really sure what Menasse means with "without regard to life." Does it imply one's powerlessness as time mercilessly moves forward without regard for the individual? I can't really agree to that; it's too fatalistic for my taste. I agree that the future cannot be known nor directly influenced, but it sounds like an excuse for remaining passive to me. Do not produce the future in the future. What if one would say: "With regard to life, the past informs the future." With that, the human being is the actor who deals with what is coming. By combining his experiences with his hopes for a vision of a future, he is motivated to navigate these unknowable waters. I think I like it better, because I don't believe in "the future" as something apart from human's capacity to define time.

ZK   I honestly would not have imagined that I'd feel this contemporary digital revolution as intensely as I do—despite the often-visionary projects we did, to quote you there. The apparatuses we designed for our *Mindexpanding Program* had the intention to spark communication and the ambition to transcend awareness. Fifty years later we are at the verge of a superintelligence developing with an artificial dynamic, that will open up possibilities for our cognitive and sensory functions that will surely surpass the imaginable. Architecture and design will be essential to shape the processes that inform this superintelligence. I don't get the sense that people as society really partake. Take our dystopian scenario for *Cover—Survival in a Polluted Environment* in Krefeld for example, where we covered the Mies van der Rohe villa with an air-inflated tent to create a synthetic reserve. It seems more relevant then ever when we look at the metropolises in China or even the air pollution problems we face here in Germany. Again, external effects of a man-made future!

LE   It's interesting to talk about the effects of future-oriented acting that no longer can be controlled like climate change or artificial intelligence. The uncontrollable consequences of human acts are based on well-intended visions from the past, no? What's still left of the utopias that have inspired you? Or to put it differently: do you still think that utopian thought can productively engage with world affairs?

ZK   Definitely! [Vladimir] Tatlin's Monument for the 3rd International with its geometric parts rotating at different speeds, and El Lissitzky's weightless constructions floating in nothingness are still relevant examples of the historical discussion about object and space and [to this day] shape my conscious. Visionary construction was always an integral part of my projects. The construction of utopias is part of an aggressive worldview that refreshes our actions with speculative moments, foils our realities.

LE   But how does it feel to leave so many of your ideas unrealized? Was your job rather to refresh our action with speculative moments than to build stuff?

ZK   The idea or message that is attached to a building or a design was always the most important part to me. When ideas are being realized, they are being steadied; they reach the final point of their becoming. Take my *Neanderthal Museum* for example. It is built time, or the attempt to make time visible at least. If ideas continue to live on as ideas, they remain open windows through time. Many ideas open many windows; they are life's oxygen. I love ideas.

1988 In October, we move our office from the Rhine's left bank back to the center of Düsseldorf and onto Friedrich-Ebert-Strasse near the main station. The sixth floor of an office building from the 1950s has been divided into two offices: one for Zamp Kelp and the other for Ortner und Ortner. The administration is located in my office and will be used in various ways from now on. At the same time, my work as a professor at the UdK begins. The first project is about conceiving and designing a TV station in Berlin. Around fifteen students developed solutions for different situations in West Berlin. The project is accompanied by a series of lectures, one of which is led by Norbert Bolz in the field of media science.

Kristin Feireiss in conversation with Zamp Kelp

Kristin Feireiss (KF) Zamp, we have known each other since the early 1980s when Aedes was invited to curate the show *Architekturvisionen* at Kunsthalle Hamburg. Next to Raimund Abraham, Peter Cook, Peter Eisenman, Zaha Hadid, John Hejduk, and Rem Koolhaas, we invited you—that is, Haus-Rucker-Co—with Linear House to contribute to the show. Ever since, you have remained a fascinating figure to me, a visionary force as an architect, artist, and teacher. We've also collaborated on multiple projects at Aedes since then. *Neanderthal Museum* and *Mediale Aureolen für die Stadt* come to mind and the presentation of *Time Loops*, projects of your students at UdK [University of the Arts Berlin]. There were many more of course. You seem to be—still—a step ahead of the times, thus remaining true to yourself. But tell me, how did everything begin?

Zamp Kelp (ZK) Thanks, Kristin, that's really a quite favorable description of me that you give here. As you know, we started in Vienna. Looking back, I would say 1967 was a year of conclusion and restart, a personal demarcation line. I had just graduated from Technical University in the spring and got a job as one of Karl Schwanzer's assistants at the same institution. At the time, it felt as if there were unused potentials accumulating and I was looking for ways to put these energies into effect. Usually, after graduation, one would start at an architecture office for five years to become a certified architect, but I felt that wasn't really for me. Instead I felt the urge to immediately intervene into everyday life.

KF How did you then intervene into everyday life? I'm asking this as if what you are going to answer now isn't common knowledge…

ZK Well, common knowledge, I don't know. Maybe among die-hard expert circles … anyway … in the summer of 1967, I participated in the competition *Interdesign 2000 / Lebensraum Zukunft* with a group of friends. Our contribution was a big public success and was picked up by the media quickly. Shortly afterwards a group of like-minded individuals, namely Laurids Ortner, Klaus Pinter, and myself, formed Haus-Rucker-Co.

1989 Heinrich Klotz has since moved from the Architecture Museum in Frankfurt to Karlsruhe in order to establish the Center for Art and Media Technology (Zentrum für Kunst und Medien, ZKM). At the beginning of the year, he sends out an invitation for a contest to develop the building concept of a property near the main station. It will be the last project to be submitted under the name Haus-Rucker-Co. I see it as a chance to use the interpretation of the Kaaba in Mecca for this task about an art and media hub—an idea that has been on my mind since the Städel project. In my office, Julius Krauss, Barbara Bruder, and I work on ideas. At the center of the concept is a cubic, multifunctional interior with a side length of thirty meters that opens up to Karlsruhe's cityscape by means of a generously dimensioned rolling door on its eastern side. As a stage for the public, experiments are to take place here that combine familiar, analogously determined processes and medial, digitally determined worlds of cultural development. So far, so good. The project is submitted in time and I make my way to present in Karlsruhe, where all the projects are on display. I am a little startled by the resemblance of our project's outer appearance to that of OMA, which will win the competition. At the time, none of the participants knew that the contest's winning design would not become a reality, because the vacant ammunition factory's enormous space would actually become the institution's new location instead.

Crossing Bridges, Berlin

1989 In Berlin, there is a need for a pedestrian and cyclist bridge on the former tracks of the railway station Anhalter Bahnhof near the Museum of Technology. The museum's proximity brings me to participate in the respective contest and propose a special kind of traffic situation. I plan *Crossing Bridges*, or the pervasion of two functionally independent bridge structures, by crossing the existing S-Bahn bridge's steel framework with the newly envisaged pedestrian and bicycle bridge that's designed to be an arched bridge. Additionally, the traffic on the left and right side of the Landwehrkanal will run underneath the construction. This creates a mixture of roads with a sculptural character and an intention to generate an indicative signal in front of the museum building. Interestingly, the people in charge at the museum do not want to implement the proposal. Apparently, they bank on a Raisin Bomber from the Second World War, which looks as if it were in a crash landing, is supported by a rope construction, and decorates the museum entrance today. At least our project comes in third. Yet again, none of the contest contributions are implemented.

KF Why Haus-Rucker-Co?

ZK The name is derived from a programmatic and geographic approach. The combination "Haus-Rucker" is borrowed from Austrian dialect: "shifting a house" in the sense of advancing the meaning of the term "house" itself. At the same time, "Hausruck" is a landscape in the Innviertel of Upper Austria, a nod to our origins as we were all brought up in this region.

KF Haus-Rucker-Co existed for twenty-five years. What were the reasons to end the partnership after such a long time in 1992?

ZK How much time have you got? I'd need hours for a good answer. But to make it very short: there are two important partnerships in my life. Most importantly, my marriage to Lilly Kelp. Since almost forty years, Lilly is my emotional balance and takes care of all our things—both business and private. The second most important relationship in my life for over twenty-five years was Haus-Rucker-Co.

KF Sorry for insisting, but I would like to know a little more. When did the dissolving of Haus-Rucker-Co start?

ZK Probably around 1987. By then the direct communication between us had shifted to indirect communication through our employees. Some specific interests came to the fore, the three partners gradually advocated for change. The ambition to try out new and different ways was finally realized in an exhibition at Kunsthalle Wien in 1992: end and restart. It was some time before that when we already had separate offices on the fifth floor of an office building on Friedrich-Ebert-Strasse in Dusseldorf.

KF Alright, let's leave it at that and let's go back to the beginning once more. Haus-Rucker-Co's first work series was called the *Mindexpanding Program* and intended to expand consciousness through spatial experiences...

ZK The *Mindexpanding Program* was conceptualized to transcend and expand conventional ways of perception. In this context, we developed prototypical spatial constellations and tools, intending to irritate the day-to-day habits of perception, delivering thought-provoking impulses for how to look at the common public space under new perspectives.

KF How do you define the relationship of consciousness and space?

ZK As a human being I'm part of a biological habitat, which superimposes, stimulates, and stages architecture—understood as geometrical space. This classical bipolar comprehension of habitat is furthermore enhanced by information and its dissemination through various media. This spatial trinity of biological, geometrical, and projective factors merges spaces and situations into authentic moments of cognition, letting events and places appear unique and irreproducible.

KF Well said! I'm just thinking of the square format of the exhibition catalogue for *Haus-Rucker-Co LIVE*. Was that a subtle avowal to this archetypical form?

ZK In those days, we were more into spheres than into squares. The square format of the catalogue was rather the attempt to borrow from the youth culture we felt we were part of. Bands like The Beatles were already very prominent and reflected our generation's attitude towards life. As architects and artists, it was our main interest to express this attitude by space-related interventions and to reach, as much as possible, contemporaries by media transport like the pop bands did. The medium of choice for pop music was the vinyl record with its square-formed sleeve, which we adopted for our catalog, containing documents about space and concreteness instead of music.

KF Flirting with the beat and rock music scene!

ZK Sure, we also wanted to be rock stars!

KF In 1971, you installed *Cover – Survival in a Polluted Environment* at Haus Lange in Krefeld. You covered the villa built by Mies van der Rohe with an air-inflated tent and thus created a synthetic, climate-controlled reserve. The premise of your intervention was to highlight the toxic quality of the air outside. How did your worldview change within just a couple of years from optimistic to dystopian?

ZK The moon landing in 1969 changed our generation's approach to life. We were left in a vacuum of expectation that was quickly filled by the events around the first oil crisis that sparked an economic recession and induced a common reflectiveness in us. In addition, the Club of Rome's widely perceived insights and predictions for our global society laid bare the aberrations of our doings on many different levels. Topics like climate and nature were suddenly connected to upcoming

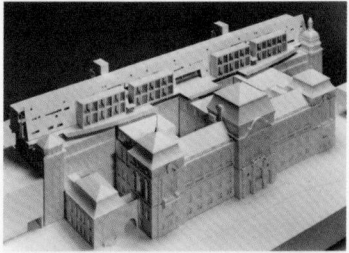

Loft Conversion, UdK Berlin

1989 Following the fall of 1989, in terms of seasons as well as walls, a new era begins in the Federal Republic of Germany and in Berlin. During this year, I develop a project for the loft conversion of the UdK's main building on Hardenbergstrasse in the context of an internal competition among the teachers. Due to a change in budgeting, none of the designs are realized.

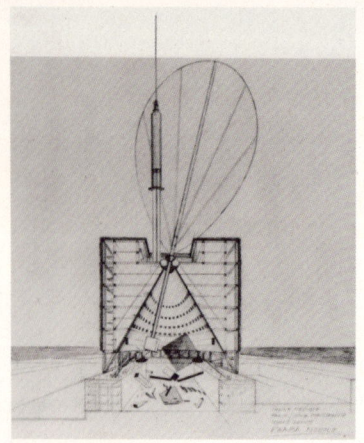

Mekka Medial

1989 We receive a letter from Kristin Feireiss asking us to participate in an exhibition called *Architecture and Utopia* at the Pavillon de l'Arsenal in Paris. The exhibition system is designed by Nalbach+Nalbach and mainly consists of horizontally and vertically positioned table surfaces, each around two meters long and one meter wide, on which the participants will spread out topic proposals under plexiglass. I am still motivated by the ZKM-contest and feel ready to develop another interpretation of the subject of religion and media. *Mekka Medial* has to be conceptualized within a week, as I am planning a two-week trip for before then. So, I leave the drafting to Andreas Hanke, an employee of the office at the time, who turns them into two and a half drawings in tabletop format. The main focus of the unquestionably utopian draft is a cubical building that can be moved via four caterpillar tractors through a network of forty rooms, which are all recessed in the ground and open to the top. Like a queen bee fertilizing individual honeycombs, the cube hovers over the rooms at certain intervals of time to develop topic-related scenarios inside them, which then become omnipresent throughout Europe via a TV station integrated into the building. Simultaneously, the media hub is open to visitors; every European should witness the tangible place that provides European societies with cultural sequences at least once in their life. After Paris, the exhibition is displayed at the Bikini-Haus at Kunsthalle Berlin. There is an accompanying model for the building. In 1996, I showcase the project during my exhibition in the Aedes Gallery on the Hackescher Markt, and in 1997, at the Nederlands Architectuurinstituut (NAI) in Rotterdam.

problems produced by our civilization. Environmentalism was on the rise, and things like air pollution were real, not hypothetical, problems we were facing. Also, Haus Lange as a secluded villa was an ideal backdrop for showcasing a *Synthetic Reserve*.

KF How would you describe the role of the public in your works back then?

ZK If I exemplify "back then" on to the exhibition *Haus-Rucker-Co LIVE* at Museum des 20. Jahrhunderts in Vienna in 1970, it was our ambition and vital conceptional intention to communicate and interact with the public, represented by the visitors of the event. In *Haus-Rucker-Co LIVE* you could say interaction was the important concept of the exhibition. Most of the exhibits were interactive, not to look at but to play with, dominated by *Giant Billiard* as central object. We also moved our apartments' furniture into the museum and lived there for a couple of days. Back then still a provocation. These two premises—interactive installations and living in the museum—challenged the status of the museum for the time of our show, turning a temple of art into a platform of interactive communication.

KF And later on? After Haus-Rucker-Co?

ZK I consider the *Neanderthal Museum* in Mettmann near Dusseldorf from 1996 my most important building after Haus-Rucker-Co. It is a building that broaches the issue of time. The museum shows the evolution of humankind with specific stages manifested in segments arranged along a slowly ascending spiral. At its high point, the spiral is tangentially cut, propelling time into an uncertain future. It's a built model of time, really. The historical model of a society that moves upward in time loops from past into the future is questioned at the end and sensitizes for the coming turn of times.

The Club of Rome is an association of experts from various disciplines from more than thirty countries and was founded in 1968. It advocates sustainable development and the protection of ecosystems.

KF Toward what kind of future are we heading?

ZK The metaphor of the time loop I used for the *Neanderthal Museum* does not provide answers for how the future will look like. But I expect a future in which digital projections will overlay the surfaces of our geometrical and haptic spaces. If mankind wants to follow up with the historical narration of time furthermore, as suggested by French philosopher Paul Ricœur, and in this way prevent a takeover by artificial intelligence, a symbiosis between the world of digital projection and the one of concreteness will be essential. In this sense, I call on all architects, artists, philosophers, sociologist, and futurologists to collectively engage in shaping vision and reality of a future commonality.

1989 The same year, I rent an office space on the vacant sixth floor of an office building by Max Taut at the Oranienplatz in Kreuzberg. On November 9, the borders to the GDR open and the dividing wall between East and West Berlin begins to fall. A new era for Germany.

1990 We are involved in the processing of submissions to the competition for the Austrian Pavilion at the 1992 Expo in Sevilla in cooperation with the Viennese architecture office Hoppe Partner. The identifying element is a cylindrical ring, four meters high and fifteen meters in diameter, which floats above the area on a rope construction and shows a panoramic view of the Austrian Alps on its inner surfaces. Escalators leading diagonally to the upper level cross the ring and offer ascending visitors the chance to perceive the panorama, accompanied with sound sequences from the Alpine region as an introduction to the pavilion's Austrian-related themes. Both this project and another are currently being reworked. The *Panorama Pavilion* is checked for its technical feasibility for the time after the Expo, but the majority of the jury does not vote for the project's realization.

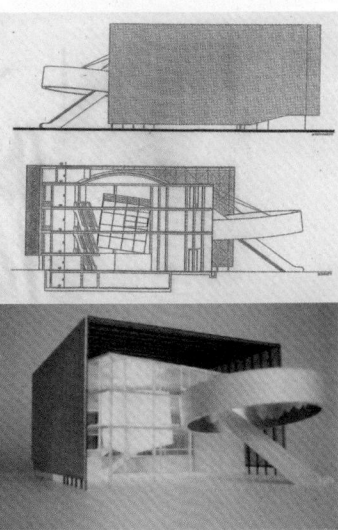

Panorama Pavillon

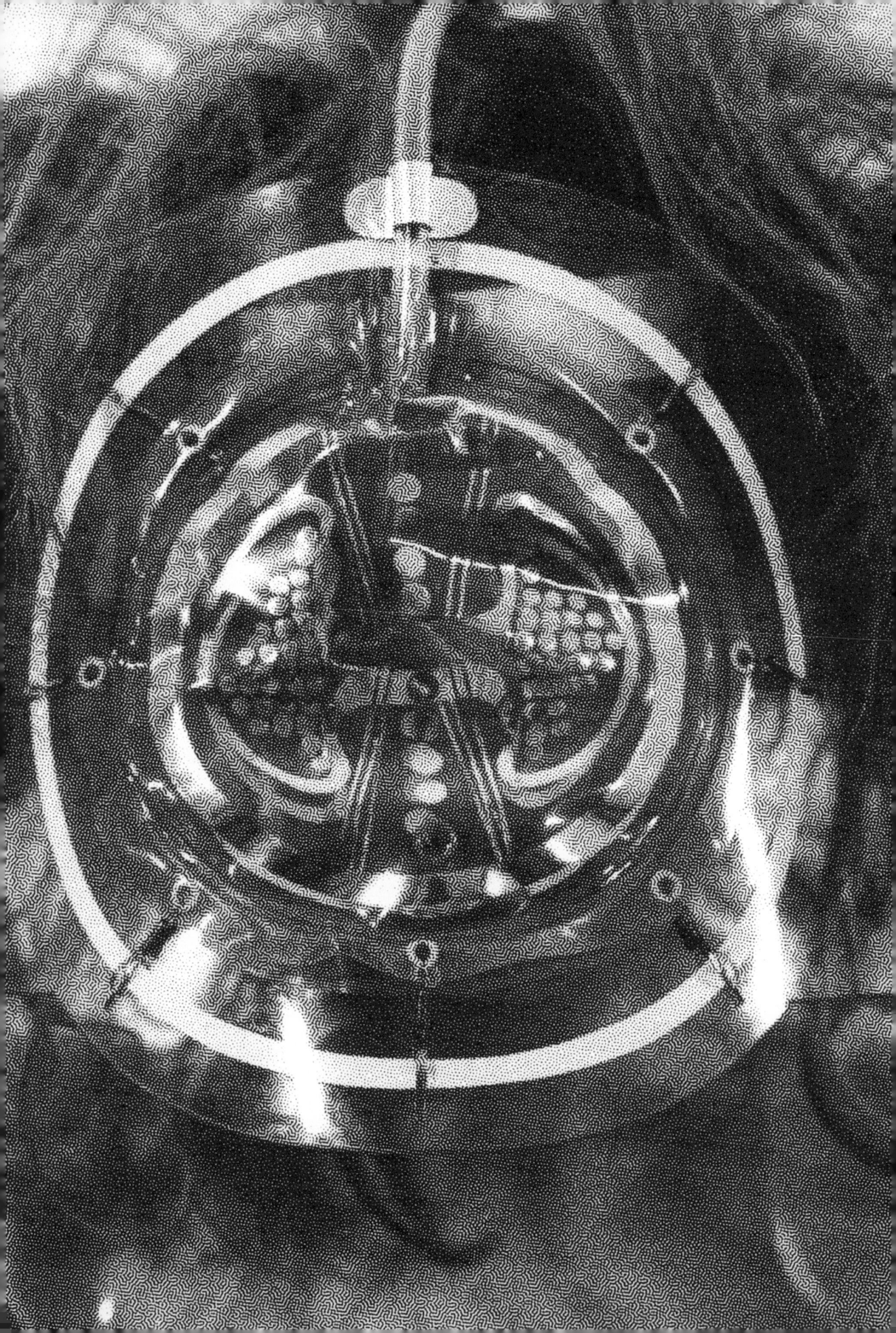

Utopia and Function

by Christoph Kelp

Utopias permeate cultural space. We can find them, for instance, in philosophy, literature, art, religion, and architecture.

Plato's *Republic* is one of the first utopian pieces. In it, Plato describes Kallipolis, a place of perfect justice and virtue, which is ruled by philosophers. It is worth noting that already Plato's utopia was criticized for making assumptions that are completely unrealistic. For instance, Aristotle objected that Kallipolis is at odds with human nature and rejected Plato's proposal as not only psychologically impossible but also simply undesirable (Aristotle 2009).

This kind of criticism of utopias remains popular. In fact, "hopelessly utopian" has established itself a catchphrase for everything that is regarded as too unrealistic. At the same time, we continue to be attracted to utopias as a means of expression. We produce and discuss them today as we did back in antiquity. Is the reason for this that we have an irrational propensity for daydreaming? Or do utopias play a more important role in our lives as means of expression and, if so, what might that be? These questions will be the focus of this paper. To answer it, I would first like to distinguish between two types of functions.

The first type of function is known as "design function." It is well known among architects and designers. A design function of an item is its intended purpose. A central design function of an architectural plan for an art gallery is typically the design of a space that is suited for the exhibition of artworks. A central design function of a coffee maker is typically the production of good coffee.

Utopias have design functions which can be very ambitious, or at the very least they can be perceived as being very ambitious. They are particularly likely to be thus perceived when the intended purpose of the utopia constitutes a radical breach with the status quo. Paradigm examples are political utopias aimed at establishing radically new societal structures. By way of illustration, let's consider one concrete example. In the 18th century, Samuel Taylor Coleridge and Robert Southey developed the idea of an egalitarian society in which everyone is working towards the common good and in which there is no private property (McKusick 1998). If we assess utopias such as Coleridge and Southey's "pantisocracy" only in terms of their design functions, it is only natural that we should conclude that they are "hope-

Bunker transformation, Cologne

1990 Following an impulse of Felix Droese, I contribute to the intervention *Space Transformation* with a significant superstructure of a bunker in Cologne Ehrenfeld. The planned integration of an art piece by Droese leads to incorporating the bunker building's model in his piece *Ich habe Anne Frank umgebracht* (I killed Anne Frank), which today belongs to the Kunsthalle Hamburg.

Publisher: Jürgen Häusser

1990 On the day of the Frankfurt Book Fair, the text I had written, edited by Heinrich Klotz, will be published by Jürgen Häusser. It includes reflections on the relationship between architecture and mediality, complimented with the documentation of projects related to it.

1990 We start preparing for the final exhibition of Haus-Rucker-Co in the Kunsthalle Wien, curated by museologist Dieter Bogner in cooperation with Martina Kandeler-Fritsch. Possible cooperation with cultural institutes in North Rhine-Westphalia are scouted.

lessly utopian." The idea that our interest in utopias is based on an irrational propensity for daydreaming may look more plausible than ever.

A central thesis of this paper is that it would be a mistake to assess utopias only in terms of their design functions. The reason for this is that there is a different kind of function which supports a more optimistic view of utopias. The kind of function I have in mind is known as an "etiological function" (Millikan 1984, Wright 1973). In a nutshell, etiological functions are effects that contribute to the continued existence of their bearers. The classical example of something with an etiological function is the human heart. A central function of the human heart is to pump blood. This function is an etiological function. The fact that human hearts pump blood contributes to the explanation of the continued existence of humans and, by the same token, of the human heart itself. What we have here is a feedback mechanism such that an item has a certain effect and the effect, in turn, contributes to the continued existence of the item. Since the item continues to exist, it continues to produce the effect. And this, in turn, leads to the continued existence of the item, and so on.

With these two types of function on the table, let's ask how they relate to one another. To begin with, consider design projects, i.e. projects that aim to develop items with design functions. Note that, typically, design projects are successful when the item's design function becomes its etiological function. Recall the case of our coffee maker, which has the central design function of producing good coffee. The project of developing a coffee maker will be successful when the coffee maker does in fact produce good coffee and, as a result, is bought by consumers, which, in turn, means that further instances of the type of coffee maker continue to be produced. The production of good coffee is an effect of the coffee maker, which contributes to keeping the type of coffee maker in demand, which contributes to its continued existence. The continued existence of the type of coffee maker means that good coffee continues to be produced, and so on. It is easy to see that we have exactly the kind of feedback mechanism that is characteristic of etiological functions. The coffee maker's design function has become its etiological function. The design project was successful.

Unfortunately, it is hard to see how these considerations might help us achieve a more optimistic view of utopias. After all, utopias rarely become reality. And for utopias that are aimed at (i.e. have as their design function) a radical breach with the status quo, this means that they don't even get the chance to transform their design functions into etiological functions in the first place. If a utopian project's success depends on this kind of transformation, utopias may now seem more hopeless than ever. They may even appear to be doomed to failure from the very beginning.

To make good on the promise of a more optimistic view of utopias, I will now argue that the two types of functions are importantly different (Graham 2010). For instance, it is possible for something to have an etiological function but not a design function. The human heart is a case in point. No one designed the human heart. And even if we want to leave relevant religious questions open, at the very least it would seem possible that no one designed the human heart. But if it doesn't have a designer, then it doesn't have a design function. It is thus at least possible that the human heart doesn't have a design function. At the same time, it is clear that this organ has an etiological function. It is also hard to deny that it could have this etiological function even if it hasn't been designed and so doesn't have a design function. In this way, there is reason to think that something can have an etiological function without having a design function.

On the other hand, it is also possible for something to have a design function without having an etiological function. The Museum of Failure is gold-star evidence for this. Its exhibits illustrate clearly just how many items with design functions don't have etiological functions. We develop things that simply don't have effects that contribute to their continued existence. In fact, this happens all the time. One reason for this is that the items simply don't produce the intended effects; another that the effects are too insignificant to contribute to the continued existence of the items.

These considerations provide excellent reason for thinking that design functions and etiological functions are importantly different. In addition, there is also reason for thinking that they can be acquired independently of one another. In particular, it is possible for an item with a design function to acquire an etiological function that differs and is independent from its design function. To take a concrete example, consider heroin. When the Bayer Company launched heroin around the turn of the twentieth century, its intended purpose (i.e. design function) was to be a nonaddictive kind of pain and cough relief. It goes without saying that the design function of heroin did not transform into its etiological function. It is also clear that heroin does have an etiological function, i.e. an effect that contributes to its continued demand and production. True, it may well be that the typical route from design function to etiological function is via transformation of the former into the latter. What the case of heroin forcefully indicates, however, is that it doesn't have to be this way. Etiological functions can be acquired independently of design functions.

House for Steirischer Herbst

1990 I accept Andreas Brandolini's invitation to take part in the initiative *Platz Machen* (Making Room) in celebration of this year's Steirischer Herbst, the fall festival in Graz. I create the project *House for Steirischer Herbst* with the intention to transfer the institution from its baroque palace to a respective new building on the Fischplatz square. At the time, I write about the project: "In the harmony of Graz's old town, the Fischplatz is a place of disharmony. Half bus stop, half gas station, the ground underneath is honeycombed with parking spots for private transportation. A reloading point for humans. Here, locality is developed through superimposition. Superimposition as the source of vitality. My project deals with the complexity of the location 'Fischplatz,' which becomes more complex through the establishment of a house for the institution 'Steirischer Herbst.' The chosen shape of the building, in the form of an inverted cone standing on its tip stems from the ambition to use up as little floor space of the existing square as possible, while signifying the delicate dynamic of a rotating spinning top, which is known to only be able to maintain in this state through a permanent supply of energy. In this respect, the outward appearance of the house serves as a synonym for the annual cultural events in the city of Graz, which are prepared and overseen from there."

View into the World of Conceptions, Zamp Kelp, Berlin, 2008

1991 *Daidalos* publishes my text "Monument oder Ereignis" ("Monument or Event") in the fortieth edition, where I write, "The scope of duties in architecture has become more diverse in the field of social tectonics, but the profession is not yet fully aware of this. The result is a new multilayered relationship between society, space, architecture, and design. A space thereby gives up its right to finality. Houses are no longer monuments, but instead are perceived as events. Well-functioning space, i.e. space that is differentiated in relation to society, is assimilated to film productions in the future, orchestrated by a team of diversely trained experts. Consequently, there will be a range of tasks and specialists in the above-described field, from architectural and context designers, product designers and social tectonicians, to those who turn concepts of concerted action into reality. Whether the architect takes on the role of a director in doing so ultimately depends on whether they are able to surrender their anachronistic position as a sociable, yet inflexible 'building block.'"

As I will argue momentarily, this insight is crucial for the more optimistic view of utopias that I promised to develop. However, I'd first like to introduce one further distinction. On the one hand, items with etiological functions can have one main function. This happens when the continued existence of the item depends on the production of the functional effect. The human heart is yet again a case in point. If human hearts didn't pump blood, they would cease to exist before long. On the other hand, items with etiological functions may have a range of functions rather than one main function. Multipurpose tools are the paradigm example here. No individual tool (pliers, file, etc.) constitutes the main function of your Swiss Army knife, say. After all, the product would still sell if it didn't have this one particular tool. Rather, what's happening here is that all of the tools contribute to the item's etiological function.

With these points in play, let's return to utopias and my attempt at a more optimistic view of them. The bad reputation of utopias is generated by its lofty design functions, which don't transform into etiological functions. At the same time, I argued that design functions and etiological functions are importantly different. In particular, etiological functions can be acquired independently of design functions. This raises the question as to whether this might be the case for utopias. And if the answer to this question is positive, a further question that arises is whether utopias have one main function (as the human heart does) or whether they have a range of functions (like your Swiss Army knife).

My hypothesis is that utopias are often like Swiss Army knives. They can have a range of etiological functions, which may differ from one utopia to the next. What's more, these functions have value. They are not irrational, as critics would have us think. The last part of this paper will briefly survey a range of possible functions of utopias.

An important function of many utopias is to engage our imagination. Now, this may look like I am trying to repackage the idea of irrational daydreaming and to sell it as something positive. And, in a way, that is what I am doing. Utopias can be daydreams. However, the important point is that this kind of daydream doesn't have to be irrational. Utopias can offer welcome refuges from tough realities, at least for short periods of time. The utopia of Cockaigne might have acquired this function in the Middle Ages. What's more, utopian daydreaming can inspire and motivate focused courses of action. For instance, as Zamp Kelp's contribution to this book forcefully indicates, the "utopia of landing on the moon" is a case in point. After all, it was Méliès's film and Verne's book that provided the key motivation for Oberth to work on rocket technology. Utopias can have value, even when they are daydreams.

Another function of many utopias is to question the status quo or to challenge us in one way or another. This is a function that we often find in utopias in architecture. Consider Haus-Rucker-Co's *Blickzerstäuber*, an excellent example of a utopian piece of architecture that questions existing forms of perception and challenges us to take into consideration radically different perspectives of the world.

The last type of function I'd like to mention here is of particular interest to me as an epistemologist. Utopias have considerable cognitive potential. They typically embody values. It will come as no surprise then, that utopias can help us come to know what we value. And, of course, this kind of knowledge is important even if the utopias in question never become realities. After all, this kind of knowledge is key to acquiring further knowledge about whether and to what extent reality corresponds to what we value. What's more, utopias can play a key role for tracking changes in our values and registering moral progress. Take Thomas More's *Utopia*. While More's utopia embodies certain values that are still popular, others have

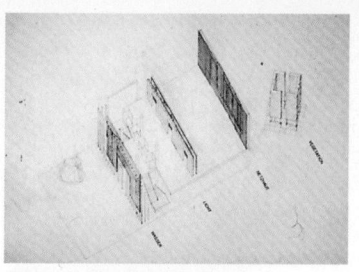

Water—Light—Vegetation

1991 I participate in a contest for the artistic design of the recently built ceremonial hall building at the University of Veterinary Medicine Vienna. The proposed idea to creatively superimpose the building with the theme "Water — Light — Vegetation" as a starting point for human and animal life convinces the jury, and I am awarded the contract for the realization, which is finished in 1995.

1991 I am one of the jury members for the documenta Hall competition. One bizarre detail is the fact that the draft by Jourdan Müller wins, even though it is planned outside of the given buildable area. Contrary to the predefined urban planning agreement, the project keeps the view of the so-called Schöne Aussicht ("Beautiful View") into the Aue meadow largely unobstructed. The *Framebuilding* also remains intact as an important emphasis and indicator in the surroundings of the hall. These two aspects are what convince the jury after thorough discussion.

1992 In the fall, Haus-Rucker-Co's existence comes to an end with an exhibition at the Kunsthalle Wien. The location is the provisional construction by Adolf Krischanitz on the Karlsplatz square near the Secession building in the fourth district. In celebration of the exhibition, Dieter Bogner and Martina Kandeler-Frisch publish the book *Haus-Rucker-Co: Denkräume Stadträume* (conceptual spaces, urban spaces). The exhibition opens on September 9. A few feuilletonists complain about the conceptual secrecy of the show, in which we present piles of framed images inaccessible to the eyes of the viewer. One even writes about a wasted opportunity to make our work prominently public. Students of the HdK and I visit the exhibition in the course of a field trip to Vienna. On December 2, and during the concluding finnisage, I sign countless copies of the book published by Bogner.

become subject to severe criticism. Slavery is the most striking example here. One central component of More's utopian society is that every household has two slaves (More 2012). There is reason to think then, that More valued the institution of slavery. It goes without saying that there is no room for slavery in contemporary utopias. In this way, utopias can be an important tool for tracking changes in our values and for registering moral progress.

My final hypothesis is that these functions are often enough etiological functions of particular utopias in the following sense. The fact that they produce the effects in question explains why we continue to think about and discuss utopias. In this way, the effects in question contribute to the continued existence of utopias. And the fact that these utopias continue to exist leads to them to continue to have these effects. This means that the effects of utopias under consideration are the etiological functions that they have. Whether they are also their design functions is of little consequence.

References

Aristotle 2009. *The Politics*. Oxford: Oxford University Press.

Graham, P. 2010. "Testimonial entitlement and the function of comprehension." In Pritchard, D., Millar, A. and Haddock, A. (eds.) *Social Epistemology*. Oxford: Oxford University Press.

McKusick, J. 1998. "'Wisely forgetful': Coleridge and the politics of pantisocracy." In Fulford, T. and Kitson, P. (eds.) *Romanticism and Colonialism: Writing and Empire 1780-1830*. New York: Cambridge University Press.

Millikan, R. 1984. *Language, Thought, and Other Biological Categories*. Cambridge: The MIT Press.

More, T. 2012. *Utopia*. London: Penguin.

Plato 2008. *The Republic*. Oxford: Oxford University Press.

Wright, L. 1973. *Functions. The Philosophical Review* 82: 139–168.

Register chronology

Register chronology for selected projects and activities within the scope of personal works, works in the frame of Haus-Rucker-Co, and in cooperation with others.

1965

ARCHITRAINER
Günter Zamp Kelp
School of Architecture, delegated by the chair of Prof. Karl Schwanzer to take part in a student competition on the occasion of the International Union of Architects (UIA) Congress
Paris, 1965

1966

SAINT ELIAS
Günter Zamp Kelp
Project of a church for the patron saint of aeronautics

ARCHITECTURE SLING
Günter Zamp Kelp
Rotating reflector composed of 6 mirrors on tripod with electric motor, Kodak carousel of +80 slides, poetic statements from audiotape.
Vienna, Fall 1967

1967

FOUNDING OF HAUS-RUCKER-CO
by Laurids Ortner, Günter Zamp Kelp, Klaus Pinter
Vienna, Fall 1967

MINDEXPANDER 1
HAUS-RUCKER-CO, Laurids-Zamp-Pinter
Angela Hareiter, Edith Ortner, Herbert Schweiger
Communicative chair for 2 persons
polyester, plexiglass, pvc
Vienna, Spring 1967

PNEUMACOSM
HAUS-RUCKER-CO, Laurids-Zamp-Pinter
Manfred Ortner, Helmut Grasberger
Pneumatic living unit for 10–15 residents
Vienna, Spring 1967

Expanding Space

1992 In Meinerzhagen in Germany's Sauerland region, Christoph Kessler and I develop the project *Expanding Space* for a local furniture store. The space is an empty area between two buildings with show rooms for design furniture from the 1950s and 1960s. By installing an interior space that opens up outwardly, the gap makes an interpretative reference to the current expansion of the social field of perception and becomes the furniture store's identifying mark. In autumn of this year, the project *Expanding Space* is finished and handed over to the building contractor.

1992 I move my atelier in Düsseldorf to the Rathausmarkt right across the street from the town hall, which I took over from Konrad Beckmann, the architect I interned with in 1964.

1993 North Rhine-Westphalia tenders a contest for a new building at the *Neanderthal Museum*. Several internationally known architects and members of the local Chamber of Architects can participate. One day, Julius Krauss calls and asks if I would like to take part in the competition with him. Since I had successfully cooperated with Krauss at the ZKM, I agree to it. For one of the first meetings, he is accompanied by Arno Brandlhuber, unknown to me but coming as Krauss's recommendation for additional help. We agree on a group of three, in which I account for 51% of all decisions throughout the project. After thoroughly examining the bidding and location in the Neander Valley, we begin with conceptual ideas regarding the museum building's function and message. This process is characterized by the metaphor of the double helix as an archetype of all life, which, in the form of a spiral-shaped pathway, gives access to the exhibition. In the text for the submitted draft, I explain, "A museum about human evolution has to fit the myth of its location in the Neander Valley and represent the contents presented in it. In the proposed project, the idea of the location superimposes the distinct exhibition theme and the building to create a unique scenario. The building's central theme is the spiral-shaped ramp, which is used to access different sections of the exhibition and provides the museum with character. The loop-like ramp as a synonym for infinity makes the building a spatial parable for the development of mankind, which is, after all, part of this infinity." As a person who aims for the top, I react to winning second prize with disappointment at first. But the phone call I receive from a member of the museum trust a few days later raises a faint hope. The member appears interested in a talk at my office and indeed, a reworking of the first and second place projects is planned in order to achieve a thirty percent reduction of the construction volume.

BALLOON FOR 2
HAUS-RUCKER-CO, Laurids-Zamp-Pinter
Pneumatic construction out of pvc film, diameter 3.5 meters, steel pipe scaffold, blower
Vienna, Fall 1967

LIVING ROOM
HAUS-RUCKER-CO, Laurids-Zamp-Pinter
Pneumatic bubble out of pvc film with sprayed-up color motives, blower
Vienna, Winter 1967

    New—as *Shindai Room*,
    Düsseldorf 1971

CONNEXIONSKIN
HAUS-RUCKER-CO, Laurids-Zamp-Pinter
Pneumatic construction, derivative object on the base of *Balloon for 2*
Vienna, Fall 1967

YELLOW HEART MODEL
HAUS-RUCKER-CO, Laurids-Zamp-Pinter
2 plexiglass spheres, one red, one transparent, sluice out of foam rubber, steel stakes with chrome-plate, couple as miniature inside
Vienna, 1967

1968

YELLOW HEART
HAUS-RUCKER-CO, Laurids-Zamp-Pinter
Breathing pneumatic space for 2 persons
Pvc film with sprayed-up color motives, blower, steel pipe-construction
Vienna, 1968

MINDEXPANDER 2
HAUS-RUCKER-CO, Laurids-Zamp-Pinter
Chair with seat shell in blue or yellow,
Lowered cupola in transparent red-and-blue plexiglass,
Multiple (4 Pieces)
Vienna, 1968

ELECTRIC SKINS
HAUS-RUCKER-CO, Laurids-Zamp-Pinter
ES 1, pantsuit red transparent pvc film with applications
ES 2, wrap-dress out of blue, red, silver pvc film
measurement 2 × 1.5 m
ES 3, wrap-dress, analog ES 2
measurement 1.6 × 1 m
Vienna, 1968

ENVIRONMENT TRANSFORMERS

FLYHEAD, VIEWATOMIZER, DRIZZLER
HAUS-RUCKER-CO, Laurids-Zamp-Pinter
Vienna, 1968

1969

VANILLA FUTURE
HAUS-RUCKER-CO, Laurids-Zamp-Pinter
Event at the gym in Schleifmühlgasse, Vienna 4th district
Presentation of the objects: *Battleship*, 2 examples of *Mindexpander 2*, *Roomscraper*, *Viewatomizer*, *Drizzler*, *Kiss-Cupola*
Vienna, 1969

STAND FOR AUSTRIAN INSTITUTE OF DESIGN
HAUS-RUCKER-CO, Laurids-Zamp-Pinter

    1. Draft: SIGNIFIER (not realized)

Oversized index finger, movable, air supported construction with integrated information area

    2. Draft: DESIGN MARK (realized)

Pneumatic construction, out of rings and cylindrical elements, stuck into one another, produced out of translucent pvc, total height = 7 meters

ROOMSCRAPER
HAUS-RUCKER-CO, Laurids-Zamp-Pinter
Air-supported cylinder with silkscreen print of an oversized female finger, base of a carton cylinder with integrated light source and air pump, diameter = 0.35m, height = 2.20m

1993 Andreas Hanke, Diego Rodriguez, and I take part in the contest for the *Dortmunder U*. When proposing a reinterpretation of the brewery site, the tower with its "U" becomes the subject of the urban planning arrangements due to the multiplication of its volume. The day of the presentation, I meet Richard Rogers in person. In a friendly chat, he reacts to our project by proclaiming: "This is it." When the jury meets some time later and the results are announced, Richard Rogers wins. His proposal is never realized.

1994 The revision phase for the *Neanderthal Museum* takes shape. We achieve the reduction of the building volume by functionally expanding the spiral-shaped accessway to the exhibition space, which winds its way up around a central staircase without altering the building's outer appearance. The revised project eventually receives the necessary funding, and we keep working on it until the building application is submitted. After the design planning is finished, I notice my project drafts in the trash bin and save them from being thrown away at the last minute.

1994 In the fall, a collaboration with Saulius Vallius creates the exhibition *Ansichten und Grundrisse* (Elevations and plans) for Lindinger + Schmid in Regensburg. It includes four projects that have not been realized yet, and model photos that are vertically arrayed on a wall with the associated layout horizontally on the floor beneath it. The projects are from the draft for a *Panorama Pavilion for Sevilla*, the *House for Steirischer Herbst* for Graz, the *House Behind Riverscape* for the town Meerbusch near Düsseldorf, and the planning for the construction of a Second World War bunker in Cologne Ehrenfeld. The large formats of the elevations and floorplans on the wall and floor are each created by the multisheet presentation of seventy-five A3 sheets, generated from a cardboard box measuring 43 × 31 × 5.5 centimeters each.

1970

HAUS-RUCKER-CO LIVE
Solo exhibitions at Museum of 20th Century, Vienna and Museum of Contemporary Crafts, New York

> Event:
> *Giant Billard* on 53rd Street Manhattan, on the occasion of the opening and of the annual congress of the American Association of Museums

TARZAN
HAUS-RUCKER-CO, Laurids-Zamp-Pinter
Scenery for the Tarzan book presentation,
Built to order of publishers Bärmeier und Nickel
Frankfurt Book Fair/Main, 1970

1971

COVER — SURVIVAL IN A POLLUTED ENVIRONMENT
HAUS-RUCKER-CO, Laurids-Zamp-Pinter
Synthetic Reserve over Haus Lange, Krefeld
Built 1928 by Ludwig Mies van der Rohe, superimposed 1971 by Haus-Rucker-Co with an air-inflated structure
Krefeld, 1971

> April:
> Zamp Kelp starts a one-year stay in New York City

BROADWAY SILKSCREEN SERIES
HAUS-RUCKER-CO
5 Silkscreens with integrated montages of "Live-Cells"
Rooftop Garden (Zamp-Pinter), *Joe's Bar* (Pinter), *4 seasons Hotel* (Zamp), *Cocoon* (Pinter), *Fresh Air Reserve* (Zamp)
New York, 1971

> July:
> Manfred Ortner
> joins HRC-studio in Düsseldorf

FINGERPOST
HAUS-RUCKER-CO, Laurids-Zamp-Pinter and Manfred Ortner
Air-supported oversized finger at the Nuremberg Airport
Nuremberg, 1971

FOOD CITY 1
HAUS-RUCKER-CO, Laurids-Zamp-Pinter and Caroll Michels
Edible model of a city structure at Walker Art Center on occasion of the City Art Festival
Minneapolis, 1971

FOOD CITY 2
HAUS-RUCKER-CO, Laurids-Zamp-Pinter
and Caroll Michels
Edible model of downtown Houston, invited the by city government
Houston, 1971

PIECE OF NATURE/SKI SHOW NY
Haus-Rucker-Co, Laurids-Zamp-Pinter
and Caroll Michels
Stand for the Austrian Trade Delegation, prospect with panorama of the Alps, lettering AUSTRIA at information desk
New York, Columbus Circle 1971

WALKING SCHOOL
HAUS-RUCKER-CO, Laurids-Zamp-Pinter and Manfred Ortner
Temporary installation at the Graben in Vienna, parkours to irritate everyday walking habits
Vienna, 1971

Stone Animals

1995 The ceremonial hall building at the University of Veterinary Medicine Vienna is completed. It was my job to use artistic interventions to address the topic "Water — Light — Vegetation" as a basic requirement for animal life in both the surroundings of the hall building and its interior. The *Stone Animals* on display in the foyer—findings of various sizes, each standing on four tubular steel telescopes and reminiscent of a pack of pets—are especially popular.

1972

OASIS NO 7
HAUS-RUCKER-CO, Laurids Ortner-Günter Zamp Kelp-Manfred Ortner with Klaus Pinter
Air-supported structure as Synthetic Reserve at the façade of Fridericianum in Kassel on occasion of documenta 5
Kassel, 1972

CENTENIAL CITY HALL VIENNA
HAUS-RUCKER-CO, Laurids Ortner-Günter Zamp Kelp-Manfred Ortner with Klaus Pinter
Provisional staircase as a direct path from the fore court to the mayor's office, avoiding the way through the authorities, project
Vienna, 1972

1973
HAUS-RUCKER-INC, New York, Klaus Pinter and
Caroll Michels
declare independence from Haus-Rucker-Co, Düsseldorf

1995 The beginning of the year marks the start of construction at the *Neanderthal Museum*. Prior to this stage, a committee of experts and a group of architects and art historians from Strasbourg called "Creamuse" had decided on the museum's contents. Since the committee cannot picture a spiral room for the exhibits, a meter-long 1:10 paperboard model is built. I cannot say whether it truly helped the members of the foundation to understand the spiral space or not, since they only confessed after the building's completion that they would have saved themselves several sleepless nights if they had been aware of the twined, slightly rising room's quality.

DRAWER HOUSE
HAUS-RUCKER-CO, Laurids Ortner-Günter Zamp Kelp-Manfred Ortner
Apartment house, Düsseldorf Inselstrasse 32
Façade with drawer-like oriels
Düsseldorf, 1973

VALLEY
HAUS-RUCKER-CO, Laurids Ortner-Günter Zamp Kelp-Manfred Ortner
Oversize hammock for up to 10 persons, Educational Center, Berlin-Lichterfelde
Düsseldorf/Berlin, 1973

GREEN LUNG
HAUS-RUCKER-CO, Laurids Ortner-Günter Zamp Kelp-Manfred Ortner
Installation in the rotunda of the Kunsthalle Hamburg, object with a connection to an outdoor "breathing zone" at the vestibule of the museum
Hamburg, 1973

1974

BOSCH MOTORCYCLE-SCENARIO
HAUS-RUCKER-CO, Laurids Ortner-Günter Zamp Kelp-Manfred Ortner
Fair stand designed as oversized bust of a motorcyclist with incorporated presentation of products by Robert Bosch GmbH
Cologne, IFMA, 1974 and 1975

RIPPLED GRASSLAND WITH LUMINARY ROD
HAUS-RUCKER-CO, Laurids Ortner, Günter Zamp Kelp, Manfred Ortner
Open space project at the Ministry of Education, Research and Science, Bonn
Bonn-Bad Godesberg, 1974

PEDESTRIAN ZONE LINZ
HAUS-RUCKER-CO, Laurids Ortner, Günter Zamp Kelp, Manfred Ortner in cooperation with D.S. Hoppe and Christoph Langhof
Project with a streetcar-trace integrated in an expanse of water as an element of pedestrian security
Düsseldorf, Vienna, 1974

URBAN OASIS

Haus-Rucker-Co participates in an exhibition about spaces of urban regeneration with an entrance design in the form of an enlarged drawing by Haus-Rucker-Co, showing urban scenery, which is penetrated by a stair construction leading to the exhibition space where, among others, a photomural of *Oasis No 7* is exhibited
Munich/Vienna/Zurich, 1974

SUNDOWN

Haus-Rucker-Co, Laurids Ortner-Günter Zamp Kelp-Manfred Ortner
Exhibition dealing with nature and urbanism
Major installation: painted scenery of the Matterhorn with integrated wire-mechanism to wind the peak down to the observer
Braunschweig, Haus Salve Hospes, 1974

1975

WAY TO LILLYPUT

HAUS-RUCKER-CO, Günter Zamp Kelp
Collage dealing with the fragmented perception of natural, cultural, and urban landscapes
Düsseldorf, 1975

PENDING MUSEUM

HAUS-RUCKER-CO, Laurids Ortner-Günter Zamp Kelp-Manfred Ortner
Project for the entrance hall of an educational center Kiel-Mettenhof
Düsseldorf, 1975

WALLRAF-RICHARTZ-MUSEUM COLOGNE

HAUS-RUCKER-CO, Laurids Ortner-Günter Zamp Kelp-Manfred Ortner
Project in cooperation with Prof. Karl Schwanzer and Angela Hareiter
Düsseldorf, 1975

ART COLLECTION NORDRHEIN-WESTFALEN

HAUS-RUCKER-CO, Laurids Ortner-Günter Zamp Kelp-Manfred Ortner
Project in cooperation with Prof. Karl Schwanzer
Munich/Düsseldorf, 1975

Swarm of Birds

1995 The construction company Hochtief commissions me to improve the entrance of the new E-Plus administration building at the Düsseldorf Airport by means of identity-formation measures. I propose a wall of green glass through which one can enter, and whose alignment optimizes the building's position in its surrounding area. Because the construction management swears that there is no suitable green glass, the wall is initially erected using colorless glass with a sandblasted flock of birds on it, inspired by the corporation's carrier pigeon logo. The director of the mobile telephone provider appears disappointed about the color and demands green. Without further ado, the wall is redone yet again and this time, in green. Procuring the tinted glass turns out to be completely unproblematic.

1995 The "Tempelhof 2030+1" project is taking place in the study program Building Planning, Spatial Design, and Conveyance Technology (GRuV) of the UdK.

1996 The implementation of the *Neanderthal Museum* is nearing completion. One Saturday afternoon in May, just before the exhibits are to be installed, I present the building and its still-empty interior to experts and friends. In October, the museum opens with great security precautions, as even the President of Germany, Roman Herzog, visits the building and its contents and elaborates on his perspective of the positions of homo sapiens and homo neanderthalensis over the course of global society's historical development. Minister-President of North Rhine-Westphalia, Johannes Rau, inspects the building, talks about Neanderthals, and how the new building came to be. Crucial for the project's implementation is the sponsorship of the energy company RWE, who has contributed significant funds in addition to the money provided by the state of North Rhine-Westphalia.

1996 In the fall, I receive an invitation from the faculty of Structural Engineering at the Architecture department of the TU Vienna in the context of a professorship at the Institute for Structural Engineering and Design to work with students on an art museum near the Karlskirche. At the time, the department is going through a critical phase, as the new chairholder Will Alsop begins to abolish the decade-old specialized library.

BURGPLATZ DÜSSELDORF
HAUS-RUCKER-CO, Laurids Ortner-Günter Zamp Kelp-Manfred Ortner
Design concept for the right bank of the Rhine river
Düsseldorf, 1975

1976

INCLINED PLANE
HAUS-RUCKER-CO, Laurids Ortner-Günter Zamp Kelp-Manfred Ortner
Walkable object at the entrance of "Supersommer" at Naschmarkt in Vienna
First realization of "Provisional Architecture"
Düsseldorf/Vienna, 1976

KÖNIG BREWERY DUISBURG
HAUS-RUCKER-CO, Laurids Ortner-Günter Zamp Kelp-Manfred Ortner
Conceptual study for the image of brewery's administrative center and its periphery
Düsseldorf, 1976

WIND ROSE
HAUS-RUCKER-CO, Laurids Ortner-Günter Zamp Kelp-Manfred Ortner
Project for the outdoor areas of an officer training base in Fürstenfeldbruck
Düsseldorf, 1976

OPEN HOUSE
HAUS-RUCKER-CO, Laurids Ortner-Günter Zamp Kelp-Manfred Ortner
Outdoor spatial extension at the community center in Bremen/Vegesack, 1976

1977

L'ARCHEOLOGIE DE LA VILLE
HAUS-RUCKER-CO
Opening exhibition at Centre Pompidou / Centre de Creation Industrielle
Paris, 1977

> Haus-Rucker-Inc New York closes with the exhibition at Centre Pompidou

FRAME BUILDING
HAUS-RUCKER-CO, Laurids Ortner-Günter Zamp Kelp-Manfred Ortner
Instrument for the perception of landscape, documenta 6
Kassel, 1977

RATHAUSMARKT HAMBURG
HAUS-RUCKER-CO, Laurids Ortner-Günter Zamp Kelp-Manfred Ortner
in cooperation with Thomas Jaenisch
Project: inclined surface of the space in front of City Hall with mobile canopy
Düsseldorf, 1977

NIKE OF LINZ
HAUS-RUCKER-CO, Laurids Ortner-Günter Zamp Kelp-Manfred Ortner
Landmark on the roof of the left bridgehead building as a signal for the new function as University of Industrial Design
Linz, 1977

HALF HOUSE
HAUS-RUCKER-CO, Laurids Ortner-Günter Zamp Kelp-Manfred Ortner
Study for the design of the fore court of a youth center
Düsseldorf/Garath, 1977

MÜHLHEIM CITY NORTH
HAUS-RUCKER-CO, Laurids Ortner-Günter Zamp Kelp-Manfred Ortner
Superstructure over a two-hundred-meter-long part of a city freeway to connect the city's north to the city's center
Düsseldorf, 1977

BOULEVARD DOOR
HAUS-RUCKER-CO, Laurids Ortner-Günter Zamp Kelp-Manfred Ortner
Project of a walkable door construction on the fore court of the office towers at the end of Königsallee
Düsseldorf, 1977

AVIARY AND GREENSPACE
HAUS-RUCKER-CO, Laurids Ortner-Günter Zamp Kelp-Manfred Ortner
Study for an open area space of relaxation at Rheinische Landesklinik, Cologne
Düsseldorf, 1977

1996 I present the projects I have been working on after the disbandment of Haus-Rucker-Co in Berlin's Aedes Gallery on Savignyplatz and the Hackescher Markt. For the project NOA (New Eco-social Ambience), I work on a commission for a housing association, which deals with a renewal of a large housing development in Dortmund Clarenberg.

1997 The NAI, the Nederlands Architectuurinstituut in Rotterdam, presents large parts of its exhibition in a solo exhibition at the Aedes Gallery. Raimund Stecker gives the introduction speech. Manu Lange, a graphic designer trained at the Köln International School of Design (KISD), who has already designed the catalogs for my Aedes exhibitions, provides the contact to the Cologne-based culture manager Andreas Grosz. He has to manage the construction of a landmark next to a stone quarry near Steinbergen in the Schaumburger Land as part of a decentralized project for the Expo 2000 in Steinbergen titled *Steinzeichen Steinbergen* (Stone Mark Steinbergen). I meet him for our first conversation at the chosen location at the edge of a quarry on top of a thirty- to forty-meter-high rock face. A first project has already been submitted by a local artist, but the Minister-President of Lower Saxony finds it unremarkable. This is probably the main reason that another project will be developed. Grosz talks to several creatives and asks me to work out a proposal that we can present to the director of the stone quarry as a potential client and to the Princely Family of Schaumburg-Lippe as the property owners. We agree to another meeting in his Cologne office in two weeks and I begin thinking about a landmark that can be seen from afar. The first idea that comes to mind is to combine the landmark with the function of a lookout. The theme of detached stairs with an observation platform at a height of twenty-five meters stems from the memory of an unrealized project, the *Big Piano*, for the documenta 5 in 1972. The name *Millennium View* is derived from the object's position in the flow of time as a calendar device at the turn of the twentieth to the twenty-first century. The main difference to the *Big Piano* is the building substance and the development of an end point at the top. In contrast to the *Big Piano*, which was a temporary structure constructed from a scaffolding system, the *Millennium View* is to be built from quarry stones from the adjacent pit. The cloud of water vapor at the top of *Big Piano*, appearing hourly, veils the upper end point of the staircase at certain intervals of time. The ten green glass frames bordering the platform of the *Millennium View* are based on the drawing *Way to Lillyput* from 1975, in which landscape motives based on a picture-in-picture-in-picture principle metaphorically represent the fragmented perception of the digital age. The *Big Piano* produces music and stands in an urban context. The *Millennium View* is an instrument for observing the landscape and manifests the transi-

PRESSEHAUS DUMONT—SCHAUBERG
HAUS-RUCKER-CO, Laurids Ortner-Günter Zamp Kelp-Manfred Ortner
Project for a publishing house with a significant slab in the façades
Düsseldorf, 1977

1978

RESTRUCTURING DISTRICT SCHNELLENGASSE
HAUS-RUCKER-CO, Laurids Ortner-Günter Zamp Kelp-Manfred Ortner with Thomas Jaenisch
Urban study with a glass-covered arcade, including a museum and residential buildings in Eschweiler
Düsseldorf, 1978

SLAUGHTERHOUSE AREA DORTMUND
Laurids Ortner, Günter Zamp Kelp, Manfred Ortner
Restructuring of the area with residential structures, fruit and vegetable gardens, central courtyard
Düsseldorf, 1978

GREEN TABLE
HAUS-RUCKER-CO, Laurids Ortner-Günter Zamp Kelp-Manfred Ortner
Design study for Schlüter-Dreieck at Kurfürstendamm: kidney-shaped table with expanse of water, surrounded by immobile chairs
Düsseldorf, 1978

LITFASSSÄULEN
HAUS-RUCKER-CO, Laurids Ortner-Günter Zamp Kelp-Manfred Ortner
Realization of interactive communication media between open-air areas at a secondary school in Düsseldorf/Benrath
Düsseldorf, 1978

PAVILION OF ELEMENTS
HAUS-RUCKER-CO, Laurids Ortner-Günter Zamp Kelp-Manfred Ortner
Realization of an apostrophized entrance situation to the visitor's center of The Ministry of Science and Research
Bonn Bad Godesberg, 1978

LINEAR HOUSE
Haus-Rucker-Co, Laurids Ortner-Günter Zamp Kelp-Manfred Ortner
Architectonic fragments are lined up along a walkway line at the Lichtwiese TH Darmstadt
Darmstadt, 1978

1979

BOWERY GATES
Haus-Rucker-Co, Laurids Ortner-Günter Zamp Kelp-Manfred Ortner
Realization of two-door staircase constructions connected by a speaking tube. Sculptural intervention in the court of the highway superstructure
Schlangenbader Strasse Berlin, 1979

NEW CONTENT FOR COALMINES
HAUS-RUCKER-CO, Laurids Ortner-Günter Zamp Kelp-Manfred Ortner and Thomas Jaenisch
Study for the revitalization of shut-down coal mines in the Ruhr area
Düsseldorf, 1979

1980

GREEN GASOMETER
HAUS-RUCKER-CO, Laurids Ortner-Günter Zamp Kelp-Manfred Ortner
Stand for Kommunalverband Ruhrarea, Hanover Fair
Düsseldorf/Hanover, 1980

ZDF PAVILION
HAUS-RUCKER-CO, Laurids Ortner-Günter Zamp Kelp-Manfred Ortner
Project of a large roof made out of a steel-glass construction in front of the Broadcast Center Mainz-Lerchenberg
Düsseldorf, 1980

GUSTAV-GRÜNDGENS-PLATZ
HAUS-RUCKER-CO, Laurids Ortner-Günter Zamp Kelp-Manfred Ortner and Thomas Jaenisch
Competition entry selected for a second stage of consolidation regarding the new interpretation of the space in front of the theater building in Düsseldorf
Significant element: pavilion with integrated thespis barrow moving along a roadbed to possible points of performing

DEVIDED HOUSES/HOUSE FRAGMENTS
HAUS-RUCKER-CO, Laurids Ortner-Günter Zamp Kelp-Manfred Ortner and Karl-Heinz Schmitz
Project for a residential area with two building types referring to each other
IBA Berlin, Rauchstrasse, Düsseldorf, 1980

tion between centuries as a landmark. Andreas Grosz and I present this proposal to the quarry's managers, to local cultural committees, and to the Princely House in Bückenburg as the landowners. Due to the generally positive mood surrounding this project, I receive consent to build.

1998 In Düsseldorf, I start planning *Zero Gravity Space*. The architectural implant in the courtyard entrance of the Schmela gallery, a building erected by Aldo van Eyck in the early 1970s, takes up the subject of a passageway in the form of a vectored cross view through two glass walls to the yard. The remaining floor, ceiling, and wall surfaces are lined with walkable, gray maple parquet to provide the space with four equally usable surfaces in the absence of gravity, thus functioning like the International Space Station. The realization follows in 1999 and later leads to the project *Zero Gravity Town*, a utopian urban planning approach I conceptualize for time travel within the weightlessness of space.

Lentos Linz

1998 This year, I also participate in the contest for the Danube museum in Linz, the realization of which is called "Lentos" today. I am again inspired by the subject of frames. Frames made from green glass, around ninety of them in a row, float above the riverbank landscape along the Danube, defining the adaptable exhibition space.

1999 The Centre Pompidou expresses its interest in objects of the *Mindexpanding Program*. In August, I present items to the head of the architecture department of the Centre Pompidou, Alain Guiheux, and his assistant, Jacqueline Stanic, who both arrived from Paris that day. Guiheux is visibly impressed and expresses his intention to buy *Mindexpander 1*, *Yellow Heart*, and the *Environment Transformer*. It takes another two years, but the Centre Pompidou eventually buys all three. The pieces are transported by assistants, who have prepared the objects for the presentation. The *Yellow Heart* is set up in one of the depots.

FORUM DESIGN
HAUS-RUCKER-CO, Laurids Ortner-Günter Zamp Kelp-Manfred Ortner and Angela Hareiter, Peter Skokan
Temporary linear exhibition structure with a café designed by Christopher Alexander as the endpoint
Linz/Wien/Düsseldorf, 1980

1981

LÜTZOWPLATZ BERLIN
HAUS-RUCKER-CO, Laurids Ortner-Günter Zamp Kelp-Manfred Ortner and Thomas Jaenisch
Significance: perspectival outdoor space, leading to the inside of the block
Residential project, IBA Berlin, 1981

GÄNSEMARKT HAMBURG
HAUS-RUCKER-CO, Laurids Ortner-Günter Zamp Kelp-Manfred Ortner and Thomas Jaenisch
Project for the redesign of the Gänsemarkt square
Significance: the Lessing statue is positioned beside its pedestal on the surface of the square
Düsseldorf, 1981

FOUNTAIN HOUSE
HAUS-RUCKER-CO, Laurids Ortner-Günter Zamp Kelp-Manfred Ortner
A glasshouse standing on 4 stands is diagonally penetrated by a stair with a water cascade, art in the urban environment, project
Berlin, 1981

AEG PAVILION
HAUS-RUCKER-CO, Laurids Ortner-Günter Zamp Kelp-Manfred Ortner
Realized provisional paraphrasis of the AEG-Turbine Hall in Berlin at Domotechnica Hanover, plus the exhibition design inside the hall
Düsseldorf/ Hanover, 1981

OBSERVATORY FOR GOOD AND BAD DESIGN
HAUS-RUCKER-CO, Laurids Ortner-Günter Zamp Kelp-Manfred Ortner
Conception for an exhibition building on the occasion of "Casa della Falsita,"
an Initiative of Focus, Furnishing House, Munich
Düsseldorf, 1981

WITH A TABLE THROUGH THE WALL
HAUS-RUCKER-CO
Scenario for the celebration of the 40th birthday of Günter Zamp Kelp. Cut-out in a garden wall, installation of a penetrating long table for thirty guests, sitting in gardens on both sides of the wall
Düsseldorf, 1981

1982

TOWN HALL SQUARE BIELEFELD
HAUS-RUCKER-CO, Laurids Ortner-Günter Zamp Kelp-Manfred Ortner
Redesign of the square surface in form of a scarf out of stones in diverse colors, combined with a formation of greenery-columns
Realized project
Düsseldorf/Bielefeld, 1982

BLOCK 7 FRIEDRICHSTADT SOUTH
HAUS-RUCKER-CO, Laurids Ortner-Günter Zamp Kelp-Manfred Ortner
In cooperation with Nalbach/Nalbach and Sartory/Kohlmaier
Design and realization of a residential area and kindergarten
IBA Berlin, 1982

FILM AND TELEVISION ACADEMY
HAUS-RUCKER-CO, Laurids Ortner-Günter Zamp Kelp-Manfred Ortner
Preliminary study for the competition Tower at *Kant-Dreieck* in Berlin
Düsseldorf, 1982

BUNDESKUNSTHALLE AND ART MUSEUM BONN
HAUS-RUCKER-CO, Laurids Ortner-Günter Zamp Kelp, Manfred Ortner with Götz Stöckmann
A project where the museum buildings are situated in the background, whereby a light-increasing fore field is generated
Düsseldorf, 1982

MUSEUMSHOP KUNSTHALLE HAMBURG
HAUS-RUCKER-CO, Laurids Ortner-Günter Zamp Kelp-Manfred Ortner
Design of a kiosk in the entrance hall, project
Düsseldorf, 1982

1999 I am invited to participate in the contest by the International Art Museum Lanzarote-Castillo de San José. The jury includes Terence Riley, Helge Achenbach, and Dietmar Steiner. Our project, *Piece of Island*, is planned in cooperation with Andreas Hanke on the grounds of a former cistern near the capital Arrecife. The theme involves a piece of land that is cut out of the island's surface and, supported by a formation of columns, floats above the ground. This effect, coupled with the generated indentation, creates a top-quality spot in the shade, from where the exhibition spaces could have been accessed via elevators and escalators.

1999 The *Millennium View* project and its planning have been developed into a park with several rest and relaxation areas. Based on this plan, the object with a viewing platform receives a building consent. From the other proposals, only a cubical room makes it to construction, in which, on the opening day, films by the artist Marcel Odenbach are projected onto a wall.

1984

3 BUILDINGS FOR A METROPOLIS
HAUS-RUCKER-CO, Laurids Ortner-Günter Zamp Kelp-Manfred Ortner
Exhibition at the Neue Nationalgalerie Berlin, model studies for mass, space, traffic, construction and surface
Düsseldorf/Berlin, 1984

FAÇADE GALLERY
HAUS-RUCKER-CO, Laurids Ortner-Günter Zamp Kelp-Manfred Ortner
Redesign of the façade of the Wertheim department store at Kurfürstendamm
Pentamerous giant show case for scenarios dealing with the city of Berlin, realized project
Düsseldorf/Berlin, 1984

CONFERENCE ROOMS TU BERLIN
HAUS-RUCKER-CO, Laurids Ortner-Günter Zamp Kelp-Manfred Ortner
Redesign and realization
Düsseldorf/Berlin, 1984

TOWER IN NEUSS
HAUS-RUCKER-CO, Laurids Ortner-Günter Zamp Kelp-Manfred Ortner
Realization as art in the urban environment in front of post office 1 at Theodor-Heuss-Platz, Neuss
Berlin, 1984

DEICHTORHALLEN HAMBURG
HAUS-RUCKER-CO, Laurids Ortner-Günter Zamp Kelp-Manfred Ortner
Project for the new interpretation of historic market halls into a cultural center right by the harbor

KUNSTHALLE AT AUGUST-MACKE-PLATZ
HAUS-RUCKER-CO, Laurids Ortner-Günter Zamp Kelp-Manfred Ortner
Upgrade of a flower market to an art institute for the ART Club Bonn
Düsseldorf/Bonn, 1984–86

1985

SUBWAY THEATER
HAUS-RUCKER-CO, Laurids Ortner-Günter Zamp Kelp-Manfred Ortner
Project to install an open-air stage in the rollover of the subway station Marienplatz
in Munich
Düsseldorf/Munich, 1985

3 SITUATIONS IN BERLIN CHARLOTTENBURG
HAUS-RUCKER-CO, Laurids Ortner-Günter Zamp Kelp-Manfred Ortner
Project for an ensemble in the area of Fasanenstrasse and Uhlandstrasse. Realization of a residential and office building right by the subway bridge
Uhlandstrasse

TOWER AT KANT-DREIECK
Project for an urban ensemble of Tower, Stick, and Helmet in the forefront of Theater des Westens at Kantstrasse
Project for a residential and office building in connection with an existing villa
Düsseldorf/Berlin, 1985

1986

STAIRWAY HOUSE
Project at the bus stop Olivaer Platz, Berlin. Information pavilion with integrated stair construction leading to an observation deck with view over Kurfürstendamm and Leibnitzstrasse
Düsseldorf Berlin 1986

KOTTBUSSER TOR
HAUS-RUCKER-CO, Laurids Ortner-Günter Zamp Kelp-Manfred Ortner
Study for a redesign of façades and open space area of a department, up-streamed to residential housing
Düsseldorf, 1986

KARSTADT AT HERMANNPLATZ
HAUS-RUCKER-CO, Laurids Ortner-Günter Zamp Kelp-Manfred Ortner
Redesign concept for the façades with integrated stairway, leading to coffee bar at the corner to Hasenheide
Düsseldorf, 1986

1999 The UdK students of the program GRuV, assisted by Jürgen H. Mayer, are working on the project "Goethe in Hong Kong. Einstein in Shanghai."

2000 On June 1, the Expo 2000 opens in Hanover. The *Millennium View* is completed in the same month, and on the day it is turned over to the client and the public, it receives a use permit from the building department in Hanover. The late approval resulted from disagreements shortly before the handover date. They occurred between the commissioned structural engineers, the Ove Arup GmbH in Düsseldorf, and the structural engineer from Hanover, who could not agree on the calculation of the project's stability against wind forces on the green glass frames.

2000 On September 23, 2000, the traveling exhibition *Cabinet of Drawing* at the Art Association of Rhineland and Westphalia in Düsseldorf opens. Reimut Stecker had commissioned me to develop an exhibition concept, which was later realized. He writes, "Zamp Kelp designed this cabinet. Protected from light but not the dark, the framed or *passe-partout* drawings hang from transparent bags on a kind of conveyance bar. Should you know which sheet you would like to look at, you can send for it, and should you not, you can look in peace. This depot, replacing the usual drawers, is thus one that not only stores but also allows for the drawings to be observed within it, which can generally be done in graphic cabinets after the presentation of the desired drawing."

KUNSTHALLE HAMBURG
HAUS-RUCKER-CO, Laurids Ortner-Günter Zamp Kelp-Manfred Ortner
Design of an additional building to expand the exhibition spaces
Düsseldorf, 1986

LOOKOUT
HAUS-RUCKER-CO, Laurids Ortner-Günter Zamp Kelp-Manfred Ortner
Art in the urban environment of University Oldenburg, project
Düsseldorf, 1986

CARILLON BERLIN TIERGARTEN
HAUS-RUCKER-CO, Laurids Ortner-Günter Zamp Kelp-Manfred Ortner
Design of a giant metronome as an urban musical instrument
Düsseldorf, 1986

1987

PFALZTHEATER KAISERSLAUTERN
HAUS-RUCKER-CO, Laurids Ortner-Günter Zamp Kelp-Manfred Ortner with Thomas Gutt
Project for a theater and concert house
Düsseldorf, 1987

CITY CENTER WITH HOUSE OF PRAYER
HAUS-RUCKER-CO, Laurids Ortner-Günter Zamp Kelp-Manfred Ortner with Thomas Gutt
Düsseldorf/Bonn 1987

CULTURAL QUARTERS MESSEPALAST
HAUS-RUCKER-CO, Laurids Ortner-Günter Zamp Kelp-Manfred Ortner
First phase of design procedure
Düsseldorf/Vienna, 1987

TOWN HALL SQUARE BIELEDFELD
HAUS-RUCKER-CO, Laurids Ortner-Günter Zamp Kelp-Manfred Ortner
Realization of competition project
Düsseldorf/Bielefeld, 1987

HOTEL VICTORIA
HAUS-RUCKER-CO, Laurids Ortner-Günter Zamp Kelp-Manfred Ortner
Project for a hotel with three hundred beds at the Victoria Insurance property on the corner Kurfürstendamm/Joachimsthaler Strasse
Düsseldorf/Berlin, 1987

MEDIAPARC COLOGNE
HAUS-RUCKER-CO, Laurids Ortner-Günter Zamp Kelp-Manfred Ortner
Urban development project for Gereons freight area, Cologne
Düsseldorf, 1987

FETISH CUBE
Günter Zamp Kelp
Realization on the occasion of the symposium *Object and Ritual*
organized by Rat für Formgebung
Frankfurt, 1987

LINEAR MUSEUM
HAUS-RUCKER-CO, Laurids Ortner-Günter Zamp Kelp-Manfred Ortner
Conceptual model, chain of exhibition halls
documenta 8, Orangery, Kassel, 1987

1988

CITY HOTEL
Günter Zamp Kelp
Expertise for ITAG: hotel building in Berlin, Charlottenburg
Düsseldorf, 1988

GREEN CUBE
Günter Zamp Kelp
Art in the urban environment, project for WIFI Vienna
Düsseldorf, 1988

RED MOON OF HAMM
Günter Zamp Kelp
Project for Santa-Monica-Platz in Hamm
Düsseldorf, 1988

1989

CENTER FOR ART AND MEDIATECHNOLOGY ZKM
HAUS-RUCKER-CO, Laurids Ortner-Günter Zamp Kelp-Manfred Ortner with Julius Krauss and Barbara Bruder
Expertise for the surroundings of the Central Station in Karlsruhe
Düsseldorf, 1989

FALLING STREAM
Günter Zamp Kelp with Barbara Bruder
Project for a transformer station, Media Parc Cologne
Düsseldorf, 1989

2000 I contribute to the contest for the BMW delivery center, also known as BMW Welt. Twenty-eight offices from two hundred and seventy-five applications are admitted to the competition. Under the label "Partner für Baukultur" ("Partners for Building Culture"), i.e. Zamp Kelp and Andreas Hanke, we submit a project that should convince less with its formal aspects than through the special nature of its functional offers. Our focus is set on the important ritual of handing over new cars and the relationship to Karl Schwanzer's *Vierzylinder*, the distinctive BMW administration building from the 1970s. The decision to go with *Skywheel*, with which the owners of the new cars can make their first experience by going for a drive in one of the gondolas together with the new car, is the functional attractor in this project and is supposed to create an additional appeal for visitors of the BMW Welt. In terms of urban planning, the *Skywheel* forms the frame for the *Vierzylinder* behind it, placing it in a Mandorla, so to speak, in a way that the two buildings relate to each other. All other functions of this place of communication are located in a rationally designed skeleton structure connected to the *Skywheel*.

House in Front of the Wind

2001 Initial proposals for an administration building in the port of Düsseldorf are being positively evaluated by the city and will eventually lead to the realization of the *House in Front of The Wind*. At the UdK, a project and an excursion to China are on the agenda. The main focus is Beijing, the city in which the student projects are planned. In Shanghai, we cross the Huangpu from the Bund to inspect the urban development area there. Around noon, we suddenly hear the sound of Johann Strauss's "At the Beautiful Blue Danube" on a square at its center, and fountains of a water begin to sway to the beat. This musical surprise motivates me to dance a waltz with one of the excursion participants. In turn, this leads to interested local spectators gathering in a circle around us and to many of the students saying that I had done quite a bit to earn extra sympathy credit.

HDK-STUDIO-ROOF
Günter Zamp Kelp with Busse Geitner
Project for the expansion of studios at the architectural department of the Art University at Hardenbergstrasse Berlin
Düsseldorf/Berlin, 1989

CROSSING BRIDGES
Günter Zamp Kelp
Project in vincinity to Museum of Traffic and Technology, Berlin
Düsseldorf/Berlin, 1989

VISION MACHINES
Günter Zamp Kelp with Wolfgang Laubersheimer
Scenario for the German car industry "Designed in Germany" in Nagoya, Japan
Düsseldorf/Nagoya, 1989

MEKKA MEDIAL
Günter Zamp Kelp with Andreas Hanke
Contribution for the exhibition City and Utopia, Pavillon d'Arsenal, Paris and Kunsthalle Berlin
Düsseldorf/Paris/Berlin, 1989

ORNAMENTA 1
Günter Zamp Kelp with Andreas Hanke
Exhibition architecture for 1. International Jewelry Exhibition, Pforzheim
Düsseldorf/Pforzheim, 1989

1990

PANORAMA PAVILION
Günter Zamp Kelp with Diether S. Hoppe
Design project for the Austrian contribution to Expo Sevilla 1992
Düsseldorf/Vienna, 1990

CULTURE KILOMETER HAMBURG
Günter Zamp Kelp
Urban study for the redesign of Deichtorplatz and an Ericusspitze
Düsseldorf, 1990

RING OF FRAMES
Günter Zamp Kelp
Design and realization of a basketball court as an art piece in a public space of Spandau
Berlin/Spandau, 1990

SHAPE TRANSFORMATION
Günter Zamp Kelp in cooperation with artist Felix Droese
Project for the functional change of an air raid shelter into a local cultural center in Cologne, Ehrenfeld
Düsseldorf, 1990

HOUSE FOR STEIRISCHER HERBST
Günter Zamp Kelp
Study for a cultural institute at Fischplatz, Graz
Düsseldorf, 1990

1991

JEWELRY MUSEUM PFORZHEIM
Günter Zamp Kelp with Rodriguez Diaz
Transformation of Reuchlin Haus into a jewelry museum
Düsseldorf, 1991

WATER LIGHT VEGETATION
Günter Zamp Kelp
Permanent outdoor-indoor installation for the ceremonial hall of Veterinary Medicine, University, Vienna
Düsseldorf/Vienna, 1991

MUSEUM FOR GERMAN INLAND NAVIGATION
Günter Zamp Kelp with Hanke/Rodriguez
Project for the redesign of an indoor natatorium into a museum in Duisburg/Rhine harbor
Düsseldorf/Dortmund, 1991

1992

HOUSE BEHIND RIVERSCAPE
Günter Zamp Kelp
Villa project including living and working spaces within the scope of a residential community
Düsseldorf/Meerbusch, 1992

PRAGER STRASSE DRESDEN
Expertise for the spatial and structural redesign of an urban development area at Prager Strasse in Dresden
Düsseldorf, 1992

EXPANDING SPACE
Günter Zamp Kelp and Christoph Kessler
Identity-producing building connection between two parts of a furnishing house
Düsseldorf/Meinerzhagen, 1992

2002 In March of this year, I transfer my office from the Marktplatz in Düsseldorf to the Charlottenburg Ufer in Berlin into the fourth floor of an atelier building overlooking the Spree river. The building project *House in Front of The Wind* at the Medienhafen in Düsseldorf on Kaistrasse is assigned a new building contractor.

2003 Friedrich Wolters, director of the project Regionale 2004, commissions Zamp Kelp neo.studio to develop a scenography for the exhibition *Nature Made to Measure* in the former coal mine Zeche Westfalen I/II in Aalen, which focuses on flood prevention.

2004 Julia Lienemayer is the new assistant for the teaching field of Building Planning, Spatial Design, and Conveyance Technology GRuV. At the UdK, we discuss the focus of the program VIENNA-ODESSA, which thematizes the anticipation of the ethnic conglomerate Europe initiated by the multi-ethnic state, the k.u.k. monarchy Austria Hungary. *Chernivtsi Tomorrow* is part of VIENNA-ODESSA and deals with the city Chernivtsi as a functioning social community, the interference of its historical past in the Austro-Hungarian monarchy, as well as the question of what extent the city has to deal with the unfamiliar, transregional, and the international in order to find its way back into the global conscience. One approach is to activate the cultural exchange as a constructive alternative to the emigration of the cultural elite. The exhibition *Nature Made to Measure* in celebration of the Regionale 2004 is opened on July 2, 2004. The main installation is the *Table of the 21st Century*, with a water basin at the center and a model of a sunken settlement arranged in the middle, on the surface of which are several electrically operated model boats that can be remotely operated from the table's edge. The similarities to the round table in Stanley Kubrick's War Room in *Dr. Strangelove or: How I Learned to Stop Worrying and Love the Bomb* become apparent through a projection onto a wall in the background that deals with environmental strategies. A first meeting with the public works department of Mainz offers the chance to discuss the possible conversion of the "boiler house" at the port of Mainz into an art hall.

1993

DORTMUND "U"
Günter Zamp Kelp with Hanke/Rodriguez
Study for an urban development to change a brewery into residential structures
Düsseldorf/Dortmund, 1993

NEANDERTHAL MUSEUM
Blueprint planning:
Günter Zamp Kelp and Julius Krauss/Arno Brandlhuber
Detailed planning:
Günter Zamp Kelp+Office, Düsseldorf Germany
Museum for History of Human Development in Mettmann
Düsseldorf/Mettmann, 1993–1996

1994

ELEVATIONS AND PLANS
Günter Zamp Kelp
Exhibition by Lindinger und Schmid, Regensburg
Presentation of four unrealized projects, showing enlarged motives of models and plans
Düsseldorf/Regensburg, 1994

1995

GREEN GLASS WITH APRON
Günter Zamp Kelp
Realized design of the entrance hall for E-plus administration at Düsseldorf airport
Düsseldorf, 1995

NOA
Günter Zamp Kelp
Study for the social-ecological re-engineering of a large housing estate in Dortmund Clarenberg
Düsseldorf, 1995

1996

RAUTENSTRAUCH-JOEST-MUSEUM
Günter Zamp Kelp
Project for a new museum building to replace the former Kunsthalle in Cologne
Düsseldorf, 1996

ZAMP KELP AT AEDES WEST
Presentation of *Neanderthal Museum*
plans and images
Düsseldorf/Berlin, 1996

ZAMP KELP AT AEDES EAST
Media Aureoles For The City + Time Loops
Project review, plans and images
Düsseldorf/Berlin, 1996

CULTURE MAGNET
Günter Zamp Kelp with D. S. Hoppe
Project for the Austrian Embassy in Berlin
Düsseldorf/Vienna, 1996

1997

MUSEUM GEORG SCHÄFER
Günter Zamp Kelp+Office
Project for an art museum in Schweinfurt
Düsseldorf, 1997

FIEGE LOGISTICS
Günter Zamp Kelp+Office
Project for an office and administration building for Fiege
Logistics at the airport Munster/Osnabruck
Düsseldorf, 1997

MILLENNIUM VIEW
Günter Zamp Kelp
Landmark with observation deck, decentral object for Expo
Hanover in Steinbergen, opened in 2000
Düsseldorf/Schaumburg, 1997–2000

1998

LENTOS LINZ
Günter Zamp Kelp+Office
Competition entry for an art institute at the Danube
Significance: structure floating above ground, generated by
ninety frames, which are part of the adaptable exhibition
spaces' outer skin
Düsseldorf/Linz, 1998

2005 Zamp Kelp neo.studio begins planning the integration of the Kunsthalle Mainz into the existing boiler house from the nineteenth century, located at the port. The construction of *The House in Front of The Wind* in Düsseldorf begins. Zamp Kelp neo.studio are invited to and take part in the contest for the Constantine the Great exhibition in Trier and subsequently, receive the contract. Initiated by the GRuV, we begin preparing for the summer academy in Chernivtsi, which will include the Polytechnic College Chernivtsi, the Faculty of Architecture of the TU Graz, the Ion Mincu University of Architecture and Urban Planning Bucharest, as well as the Architecture Faculty of the UdK.

2006 Austria celebrates the 250th birthday of Wolfgang Amadeus Mozart and the 150th birthday of Sigmund Freud. In June of this year, the ground-breaking ceremony for the Kunsthalle Mainz takes place in the empty boiler house at the Port of Mainz. The summer academy Chernivtsi takes place from July 29 to August 15. Haus-Rucker-Co contributes to the exhibition *Future City: Experiment and Utopia in Architecture 1956–2006* at the Barbican Art Gallery London, which opens on June 15, 2006, with the models *Pneumacosm*, the *Leisuretime Explosion*, and *Four Seasons Hotel* on loan from the collection of the FRAC Centre in Orléans, as well as a large print of the *Oasis No 7* from the documenta 5 in 1972.

2007 On January 26, the exhibition *Between* opens at the Kunsthalle Düsseldorf. It includes a summary of highlights from a total of the seven Betweens that have taken place there. Haus-Rucker-Co displays the *Giant Billiard* from 1970, which was installed in *Between 5*, and Gotthard Graubner shows his *Fog Spaces* from *Between 1*. On January 31, the Kunsthalle Mainz celebrates its topping-out ceremony. From May 25 to September 24, Haus-Rucker-Co joins the exhibition *Tomorrow Now* at the Mudam in Luxembourg with the works *Pneumacosm Tryptichon*, *Livingroom in Room/Shindai Room*, *Mindexpander 2*, *Roomscraper* and the screen print *Rooftop Garden/Planet of Vienna*. In June, the exhibition Constantine the Great, designed by Zamp Kelp, opens in Trier.

ZERO GRAVITY SPACE
Günter Zamp Kelp+Office
Upgrading of a passage through a gallery house, built by Aldo van Eyck in Düsseldorf, four walls covered with grey maple parquet floor, two glass walls, producing a view to the inner block.
Düsseldorf, 1998

1999

PIECE OF ISLAND
Günter Zamp Kelp+Office
Project for an International Exhibition Center for contemporary art on Lanzarote
Düsseldorf, 1999

2000

TODAY IS TOMORROW
Günter Zamp Kelp+Office
Realized exhibition project about the future of experience and construction
Düsseldorf/Bonn Bad Godesberg, 2000

BMW WORLD
Günter Zamp Kelp with Andreas Hanke
Study for a functional building with an identity-forming observation wheel in Munich
Düsseldorf, 2000

2001

LES ANNÉE POP
HAUS-RUCKER-CO
Participation at the exhibition with *Mindexpander 1*, *Yellow Heart*, and *Environment Transformers*
Centre Pompidou, Paris, 2001

HOUSE IN FRONT OF THE WIND
Günter Zamp Kelp+Office
Realization of an office building at the old Rhine Harbor in Düsseldorf
Düsseldorf, 2001–2006

2002

FLYING IMAGES
Günter Zamp Kelp+Andreas Hanke
Study for a scenario of film producer Adolf Winkelmann
Berlin/Essen, 2002–2003

2004

NATURE MADE TO MEASURE
Zamp Kelp neo.studio (Tobias Neumann, Moritz Schneider)
Exhibition architecture and scenography within the scope of "REGIONALE 2004" at the Zeche Westphalen I/II
Berlin/Aalen, 2003–2004

KUNSTHALLE MAINZ
Günter Zamp Kelp neo.studio
Start of planning for the transformation of an old powerhouse into an art institution at the Rhine Harbor Mainz
Berlin/Mainz, 2004–2008

2007

CONSTANTINE THE GREAT
Zamp Kelp neo.studio
Exhibition architecture and scenography for the major regional exhibition in Trier
Berlin/Trier, 2007

SMARTINSKA
Zamp Kelp, neo.studio, Winkens Architekten
Study for the new interpretation of an obsolete industrial region in Ljubljana
Berlin/Ljubljana, 2007–2015

2008–2019

COLD WAR MODERN DESIGN
HAUS-RUCKER-CO, Laurids Ortner-Günter Zamp Kelp-Klaus Pinter-Manfred Ortner
Participation with *Oasis No 7* (reconstruction), *Mindexpander 2*, *Electricskin 1*, drawings and collages
Victoria and Albert Museum, London, 2007

2008 On January 19, the Museum of Modern Art presents the *Environment Transformer, Flyhead* in its exhibition *Elastic Mind*. On March 1, the Kunsthalle Mainz opens with an exhibition featuring eleven artists, curated by the new director Natalie de Ligt. In the context of an urban planning competition in Ljubljana, Zamp Kelp neo.studio and Winkens Architekten are commissioned to conduct a study of the contest. The exhibition *Cold War Modern Design* opens on September 25, 2008 at the Victoria and Albert Museum. Haus-Rucker-Co exhibit the *Mindexpander 2, Electric Skin 1* as well as drawings on the subject *COVER — Survival in a Polluted Environment*. The exhibition moves on to Rovereto and then to Vilnius.

2009 The exhibition *1968 — Die grosse Unschuld (The Great Innocence)* takes place at the Kunsthalle Bielefeld. Haus-Rucker-Co is present with the *Balloon for 2* and the model of the *Pneumacosm*, on loan from the FRAC Orléans. In the fall, I end my employment at the UdK with a final dual lecture on the topic *Auf der Suche nach dem vibrierenden Nerv unserer Zeit* (In Search of the Vibrating Nerve of Our Time), with alternating lectures by Dr. Phil. Christoph Friedrich Kelp and Prof. DI Günter Zamp Kelp.

VIEWING MACHINES
Participation with images of the *Environment Transformers*

Museum für Gegenwartskunst, Siegen, 2008/2009

Müesarnok Art Hall, Budapest, 2009

Centro Andaluz de Arte Contemperaneo, Sevilla, 2009

CLIMATE CAPSULES
HAUS-RUCKER-CO, Laurids Ortner-Günter Zamp Kelp-Manfred Ortner-Klaus Pinter
Participation with *Oasis No 7* (reconstruction), *Yellow Heart* movie, *Environment Transformer*, *Viewatomizer*, and *Drizzler*
Museum for Art and Crafts, Hamburg, 2010

ARCHITECTURE-UTOPIA RELOADED
HAUS-RUCKER-CO, Laurids Ortner-Günter Zamp Kelp-Manfred Ortner-Klaus Pinter
Overview of the works from 1967–1993
Haus am Waldsee, Berlin, 2014

COSA MENTALE
HAUS-RUCKER-CO, Laurids Ortner-Günter Zamp Kelp-Manfred Ortner-Klaus Pinter
Participation with *Mindexpander 1*
Centre Pompidou-Metz, Metz, 2015

SUBLIME LES TREMBLEMENT DU MONDE
HAUS-RUCKER-CO, Laurids Ortner-Günter Zamp Kelp-Manfred Ortner-Klaus Pinter
Participation with *Protected Village*, *Protected Farmhouse*, *Fresh-air Reserve*
Centre Pompidou-Metz, Metz, 2016

URBAN TOOLS
Solo exhibition, drawings and models of provisional architecture, walkable object in the center: *Transformer/Submerger*
Art Club, Mannheim, 2019

AUSTRIAN AVANT-GARDE 1960–1980
HAUS-RUCKER-CO, Laurids Ortner-Günter Zamp Kelp-Manfred Ortner-Klaus Pinter
Participation with drawings, objects, and models
Den Bosch Design Museum, Herzogenbosch, 2021

Vita Zamp Kelp

1941	Born in Bistritz, Transsylvania
1959	Matriculation Technical University Vienna, Department of Architecture
1967	Diploma Architecture, Technical University Vienna founding member of Haus-Rucker-Co in Vienna, team of Architects and Artists
1967–69	Assistant Professor at the Institute for Design and Construction Studies, Prof. Dr. Karl Schwanzer, Technical University Vienna
1970	Transfer to Düsseldorf, Germany Member of the Architectural Association, North Rhine-Westphalia
1971–72	Founding of Haus-Rucker-Inc. New York, together with Klaus Pinter
1972	Participation at documenta 5, Kassel, with Haus-Rucker-Co
1977	Participation at documenta 6, Kassel, with Haus-Rucker-Co
1979	Kunstpreis Berlin (Fine Arts Award)
1980	Birth of Christoph FF Kelp
1981–82	Visiting Professor at Cornell University and at the Design Department, Hochschule der Künste Berlin
1987	Member of the Architectural Association, Berlin Participation at documenta 8, Kassel, with Haus-Rucker-Co
1988	Visiting Professor at the Städelsche Kunstschule, Division of Architecture University Professor at the Hochschule der Künste Berlin Department of Architecture
1993	Head of Building Design, Space Design and Communications Technology, Head of Laboratory for Computer Aided Design, Hochschule der Künste, Berlin
1995	Gustav-Meyer-Award by the City of Berlin
1996	Visiting Professor Technische Universität Wien
1997	Award Deutscher Architekturpreis Beton
1998	Member of MAD (Institute for Metropolis Architecture Design)
2001	Member at the Advisory Board of City Design in Linz, Austria
2002	Head of Architecture at the International Summer Academy, Salzburg
2004	Visiting Professor at Bauhaus University, Weimar Chair of Prof. Karl-Heinz Schmitz

2006	Chairman at the Advisory Board of City Design in Linz, Austria
2009	Final Lecture at the Universität der Künste, Berlin, with the title "In Search of the Vibrating Nerve of our Times", together with Dr. Phil. Christoph FF Kelp, Catholic University Leuwen
2014	Curator of the exhibition HAUS-RUCKER-CO: ARCHITEKTURUTOPIE RELOADED in cooperation with Dr. Katja Blomberg and Ludwig Engel at Haus am Waldsee, Berlin
2017	Presentation of Archive Zamp Kelp at Gallery Hall in Linz, Austria
2020	Handing over of Archive Zamp Kelp/Haus-Rucker-Co to Lentos Art Museum, Linz, Austria

Major buildings and projects

1965	ARCHITRAINER, Linz Zamp Kelp
1967	PNEUMACOSM, Vienna Haus-Rucker-Co BALLOON FOR 2, Vienna Haus-Rucker-Co
1968	YELLOW HEART, Vienna Haus-Rucker-Co
1972	OASIS NO 7, documenta 5, Kassel Haus-Rucker-Co
1977	FRAME BUILDING, documenta 6, Kassel Haus-Rucker-Co
1993–96	NEANDERTHAL MUSEUM, Düsseldorf/Mettmann Blueprint planning: Zamp Kelp with Julius Krauss/Arno Brandlhuber; detailed planning: Günter Zamp Kelp+Office
2001–06	HOUSE IN FRONT OF THE WIND, Düsseldorf Günter Zamp Kelp+Office
2004–08	KUNSTHALLE MAINZ, Mainz Zamp Kelp neo.studio

Vita Haus-Rucker-Co/ Haus-Rucker-Inc.

1967   founding of Haus-Rucker-Co by Laurids Ortner, Günter Zamp Kelp, Klaus Pinter in Vienna

1970   opening of studios in Düsseldorf, Germany, and New York, USA

1971   Manfred Ortner joins Haus-Rucker-Co, Düsseldorf

1973   independent studios Haus-Rucker-Co, Düsseldorf, partnership Laurids Ortner, Günter Zamp Kelp, Manfred Ortner and Haus-Rucker-Inc., New York, partnership Klaus Pinter and Caroll Michels

1977   dissolving of Haus-Rucker-Inc., New York, beginning of independent activities by Klaus Pinter as independent artist and Caroll Michels as literary writer

1987   opening of independent architectural offices by Günter Zamp Kelp and Laurids + Manfred Ortner in Düsseldorf

1992   dissolving of Haus-Rucker-Co, Düsseldorf, on the occasion of a Haus-Rucker-Co exhibit at the Kunsthalle Wien

Haus-Rucker-Co chronology from 1967–1992, anticlockwise rotation

PHOTO CREDITS

Le Corbusier, **p. 187**
Daily News, **p. 151**
C&R Eames, **pp. 68/69**
Hein Engelskirchen, **pp. 96, 98/99+**
Günther Feuerstein, **p. 36 (Kahn)**
Fluxus Manifest, **p. 134**
FRAC Orleans, **p. 44**
Fuller/Sadao, **p. 95**
Alexander Gerst, **p. 28**
Archive Haus-Rucker-Co, **pp. 51, 63, 65, 66, 67, 70/71, 72, 73, 97, 100, 108, 110, 111, 139, 141, 142/143, 144, 148, 149 154, 157, 158/159**
Harry S. Harlow, **p. 52**
Brigitte Hellgoth, **pp. 112, 113, 114/115, 116**
Ron Herron, **p. 90**
Almut Imlau, **pp. 150, 152/153**
Stanley Kubrick, **p. 85**
Lipecky, **p. 109**
MAK Wien, **p. 54**
Georges Méliès, **p. 32**
MUDAM Luxemburg, **pp. 76, 160**
Christopher Nolan, **p. 29**
Hermann Obert, **p. 34**
Michael Pilz, **p. 53, 55, 57, 144, 149**
NASA, **p. 156**
Rat für Formgebung, **pp. 178, 179**
Regionale 2004, **pp. 84, 86/87**
Thomas Riele, **pp. 26, 27**
Michael Reisch, **pp. 76, 130/131+, 132, 133, 147, 161+, 173, 174/175, 176, 217, 228**
Ben Rose, **p. 60**
Ridley Scott, **p. 181**
Lars von Trier, **p. 23**
Kenzō Tange, **p. 90**
James Wale, **p. 181**
Horst Wiedmann, **p. 58, color**
Gerd Winkler, **pp. 15+, 20, 21, 46+, 52, 56, 58, 59**
Gertraut Wolfschwenger, **pp. 35, 37, 38**
Archive Zamp Kelp, **pp. 24, 25, 26, 51, 65, 66, 67, 75, 120, 123, 124, 125, 126, 140, 180, 182, 183, 188, 200, 201, 206**
Gerald Zugmann, **pp. 31, 47, 62/63, 64, 192, 198, 204**

Digital Montages:
Bruno Torres Sunen, **pp. 15, 31, 89, 98/99, 117, 161**

(Photos with „+" have been further processed)

This book aims to be respectful of all copyright. In reproducing the illustrations and quotations, we have upheld the Amercian legal doctorin of "fair use." All the sources for the texts and images used can be found listed at the end of the book. Please contact the publisher if you find a mistake or see evidence of any copyright infringement.

IMPRINT

Edited by
Ludwig Engel

Designed by
Floyd E. Schulze

Translated by
Sara Hoss
Jan Caspers (Sci-Fi Stories)

Copyedited by
Victoria Nebolsin
Hanne Mächler

Printed and bound by
optimal media GmbH, Röbel

Published by
Spector Books
Harkortstraße 10
04107 Leipzig
www.spectorbooks.com

First edition
Printed in Germany
ISBN 978-3-95905-425-6

Distributed by
Germany, Austria: GVA, Gemeinsame Verlagsauslieferung Göttingen GmbH & Co. KG, www.gva-verlage.de
Switzerland: AVA Verlagsauslieferung AG, www.ava.ch
France, Belgium: Interart Paris, www.interart.fr
UK: Central Books Ltd, www.centralbooks.com
USA, Canada, Central and South America, Africa: ARTBOOK | D.A.P., www.artbook.com
Japan: twelvebooks, www.twelve-books.com
South Korea: The Book Society, www.thebooksociety.org
Australia, New Zealand: Perimeter Distribution, www.perimeterdistribution.com

Funded by
Bundesministerium
Kunst, Kultur,
öffentlicher Dienst und Sport

This time the journey wasn't the reward. Instead, it was more than a year of intense work and constructive communication which led to *LUFTSCHLOSSER*, which is now being published in English under the title *PROSPECTOR*.

I am writing this with a mixture of happiness and sadness as is often the case when an enjoyable piece of work is brought to completion.

My gratitude extends to everyone who was involved in this process.

First, thanks to Ludwig Engel, who played an important part in the publication of this book. He took charge not only of liaising with Spector Books, but also of the copyediting process, and he made a key contribution to selecting the title for the German version of the book. I am also grateful for his recommendation to entrust the graphic design to Floyd Schulze.

Thanks to Floyd, especially for his patience in bringing the multi-faceted tasks associated with the design of the book to a successful end.

I would also like to thank my long-standing collaborator Kristin Feireiss who presented plans, sketches, and models of the *Neanderthal Museum* at AEDES as early as 1996. The questions in her interview gave me the opportunity to reflect in more detail on a number of key projects.

Thanks to Christoph Kelp for a precise and illuminating philosophical discussion of the relation between utopia and function.

I'd also like to express my gratitude to Sara Hoss for her fantastic translations, as well as to Jan Caspers for translating the science fiction stories and also to Victoria Nebolsin for her sensible and precise work on the copyediting of the book.

Last, not least thanks to Spector Books, Anne König and Jan Wenzel, for all the excellent work on the production of *Prospector/Luftschlosser*.

Franz Kafka famously said that paths are made by walking. This book, too, was made by motion. Thanks again to everyone who came along.

Zamp Kelp